The Campus History Series

PENN STATE HARRISBURG

On the Front Cover: This photograph captures a student meeting held on the front lawn of the Olmsted Building in spring 1970, when the Capitol Campus was just four years young and its mission was to serve as a unique undergraduate and graduate center—the first of its kind in Pennsylvania. (Courtesy of Archives and Special Collections, Penn State Harrisburg Library, University Libraries, Pennsylvania State University.)

On the Back Cover: This c. 1961 aerial view of the west side of campus features Meade Heights, the former duplex housing that was originally part of the Olmsted Air Force Base and subsequently used by married students and their families at the Capitol Campus beginning in the early 1970s. (Courtesy of Archives and Special Collections, Penn State Harrisburg Library, University Libraries, Pennsylvania State University.)

The Campus History Series

PENN STATE HARRISBURG

HEIDI ABBEY MOYER
FOREWORD BY MUKUND S. KULKARNI

ARCADIA PUBLISHING

ISBN 978-1-4671-1610-7

Published by Arcadia Publishing
Charleston, South Carolina

Printed in the United States of America

Library of Congress Control Number: 2015951607

For all general information, please contact Arcadia Publishing:
Telephone 843-853-2070
Fax 843-853-0044
E-mail sales@arcadiapublishing.com
For customer service and orders:
Toll-Free 1-888-313-2665

Visit us on the Internet at www.arcadiapublishing.com

To my amazing husband, Bradley Jay Moyer, for your love, laughter, strength, and steadfast encouragement, and to Penn State Harrisburg's students, staff, faculty, friends, and over 41,000 alumni for inspiring me to write this book

Contents

FOREWORD

Penn State Harrisburg has been a vital part of the South Central Pennsylvania community for more than half a century. It began as the Olmsted Air Force Base in Middletown, Pennsylvania, where it employed many local citizens. When the base was to be decommissioned, Gov. William W. Scranton, seeking a way to lessen the economic toll of closing the base and to address the need for an academic institution near the capital city of Harrisburg, approached Penn State president Dr. Eric A. Walker with the idea of turning the site into a Penn State graduate school. Walker had a more ambitious idea: a graduate school and upper division center that would provide another higher-education option for Central Pennsylvania residents; relieve enrollment pressures at Penn State University Park in State College, Pennsylvania; complement the efforts of neighboring institutions; and allow the university to maximize its investment in faculty, classrooms, library resources, and laboratory equipment.

With the transfer of 178 acres of land and 16 buildings from the Air Force to the university, Penn State Harrisburg—or "Capitol Campus," as it was known at the time—was founded in May 1966. It was Pennsylvania's first upper division and graduate center, one of only three in the nation, with an enrollment of just 18 students. Over the next 50 years, the college grew tremendously. Penn State Harrisburg now is the largest and most comprehensive Penn State campus outside of University Park, with an enrollment that surpasses 4,500.

During the last 30 years, as a faculty member, school director, and chancellor, I have proudly witnessed much of Penn State Harrisburg's growth in enrollment, academic offerings, campus infrastructure, and many other areas. The college's current status as a thriving institution known for academic excellence can be attributed to the caliber, contributions, and continued dedication of the faculty and staff. Today, the college is known for its extensive portfolio of degree offerings, academic rigor, and highly qualified faculty. Our students come from all over the United States and all corners of the world. Academic offerings include more than 65 associate, bachelor's, master's, and doctoral degree programs in academic units divided into five schools: Behavioral Sciences and Education; Business Administration; Humanities; Public Affairs; and Science, Engineering, and Technology.

The commitment to academic excellence includes an emphasis on personal attention in the classroom and on the provision of a wide array of support services and state-of-the-art facilities. Over the past 50 years, the campus infrastructure has grown to accommodate the ever changing needs of our student body. Additions to the campus have included a 115,000-square-foot library; on-campus and apartment-style housing, including the first Leadership in Energy and Environmental Design (LEED)-certified residential building within Penn State; and expansions to many existing buildings. A recent addition to the Educational Activities Building features state-of-art engineering and faculty research labs, general purpose classrooms, and a multipurpose room for art and the performing arts. On the west side of campus, the former dining commons now houses the Select Medical Nursing Simulation Lab and the Central Pennsylvania Research and Teaching Laboratory for Biofuels, which includes an adjacent greenhouse. And, as we mark the start of our 50th anniversary in 2016, construction has begun on a 70,000-square-foot Student Enrichment Center to be built at the core of campus, providing a central location for student support services and the college's first spiritual center.

Athletics at Penn State Harrisburg are a cornerstone of our efforts to provide students with a well-rounded and full educational experience. In 2005, intercollegiate athletics resumed at Penn State Harrisburg following a decade's absence. Today, the college, an NCAA Division III member, offers 16 varsity sports that compete in the Capital Athletic Conference. In support of the revived athletics program, Penn State Harrisburg has remained committed to enhancing athletic facilities. Originally a multipurpose building housing the gymnasium, the Capital Union Building (known as the CUB) now also boasts an indoor pool and a fully equipped student fitness center. The college has also added a tennis complex and numerous athletic fields.

Penn State Harrisburg's location in Central Pennsylvania, a vibrant hub of commerce, industry, and state government, affords our students many opportunities for involvement in community service, internships, fellowships, and mentoring programs—all experiences that extend learning beyond the classroom. The college serves as an economic engine in the region, a role it has had since its founding. As part of that tradition, the college actively serves as a research and economic development partner for the Commonwealth and business and industry in the greater Harrisburg community.

It has been said that our alumni are the greatest testament to the strength of a Penn State Harrisburg education. Today, alumni number more than 41,000. Among them are distinguished business and community leaders, legislators and public officials, educators, researchers, engineers, computer scientists, historians, journalists, health professionals, and much more.

The images presented here tell the story of Penn State Harrisburg's journey—the people, places, events, and activities that have made possible its tremendous progress since 1966. The history that they illustrate is a foundation on which the college continues to build as it remains positioned for success in the decades ahead. It is my hope that through these photographs, documents, and publications, readers will share in our pride as we reflect on the past 50 years and look forward to a bright future.

—Mukund S. Kulkarni, PhD
Chancellor, Penn State Harrisburg

ACKNOWLEDGMENTS

This book is a testament to collaboration and teamwork. I extend my gratitude to the Penn State Harrisburg community, especially Dr. Mukund Kulkarni, Dr. Omid Ansary, and Dr. Gregory Crawford, who supported this book as my sabbatical research in 2014–2015; to emeritus faculty Dr. Michael Barton, Dr. Clemmie Gilpin, Dr. Irving Hand, Dr. Irwin Richman, Dr. Hall Shill, Dr. Frank Swetz, and Dr. George Wolf, who provided information about the college's early years; and to Dr. Simon Bronner, for sharing vital records about the college. I would also like to acknowledge alumni Paul Levitsky ('79) and Mark Gibson ('83) for conveying their college histories. Special thanks to the director of the Physical Plant and Maintenance Operations, Edward Dankanich; staff in the Alumni Relations and Office of Development; staff in the Chancellor's Office, particularly Sharon Blouch and Angela Larks; staff in the Marketing Research and Communications Office, notably Yvonne Harhigh, Alixandra Moyer, Sharon Siegfried, and former Public Information Manager Steven Hevner; and to Susan Hook-Smeal at Biscotti's.

To my esteemed colleagues within the Penn State University Libraries, I am grateful for your help and encouragement, including: Glenn McGuigan, director of the Penn State Harrisburg Library; Christine Avery and John "Jack" Sulzer; fellow archivists Jane Ingold, Penn State Erie, and Jackie Esposito, University Archivist at Penn State; fellow librarians Eric Delozier, Sally Feeser, Bernadette Lear, Kathy Mols, Kate Pursel, Ruth Runion-Slear, and Eileen Zagon; and library colleagues Sherry Bancroft, Angela Caldwell, Jennifer Dimeler, Keifer Kemmerly, Henry Koretzky, Alan Mays, Leslie McConnell, Gail Newcomer, Glenn Rudy, and Fay Youngmark.

In Archives and Special Collections, numerous part-time staff have spent hours scanning photographs, compiling facts, and paving the way for this book to be published. I would like to thank my former archives colleague Martha Sachs for her assistance over the years, and acknowledge the year-long dedication and phenomenal efforts of Katie Barrett, Katie Gorrell, and Ashlee Vandewater, who processed over 19,000 photographs in the College History Archives. My sincere gratitude is extended to former archives assistants Matt Anthony, Lynne Calamia, Jennifer Dutch, Jolene Fay, Rachel Ginder, Katie McGowan, Daniel Pfeffer, and David Puglia, as well as former archives interns Megan Bennett, Meghan Fitzgerald, Benjamin Hoover, Alyssa Lorance, Steve Swetz, and Rosemary Yee.

I wish to thank my friend, Agnes Baur, for giving me the courage to write another book; to Bob Rupert, for assisting with Colonel Young's genealogy; and to Peter Seibert ('87 and '92g), for generously sharing his photographs of Camp Meade. To my editors at Arcadia Publishing, Caitrin Cunningham, Ginny Rasmussen, and Abby Walker, I appreciate your assistance over the past two years.

To my parents, Ronald and Rosemary Wagaman, for their unwavering support with every project or adventure that I have ever endeavored. To my family, especially my aunt Catherine "Katie" Garrett (1947–2016), who enjoyed reading about local history and inspired me to learn more about Pennsylvania's rich traditions; this book was completed in your loving memory. To my dearest friends, the Batt, Eshelman, Long, Mervosh, Moon, and Scott families, your friendship and encouragement over the years have been invaluable to me. Thank you sincerely.

Last but certainly not least, to my patient and generous husband, Brad, and to our three wonderful sons, Liam, Adam, and Bruce, I cannot thank you enough for all of the sacrifices you have made enabling me to finish this book. Words cannot express the extent of my gratitude and love for you.

Unless otherwise noted, all images appear courtesy of Archives and Special Collections, Penn State Harrisburg Library, University Libraries, Pennsylvania State University.

INTRODUCTION

The history of Penn State Harrisburg, the "Capitol Campus," which was established in 1966, mirrors the cultural, political, and social context within which the school was born. During the mid-1960s, life in the United States was marked by upheaval and change in just about every arena—civil rights and social justice, international affairs, politics, and popular culture. Lyndon B. Johnson was elected to a second term as president, and human rights activist Malcolm X was assassinated in New York City. Some of the worst race riots in the country's history broke out in Watts, California, while the Vietnam War was escalating. Antiwar protests were prevalent across the country, and Americans were listening to the sounds of the Beatles, the Rolling Stones, and the Supremes. *Bonanza* and *My Three Sons* were hits on television, as were *Gomer Pyle, U.S.M.C.* and *Hogan's Heroes*. A gallon of gasoline cost a mere 30¢, and the average fee for undergraduate tuition, room, and board at a four-year public institution was $983 per year. Despite the challenges and turmoil of the era, forces combined to launch the educational experiment that evolved into Penn State Harrisburg. The following is an overview of the circumstances in Middletown, Pennsylvania, and at Penn State University that facilitated the establishment of the Harrisburg campus in the late 1960s. It is accompanied by a summary of how Penn State Harrisburg has advanced over the past 50 years into one of the university's most successful and dynamic college communities.

Located on the north complex of the former Olmsted Air Force Base in Middletown, Pennsylvania, Penn State Harrisburg grew out of the creative thinking and collaborative actions of Dr. Eric A. Walker, Penn State president emeritus (1956–1970), and the Honorable William W. Scranton, former governor of Pennsylvania (1963–1967) and former US ambassador to the United Nations (1976–1977). On November 19, 1964, US Secretary of Defense Robert McNamara issued a Pentagon economy order calling for the phase-out of operations at 96 military installations, including the Olmsted Air Force Base, by 1969. When Governor Scranton received the news of the Olmsted Air Force Base's imminent closure, he immediately recognized the economic devastation that it would wreak upon Middletown, Harrisburg, and surrounding communities. At the height of its operations for the Air Force, the Olmsted base employed over 17,000 civilians and nearly 2,000 military personnel. Despite several months of lobbying to save the Olmsted base, civic and community leaders and the Harrisburg Area Chamber of Commerce reluctantly accepted its gradual shutdown. However, Governor Scranton did not accept this fate.

In July 1965, Governor Scranton contacted Dr. Walker to inquire whether or not Penn State University might consider repurposing the Olmsted Air Force Base by creating a graduate school, thereby lessening the economic impact of the base's closure in the region. It did not take long for Dr. Walker to craft a response to Governor Scranton's proposal. In August 1965, Dr. Walker suggested the combined upper-division undergraduate and graduate school that still exists today. The first classes at the newly created Capitol Campus were held on October 3, 1966, on the first floor of the base's former headquarters, the Olmsted Building. The student body comprised 18 undergraduates (juniors and seniors) and 165 graduate students. Most importantly, the mission of the campus was always unique, rooted in interdisciplinary studies and focused upon balancing traditional courses with practical field work.

Over the next five decades, the Capitol Campus gradually added new faculty, created new programs, built the administrative infrastructure to strategically enhance the management of the school, redesigned the campus grounds, improved facilities, established student services and social activities, and, ultimately, increased student enrollments. In the 1970s, the campus culture witnessed the formation of several traditions, including the spring rock festival, Fertility Day, and the bathtub races. The campus community also overcame the environmental disaster brought on by Hurricane Agnes in 1972 and the technological crisis of the Three Mile Island incident in 1979. By the 1980s, the campus had six new academic divisions: Behavioral Sciences and Education; Business Administration; the Heindel Memorial Library; Humanities; Public Affairs; and Science, Engineering, and Technology. In 1986, the school officially gained college status and became known as "Penn State Harrisburg." In 1991, the 25th anniversary of the college marked a significant milestone with student enrollment reaching 3,400 and alumni totaling 16,000. From the 1990s through the 2010s, Penn State Harrisburg continued to thrive by meeting and anticipating the ever-evolving needs of students. Since 2000, the college has completed construction on a state-of-the-art library; enhanced its athletic facilities; expanded labs and resources for science, engineering, and technology programs; added new on-campus housing for over 400 students; and revamped the campus grounds to virtually eliminate any remaining traces of the former Olmsted Air Force Base.

While the details of Penn State Harrisburg's evolution are well documented in other informal histories, this book is the first attempt to visually chronicle the college's history from its 19th-century agricultural and 20th-century military roots to the present day. The story that unfolds is remarkable. For example, who would have guessed that the farmland underneath the college's buildings was once the home of thoroughbred Jersey cattle and later used to grow vegetables for the H.J. Heinz Company? Or that when the US Army Signal Corps established a training camp in the area, the land would eventually become athletic fields for the college? And who could have imagined that the Cold War bomb shelter built for Olmsted Air Force Base in the 1940s would eventually serve as inspiration for the name of Penn State Harrisburg's literary and arts magazine, *From the Fallout Shelter*? Answers to these questions—plus more information about the college's transformation—are revealed using rare photographs, documents, and publications that were previously unprocessed and unavailable for research in the school's College History Archives.

The college has grown from a small, unique, educational experiment started in the mid-1960s to become the largest Penn State campus outside of University Park—a successful, student-centered, influential, and valued part of the Penn State community poised to continue its leadership role well into the 21st century. In 1995, Interim Provost and Dean of Penn State Harrisburg, Dr. Theodore E. Kiffer, said that the Harrisburg campus is "the best-kept secret in the entire university and in higher education in Pennsylvania." Five years later, in August 2000, provost and dean (subsequently renamed chancellor) of Penn State Harrisburg, Dr. Madlyn L. Hanes, said that "we have to look to students and alumni to tell our story and help us get better so we're no longer a best-kept secret." Dr. Kiffer's and Dr. Hanes's words still ring true today, as Penn State Harrisburg prepares to celebrate its 50th anniversary in 2016.

One

EVOLVING FROM FARM TO AIR FORCE BASE

1858–1965

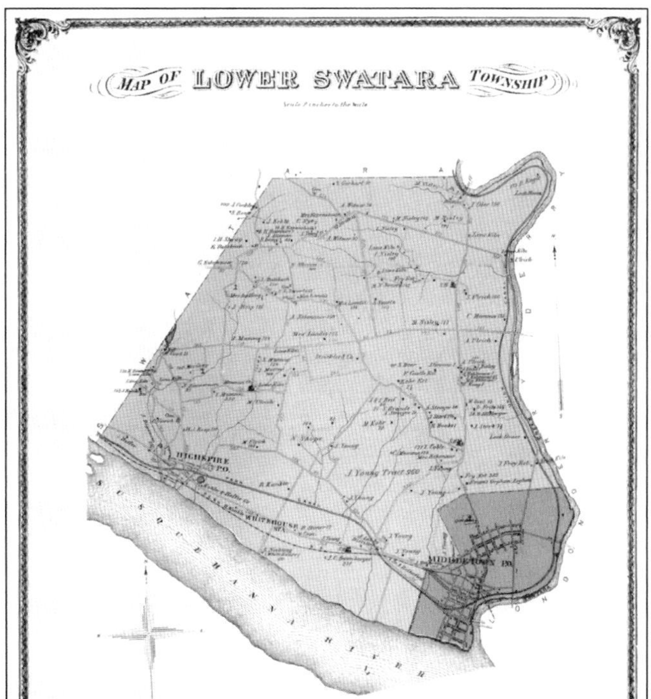

MAP OF LOWER SWATARA TOWNSHIP, 1875. This map illustrates the farms near Middletown in Dauphin County. The agriculturally rich area was home to businessman, farmer, and former Civil War colonel James Young, who began acquiring land here in 1858. Note the number of times "J Young" appears on the map. Penn State Harrisburg is located near the area labelled "J Young Tract 960." (Courtesy of the Historical Society of Dauphin County.)

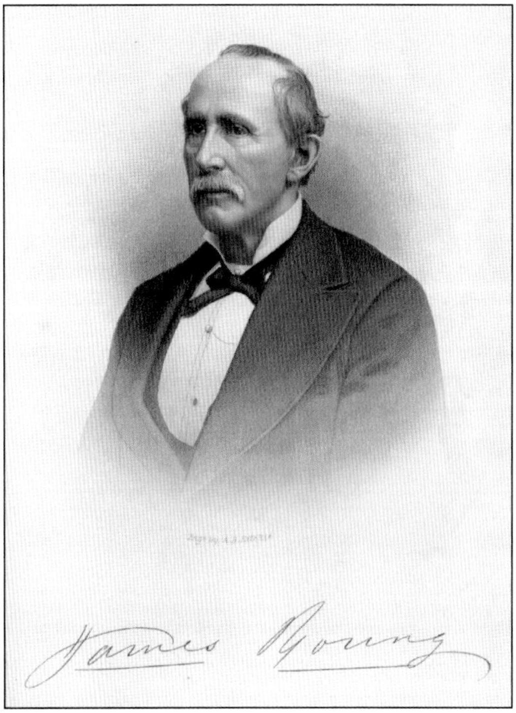

COL. JAMES YOUNG, C. 1883. Colonel Young was born July 25, 1820, at Swatara Hill, Middletown. By the time he was 63 years old, his approximate age in this image, Young had acquired over 1,400 acres of farmland and owned several businesses. He died on May 4, 1895, from injuries sustained after being thrown from his carriage. (From Egle's *History of the Counties of Dauphin and Lebanon*, facing page 606.)

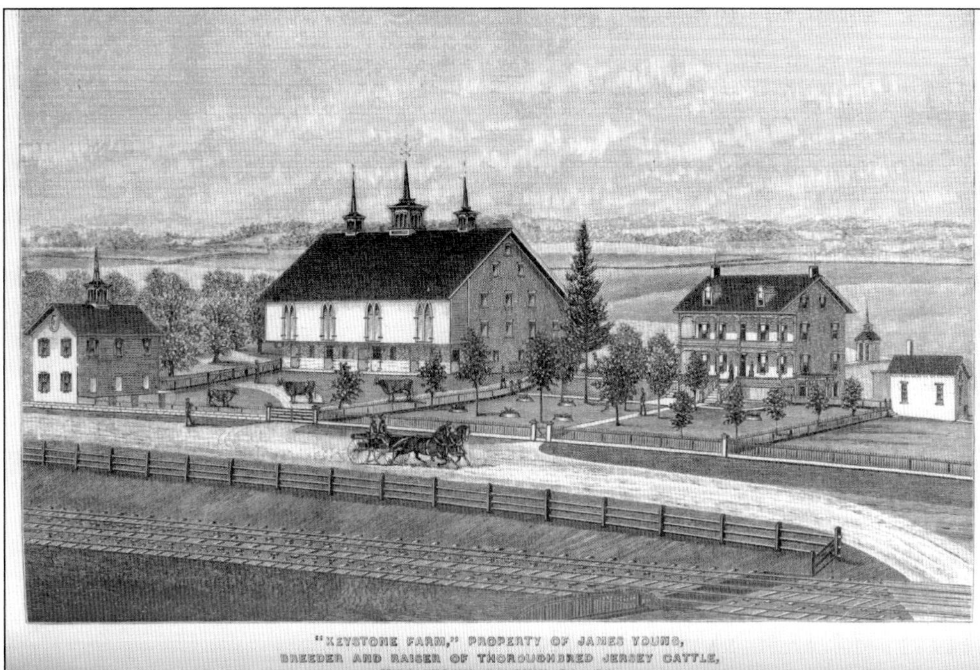

KEYSTONE FARM, C. 1883. Often described as the "prince of farmers" because of the impeccable care he gave to his livestock and land, Colonel Young was a renowned breeder of thoroughbred Jersey cattle, as shown in this early drawing of his Keystone Farm. The farm is now part of present-day Penn State Harrisburg. (From Egle's *History of the Counties of Dauphin and Lebanon*, facing page 609.)

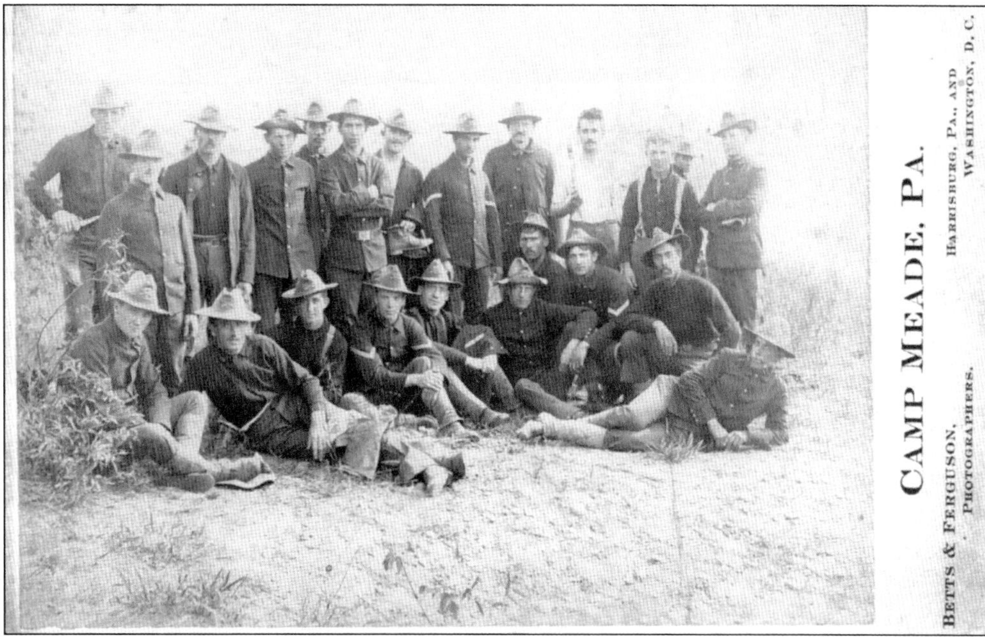

CAMP MEADE, 1898. After Col. James Young's death, 700 acres of his estate became Camp Meade, home to 30,000 soldiers during the Spanish-American War of 1898. The camp, named for George Gordon Meade, the Union army's general during the Battle of Gettysburg, occupied land that is now part of present-day Penn State Harrisburg. This photograph shows soldiers who were bathing in the Susquehanna River. (Courtesy of the Collection of Peter and Kim Seibert.)

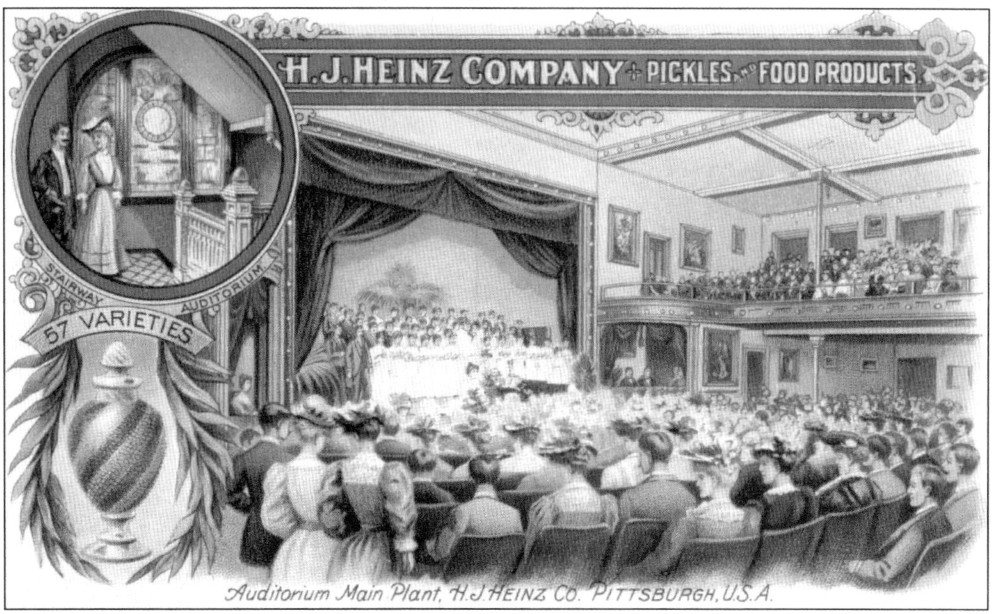

H.J. HEINZ COMPANY POSTCARD, c. 1890–1907. Before the Spanish-American War ended in December 1898, Camp Meade was deserted and returned to local landowners, including the heirs of Col. James Young's estate. The land was farmed by the H.J. Heinz Company, which grew vegetables for its now-famous 57 varieties of "pickles and food products" (as noted on this vintage postcard) until the government took over the land again in May 1917.

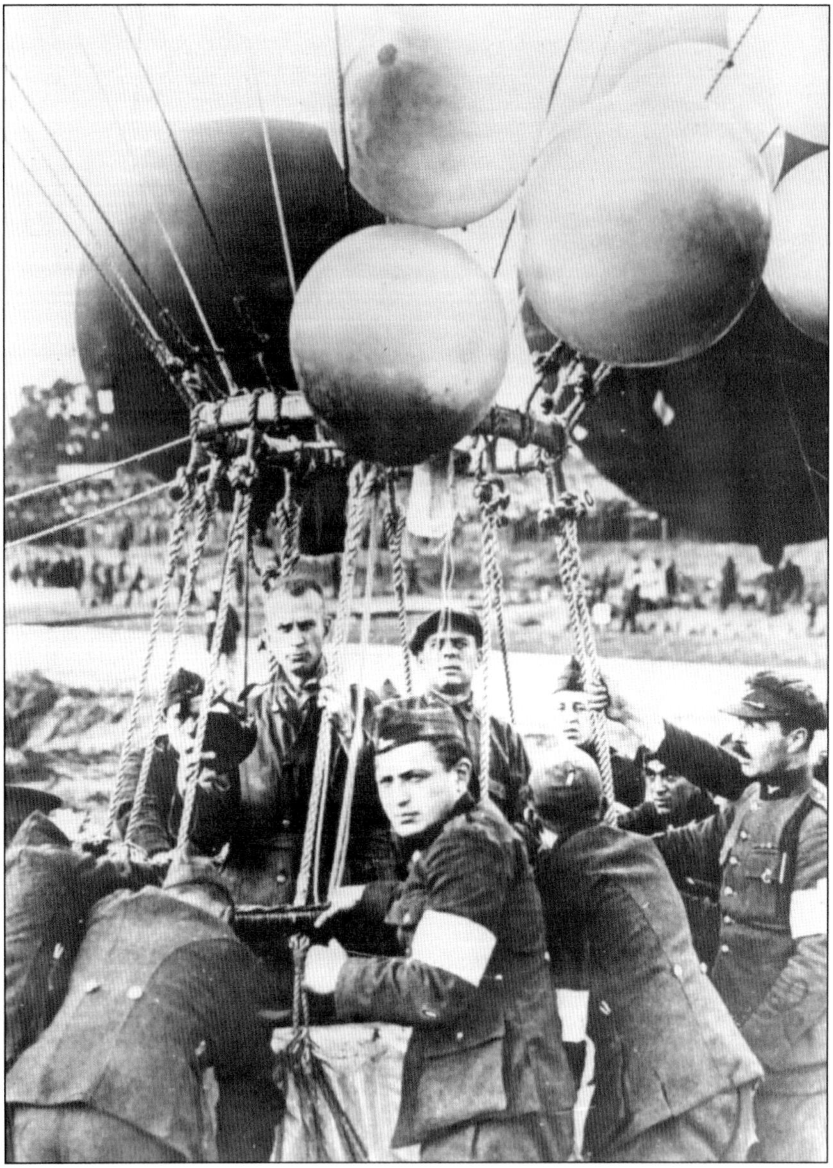

Olmsted and International Balloon Race, 1923. During World War I, part of Col. James Young's estate was the site of aviation supply warehouses for the US Army Signal Corps. The base was named the Aviation General Supply Depot and, later, the Middletown Air Depot. In 1919, 1st Lt. Robert Sanford Olmsted was serving in the Engineering Section, Balloon and Airship Division, of the Army Air Service and assigned to the Middletown depot. Olmsted and fellow officer John Shoptaw won first place in the 1923 US National Balloon Race in Indianapolis, Indiana. This victory entitled them to compete in the 12th James Gordon Bennett International Balloon Race in Brussels, Belgium, on September 23, 1923. This remarkable photograph shows 37-year-old Olmsted (left) and Shoptaw (right, wearing a cap), standing inside the basket of their Army S-6 balloon before it was struck by lightning during the race, tragically killing both over Nistelrode, Holland. In honor of 1st Lieutenant Olmsted, the Middletown depot was renamed Olmsted Field on October 20, 1923, and, later, Olmsted Air Force Base on March 11, 1948. (Courtesy of the Hagley Museum and Library.)

***Capital Collegian*, 1949**. Prior to the establishment of Penn State Harrisburg, limited opportunities existed to earn a college education in the Harrisburg area. In the fall of 1948, however, 250 men and women gathered at the Jewish Community Center on Front Street in Harrisburg to inaugurate the first freshman class of the Pennsylvania State College–Harrisburg Center. This image highlights a notable issue of the *Capital Collegian*, the semimonthly publication of Harrisburg Center's journalism club.

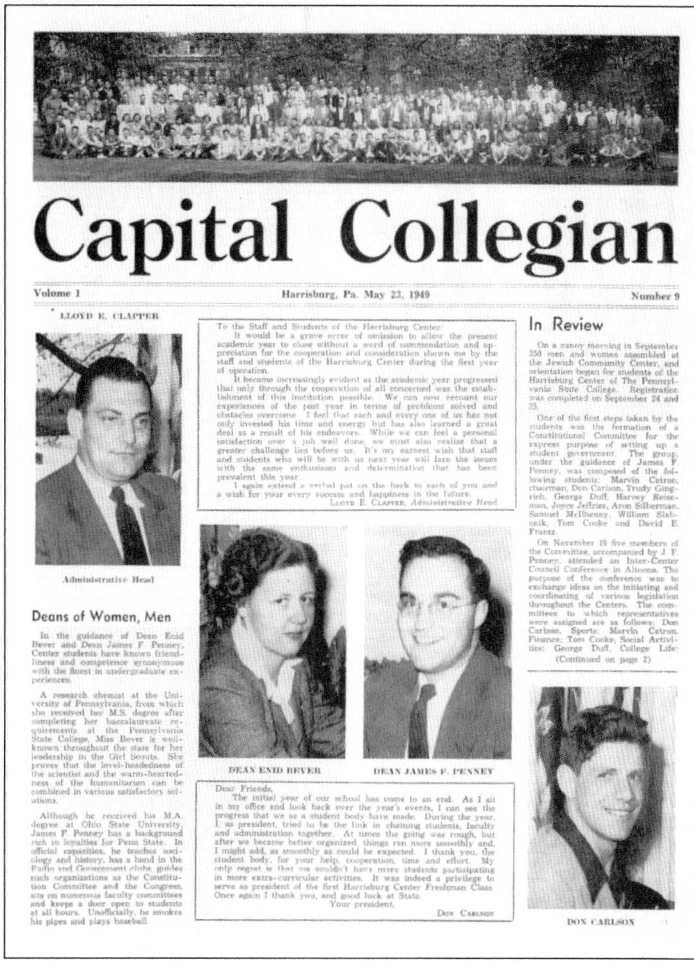

Capital Collegian

Volume 1 — Harrisburg, Pa. May 23, 1949 — Number 9

LLOYD E. CLAPPER

Administrative Head

To the Staff and Students of the Harrisburg Center:

It would be a grave error of omission to allow the present academic year to close without a word of commendation and appreciation for the cooperation and consideration shown me by the staff and students of the Harrisburg Center during the first year of operation.

It became increasingly evident as the academic year progressed that only through the cooperation of all concerned was the establishment of this institution possible. We can now recount our experiences of the past year in terms of problems solved and obstacles overcome. I feel that each and every one of us has not only invested his time and energy but has also learned a great deal as a result of his endeavors. While we can feel a personal satisfaction over a job well done, we must also realize that a greater challenge lies before us. It's my earnest wish that staff and students who will be with us next year will face the issues with the same enthusiasm and determination that has been prevalent this year.

I again extend a verbal pat on the back to each of you and a wish for your every success and happiness in the future.

LLOYD E. CLAPPER, *Administrative Head*

In Review

On a sunny morning in September 250 men and women assembled at the Jewish Community Center, and orientation began for students of the Harrisburg Center of The Pennsylvania State College. Registration was completed on September 24 and 25.

One of the first steps taken by the students was the formation of a Constitutional Committee for the express purpose of setting up a student government. The group, under the guidance of James F. Penney, was composed of the following students: Marvin Cetron, chairman, Don Carlson, Trudy Gingrich, George Duff, Harvey Reiseman, Joyce Jeffries, Aron Silberman, Samuel McIlhenny, William Slabonik, Tom Cooke and David E. Frantz.

On November 19 five members of the Committee, accompanied by J. F. Penney, attended an Inter-Center Council Conference in Altoona. The purpose of the conference was to exchange ideas on the initiating and coordinating of various legislation throughout the Centers. The committees to which representatives were assigned are as follows: Don Carlson, Sports; Marvin Cetron, Finance; Tom Cooke, Social Activities; George Duff, College Life;

(Continued on page 2)

Deans of Women, Men

In the guidance of Dean Enid Bever and Dean James F. Penney, Center students have known friendliness and competence synonymous with the finest in undergraduate experiences.

A research chemist at the University of Pennsylvania, from which she received her M.S. degree after completing her baccalaureate requirements at the Pennsylvania State College, Miss Bever is well-known throughout the state for her leadership in the Girl Scouts. She proves that the level-headedness of the scientist and the warm-heartedness of the humanitarian can be combined in various satisfactory solutions.

Although he received his M.A. degree at Ohio State University, James F. Penney has a background rich in loyalties for Penn State. In official capacities, he teaches sociology and history, has a hand in the Radio and Government clubs, guides such organizations as the Constitution Committee and the Congress, sits on numerous faculty committees and keeps a door open to students at all hours. Unofficially, he smokes his pipes and plays baseball.

DEAN ENID BEVER

DEAN JAMES F. PENNEY

Dear Friends,

The initial year of our school has come to an end. As I sit in my office and look back over the year's events, I can see the progress that we as a student body have made. During the year, I, as president, tried to be the link in chaining students, faculty and administration together. At times the going was rough, but after we became better organized, things ran more smoothly and, I might add, as smoothly as could be expected. I thank you, the student body, for your help, cooperation, time and effort. My only regret is that we couldn't have more students participating in more extra-curricular activities. It was indeed a privilege to serve as president of the first Harrisburg Center Freshman Class. Once again I thank you, and good luck at State.

Your president,

DON CARLSON

DON CARLSON

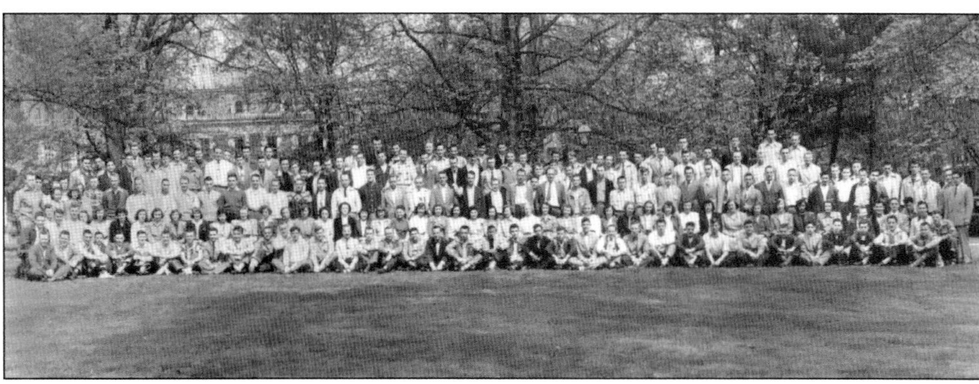

Pennsylvania State College–Harrisburg Center, 1949. This unique photograph of the Harrisburg Center's student body is from spring 1949 and was printed in the *Capital Collegian*. The Harrisburg Center predates the establishment of Penn State Harrisburg by 18 years; it operated for several years after World War II and highlights the strong interest in undergraduate education throughout South Central Pennsylvania.

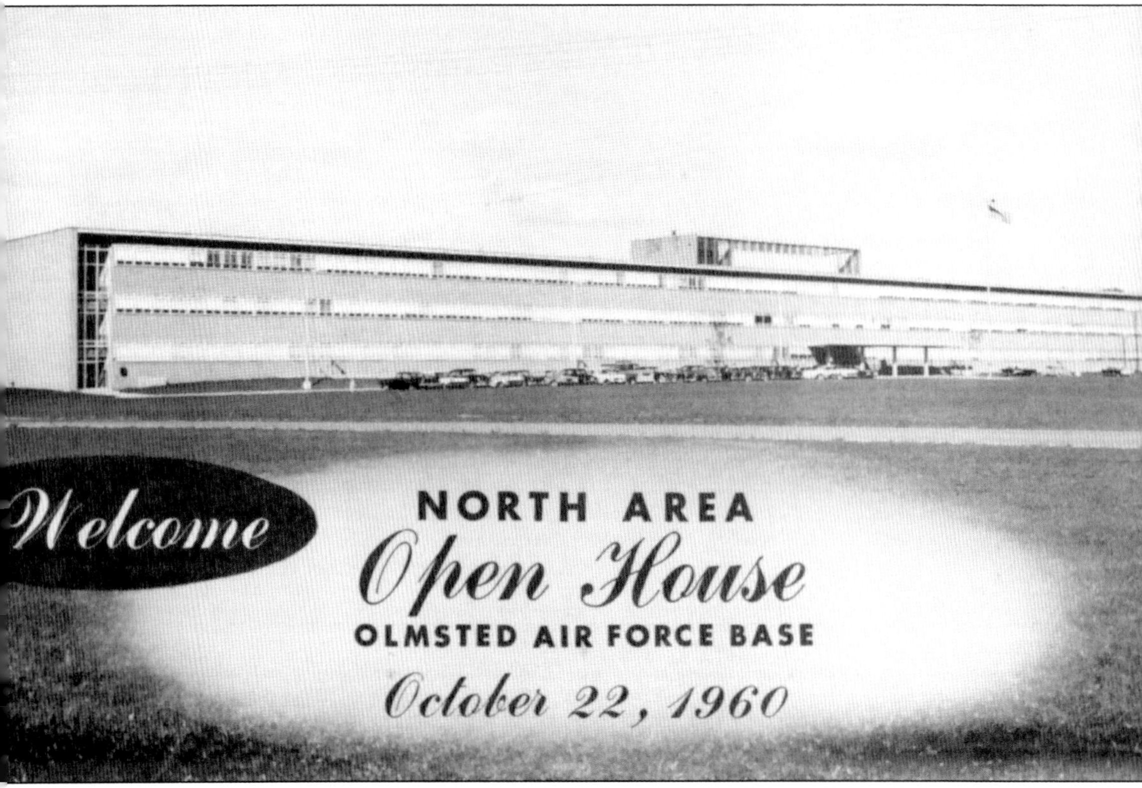

Olmsted Air Force Base, 1960. The 19th-century farming region around Middletown dramatically evolved from its use as the Keystone Farm and Camp Meade until it became the "Capitol Campus" and later, Penn State Harrisburg. From the mid-1920s until the mid-1960s, the Middletown community was home to the largest US Air Force installation in Pennsylvania, the Olmsted Air Force Base. Among its many distinctions in military history, the base was known during World War II for being the largest engine overhaul center in the world, with an October 1944 record of repairing more than 2,300 engines in just one month. The base was also responsible for maintaining supplies and military aircraft along the eastern seaboard and in 15 states. It was a major employer in the region, providing jobs to over 17,000 civilians, 300 officers, and 1,600 airmen in the 1940s. This image, which highlights an open house for the base on October 22, 1960, features the $3.5-million, three-story Headquarters (or Administration) Building, now known as the Olmsted Building at Penn State Harrisburg.

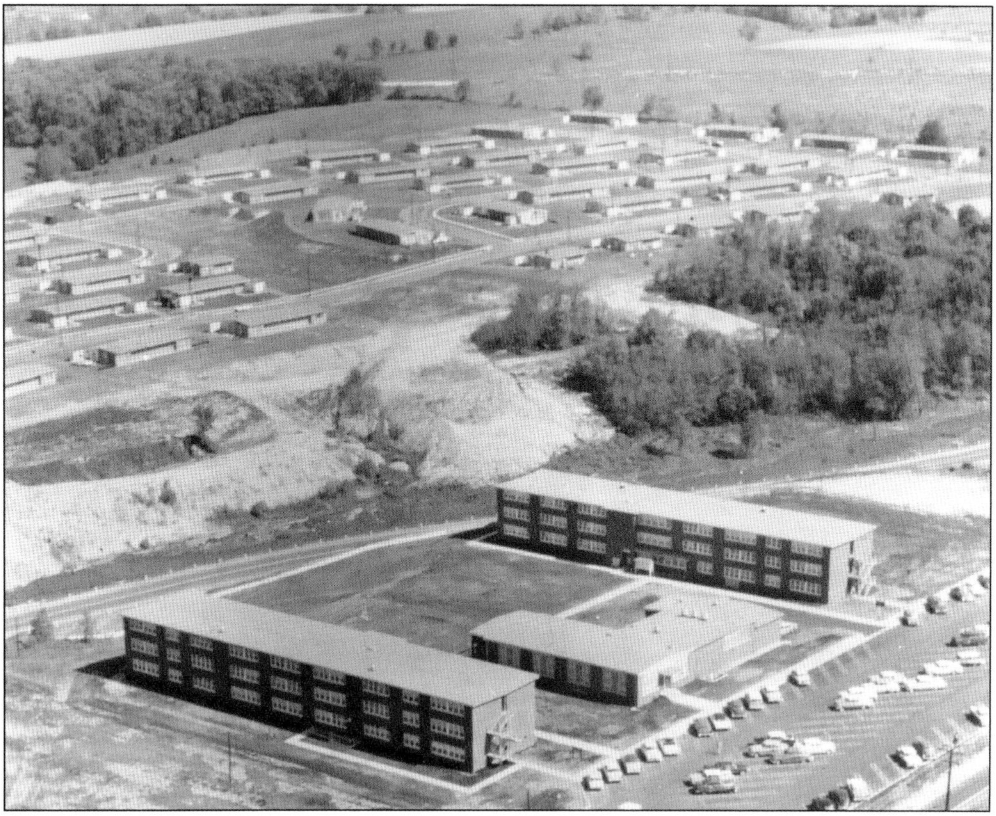

WRISBERG AND CHURCH HALLS, C. 1961. This photograph features two dormitories constructed from 1958 to 1960 on the north side of the Olmsted Air Force Base. They were dedicated on February 14, 1961. Pictured are Wrisberg Hall (left) and Church Hall (right), which were used as living quarters that could accommodate up to 400 unmarried airmen. The base's dining hall is between the dormitories.

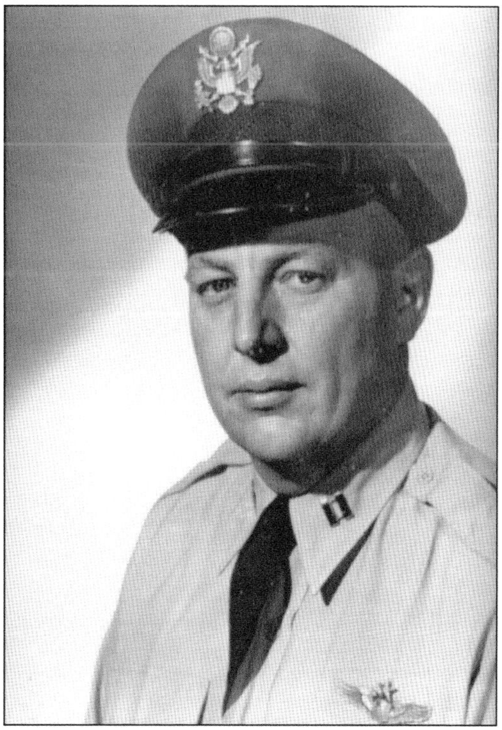

CAPT. JOHN H. WRISBERG JR., C. 1959. The airmen dormitories were named in honor of two pilots, Captain Wrisberg (pictured) and Capt. Kenneth L. Church, who were killed on May 2, 1960, while on a test flight from Olmsted Air Force Base. They both died when their C-123 airplane crashed near Loganville in York County, Pennsylvania.

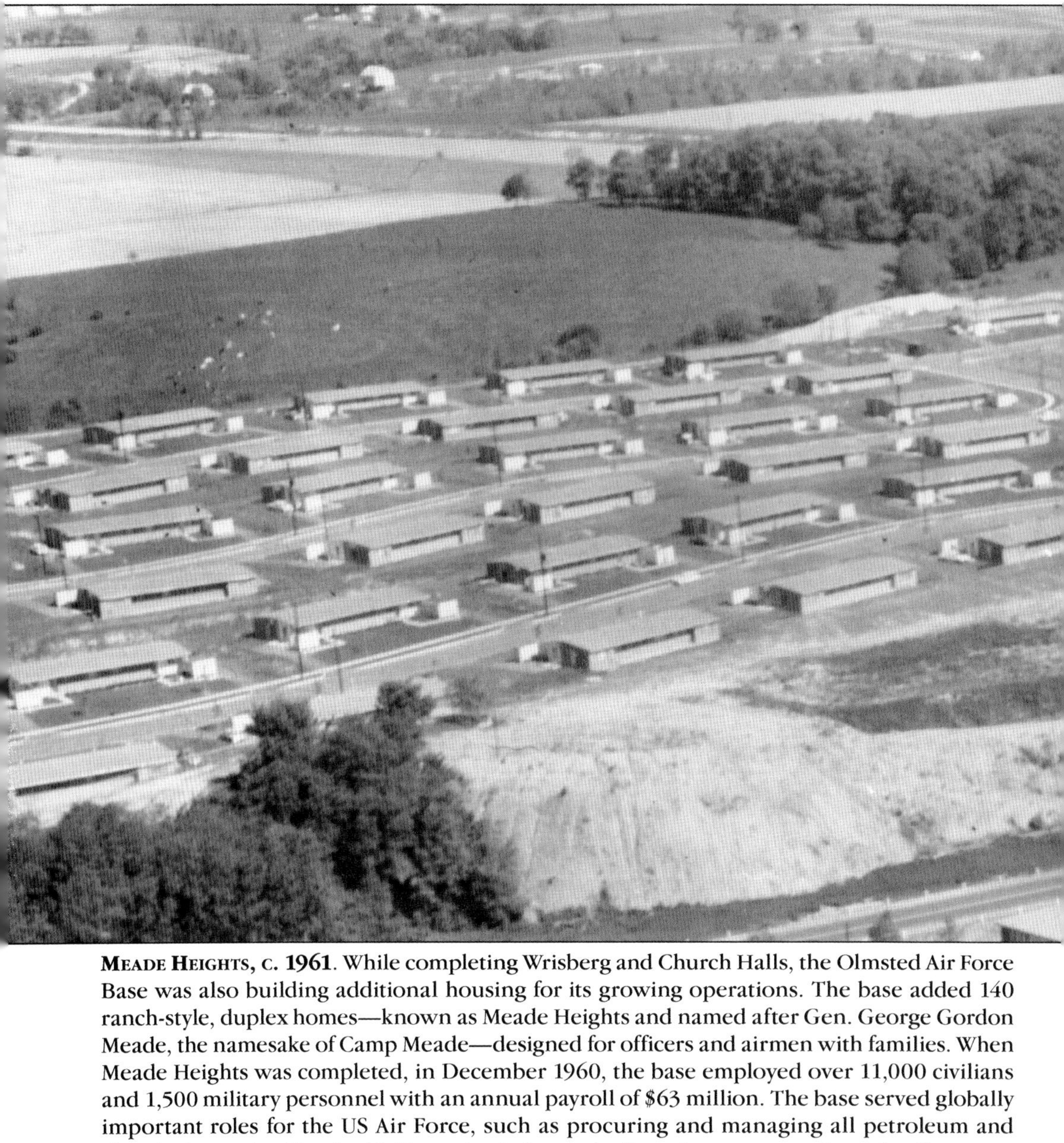

Meade Heights, c. 1961. While completing Wrisberg and Church Halls, the Olmsted Air Force Base was also building additional housing for its growing operations. The base added 140 ranch-style, duplex homes—known as Meade Heights and named after Gen. George Gordon Meade, the namesake of Camp Meade—designed for officers and airmen with families. When Meade Heights was completed, in December 1960, the base employed over 11,000 civilians and 1,500 military personnel with an annual payroll of $63 million. The base served globally important roles for the US Air Force, such as procuring and managing all petroleum and chemicals required by the Air Force, both domestically and overseas, and overhauling more than 60 percent of the Air Force's instruments. By 1962, the base occupied nearly 1,500 acres, with more than 280 buildings, and was valued at $55 million. On November 19, 1964, the US Department of Defense officially announced that operations at Olmsted Air Force Base, as well as at 95 other military installations, would be phased out for economic reasons and closed by 1969.

Two

Establishing a Campus Community 1966–1969

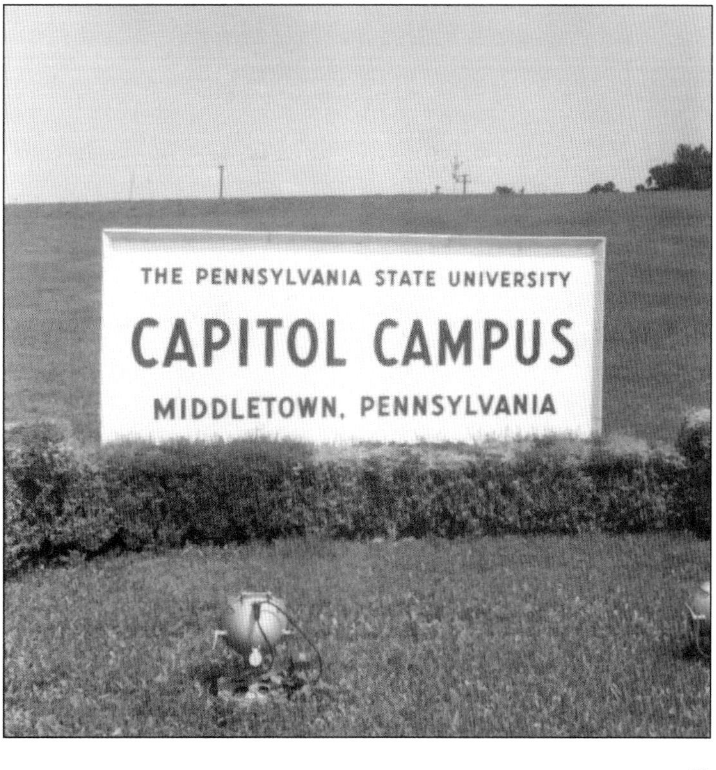

Original Campus Sign, c. 1966–1967. With the imminent closure of the Olmsted Air Force Base scheduled for December 1, 1965, Pennsylvania governor William Scranton designated the Pennsylvania State University as the applying agent for the Commonwealth of Pennsylvania to purchase the base's north complex. Two months later, on February 8, 1966, a new Penn State campus was established and named "Capitol Campus." This photograph shows an early campus entrance sign.

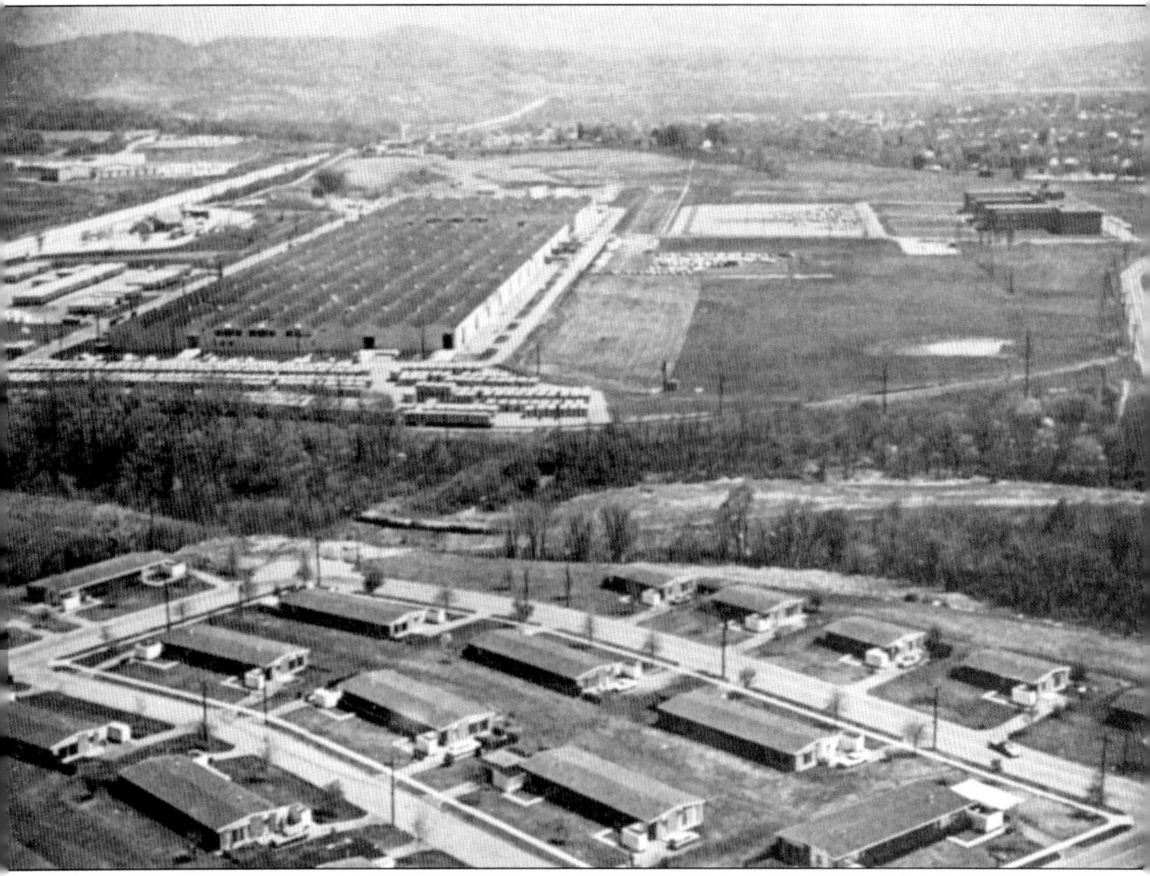

Aerial View of Campus, c. 1966–1967. Although the University announced the creation of the "Capitol Campus" in February 1966, the formal transfer of the north complex of the Olmsted Air Force Base did not take place until May 12, 1966. Penn State purchased the complex from the US Department of Defense for just $1; the sale included 177.5 acres of land as well as 16 buildings. Additionally, Penn State agreed to use the land and buildings for educational purposes for at least 20 years. In 1968, the university acquired the land and buildings on the west side of campus, including Meade Heights. This unique aerial view of the campus shows the Olmsted Building (at upper right) and Meade Heights (in the foreground).

Director Coleman Herpel, c. 1966–1967. On January 8, 1966, Herpel, the former director of Penn State Ogontz (now Penn State Abington), was appointed as the first director of Capitol Campus. In September 1966, Herpel oversaw the transfer of students to the Capitol Campus from the Susquehanna Valley Graduate Center of Penn State University in Harrisburg, which was created in January 1965 to provide graduate-level training for engineers and scientists in the Harrisburg-York-Lancaster area.

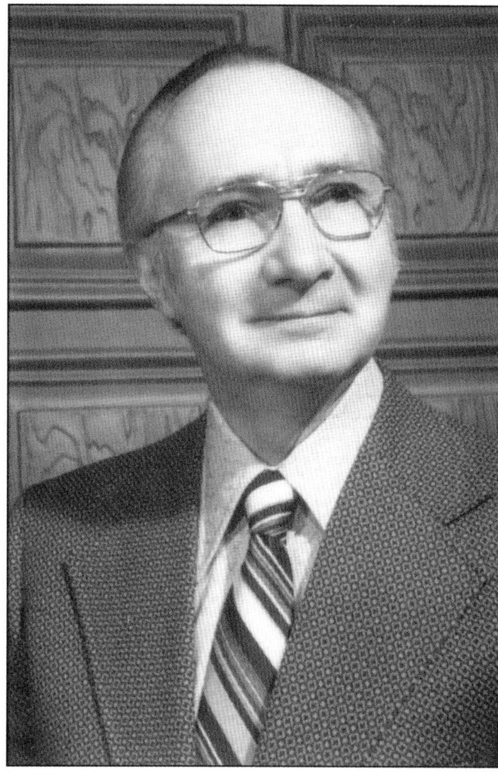

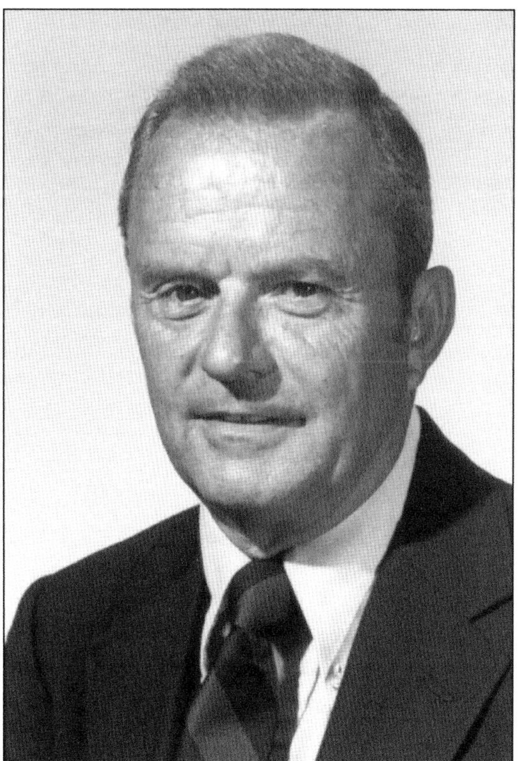

Dr. George D. Wolf, c. 1966–1973. Dr. Wolf, professor of American studies and history, was the first faculty member appointed to the Capitol Campus in September 1966. He was one of the original eight faculty members at the Harrisburg campus and served as dean of faculty from 1973 to 1978. He retired from the university in June 1983.

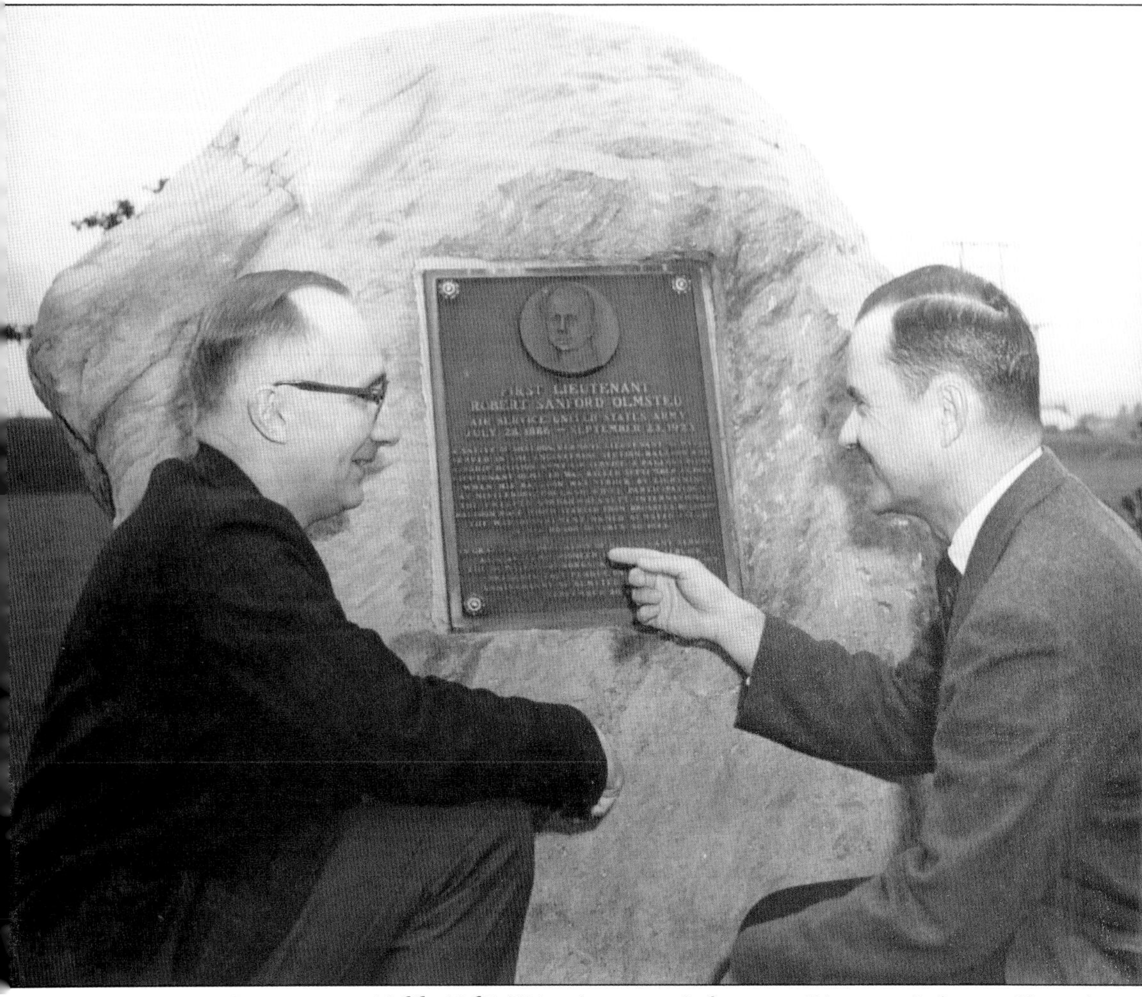

HONORING OLMSTED, c. 1966–1967. This photograph features Director Coleman Herpel (left) and Dr. George D. Wolf on the lawn in front of the Olmsted Building and next to the original *Olmsted Monument* that honors 1st Lt. Robert Olmsted. The placard and boulder, which came from Olmsted's hometown in Sheldon, Vermont, were relocated on September 20, 1987, to the 193rd Special Operations Wing, Pennsylvania Air National Guard, at the Harrisburg International Airport.

Dr. Stanley N. Miller and Dr. Daniel Walden, c. 1966–1968. Created to educate juniors, seniors, and graduate students, the Capitol Campus was the first combination upper division and graduate school established in Pennsylvania and one of only three in the United States. The first classes for the 1966–1967 academic year were officially held on October 3, 1966, on the first floor of the Olmsted Building, with a total of 18 undergraduates (juniors and seniors) and 165 graduate students. During its first year, the Capitol Campus hired eight faculty members to teach courses in English, French, history, humanities, philosophy, and social sciences. Pictured here are two of the original eight faculty members: Dr. Miller (right), who taught social sciences and education, and Dr. Walden (below), who was hired to teach classes in the social sciences and history.

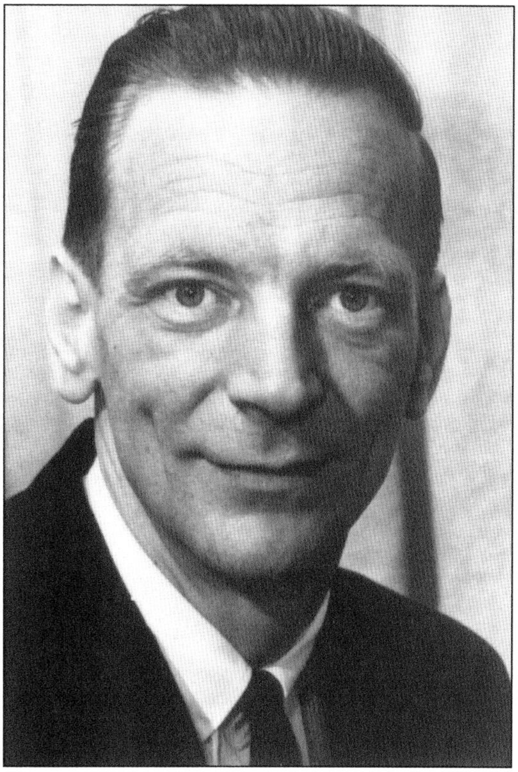

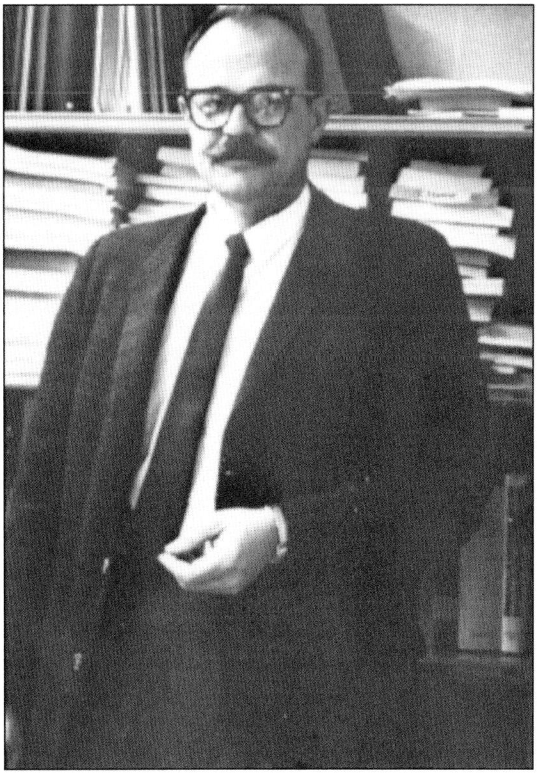

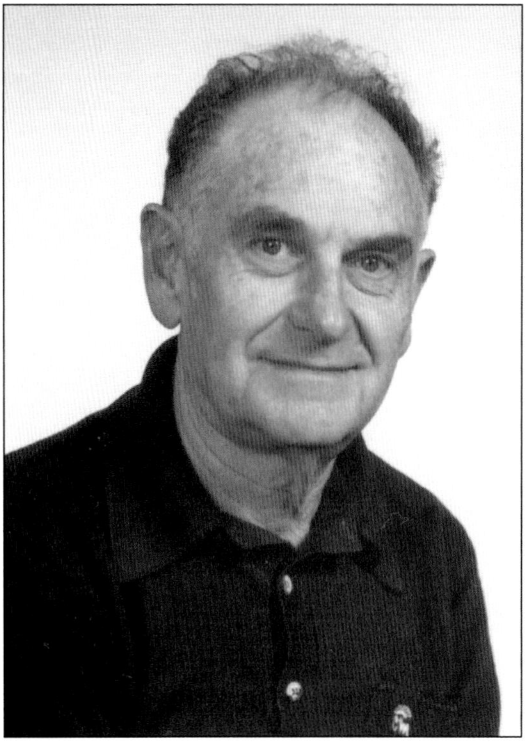

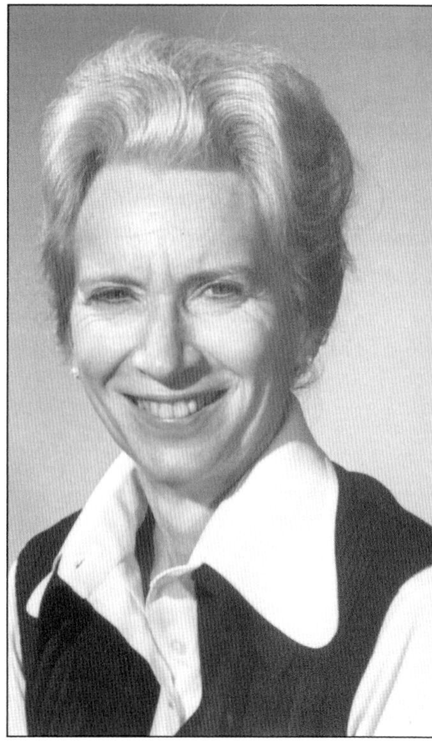

Prof. Murray Budney and Dr. Nancy Tischler, c. 1966–1969. In addition to hiring Dr. George Wolf, Dr. Stanley Miller, and Dr. Daniel Walden, the campus hired five additional faculty for the 1966–1967 academic year. They included Budney (above left), professor of French and humanities; Dr. Carl Hausman, professor of philosophy; Dr. George Larimer, professor of social science; Paul J. Reichwein, instructor in physical education; and Dr. Tischler (above right), professor of English and humanities.

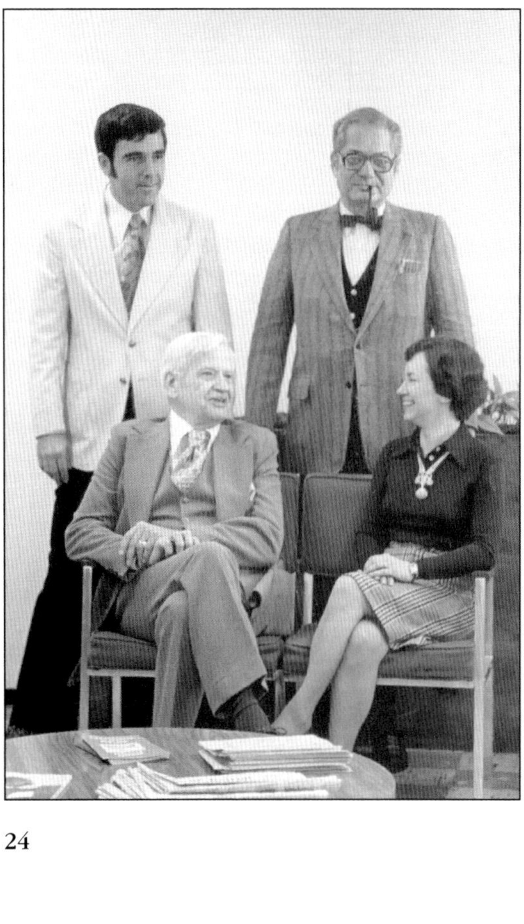

Dr. Richard H. Heindel and Dr. Irving Hand, c. 1969–1970. Pictured here are two additional faculty members who were instrumental in the early formation of the Capitol Campus. Seated at left is Dr. Heindel, who served as the first dean of faculty (from 1967 to 1973) and served the college as professor of international relations from 1967 to 1977. Standing at right is Dr. Hand, professor of state and regional planning.

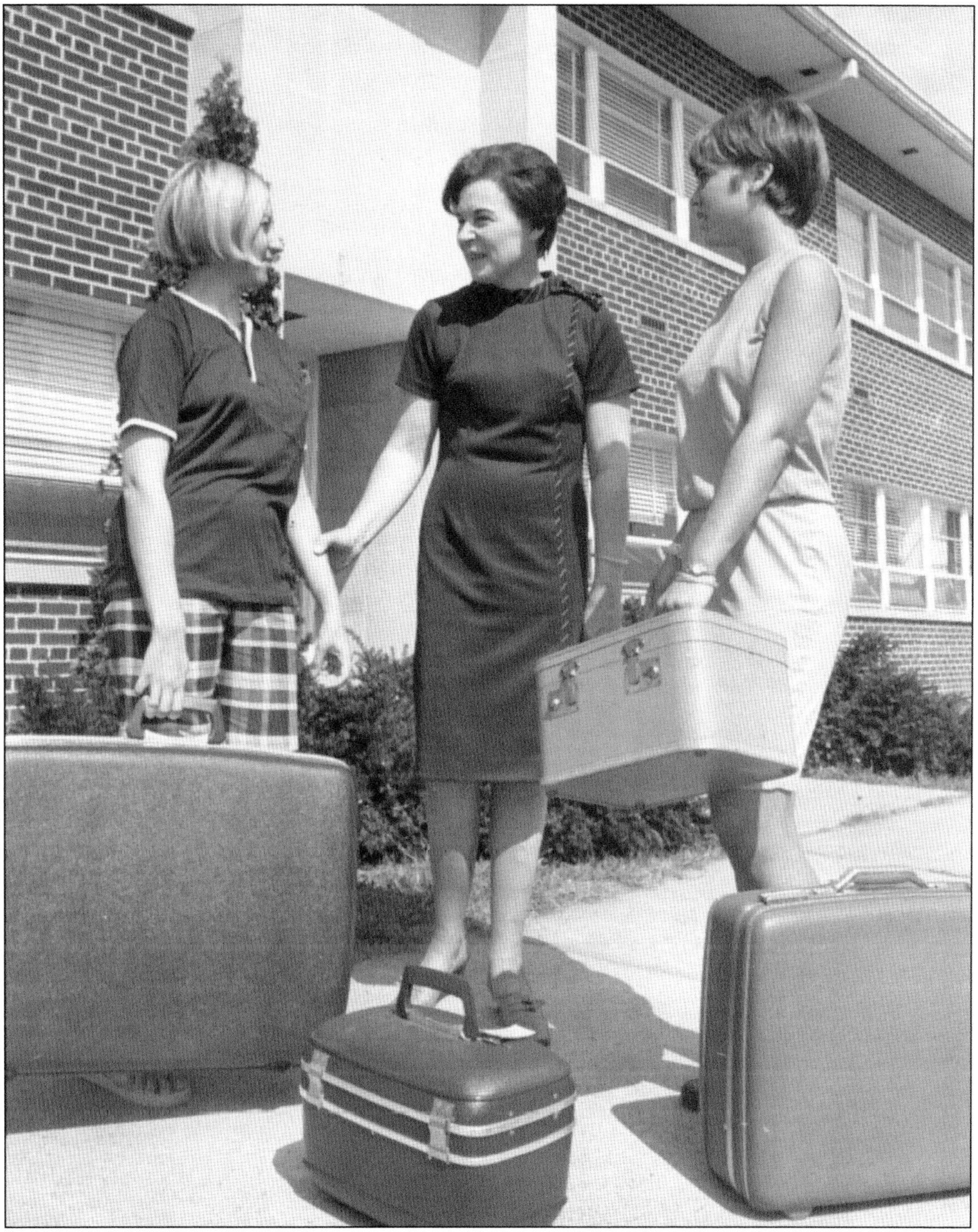

Student Orientation, 1967. When students arrived at Capitol Campus for the second academic year (1967–1968), the Meade Heights complex was not yet available as a residence hall. Instead, during fall 1967, a total of 138 male students moved into Wrisberg Hall and the third floor of Church Hall; 49 female students moved into the former Bachelor Officers' Quarters (BOQ), which the college later renamed the University Apartments. This September 17, 1967, photograph of two female students and a campus staff member provides a glimpse into college life during student orientation week. In the background is the facade of the BOQ-turned-University Apartments, which was used as a female-only residence hall and apartments for faculty. Today, it functions as the Educational Activities Building, more commonly called the EAB.

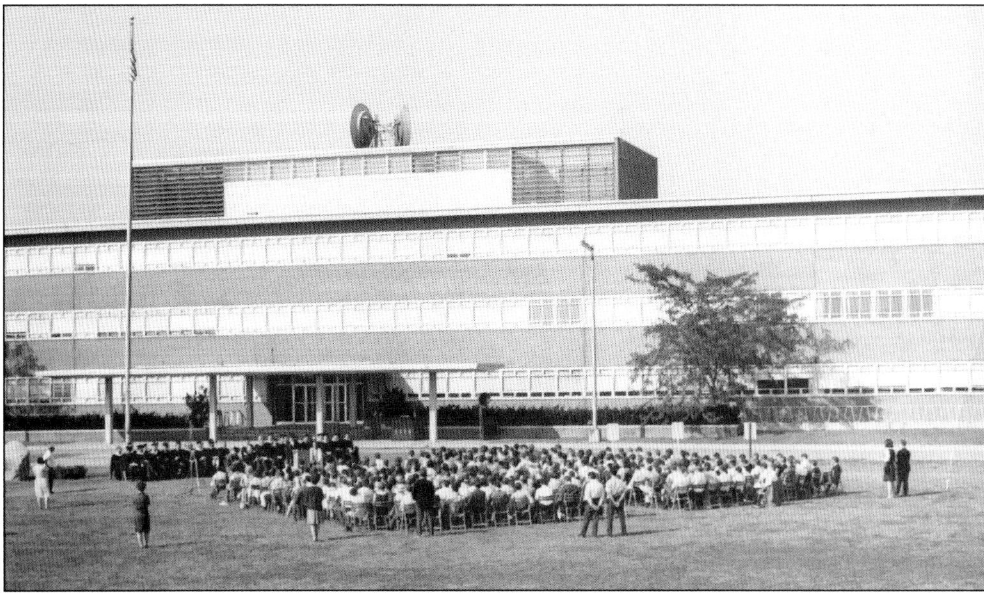

First Convocation Ceremony, 1967. The second year of classes began on September 25, 1967, with student enrollment more than tripling from 183 students (18 undergraduates) in 1966 to 564 students (337 undergraduates) in 1967. The year also marked the introduction of the bachelor of elementary education and bachelor of social science programs. On Wednesday, October 4, 1967, the school held its first convocation ceremony in front of the Olmsted Building.

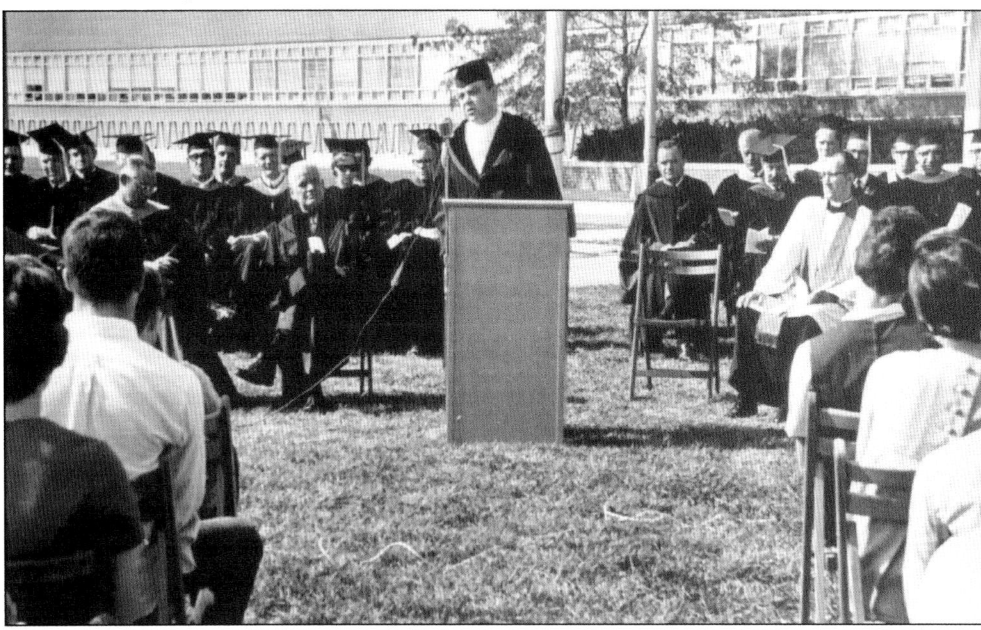

First Convocation Address, 1967. On October 4, 1967, the convocation address was provided by Dr. Luther Evans, former UNESCO director-general. In this photograph, seated to the left of Dr. Evans is Dr. Eric Walker, president of the Pennsylvania State University, and Dr. Richard H. Heindel, the first dean of faculty at Penn State Harrisburg. To the right of Dr. Evans, seated in the back row, is Dr. George Wolf.

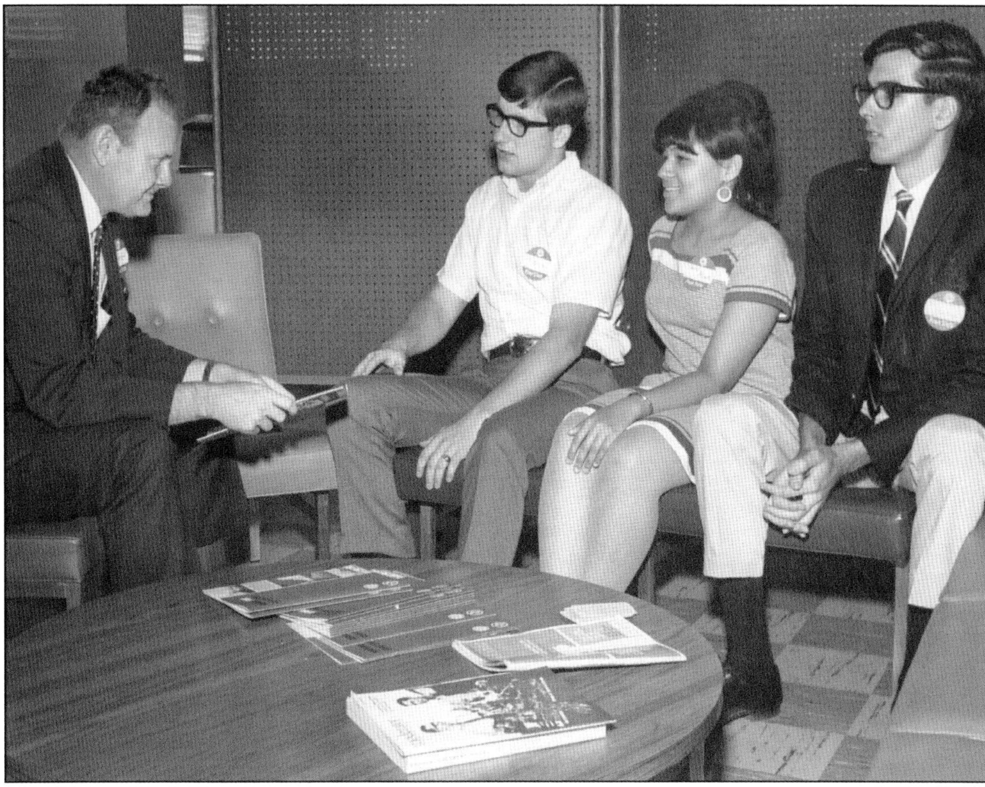

Dr. Saylor and Students, 1967. As the school continued to grow, more faculty were hired for the 1967–1968 academic year. Pictured here are, from left to right, Dr. Roger B. Saylor, professor of statistics and economics, who left the University Park campus in 1967 to establish and chair Harrisburg's business program, and several students: Jay Bowden, business; Cheryl Myers, special science; and Thomas Borstman, secondary education.

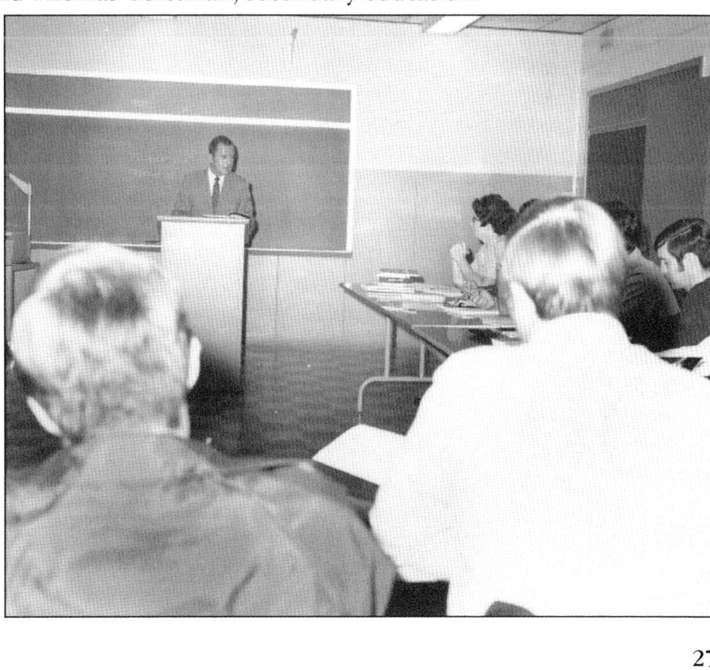

Dr. George Wolf Teaching, 1967. Students attended classes in the Olmsted Building on campus. This photograph highlights the typical classroom and facilities available to students at Capitol Campus in the late 1960s. Teaching in a pre-Internet classroom, Dr. Wolf stands at a traditional lecture podium in front of a chalkboard with an early example of an overhead projector at left.

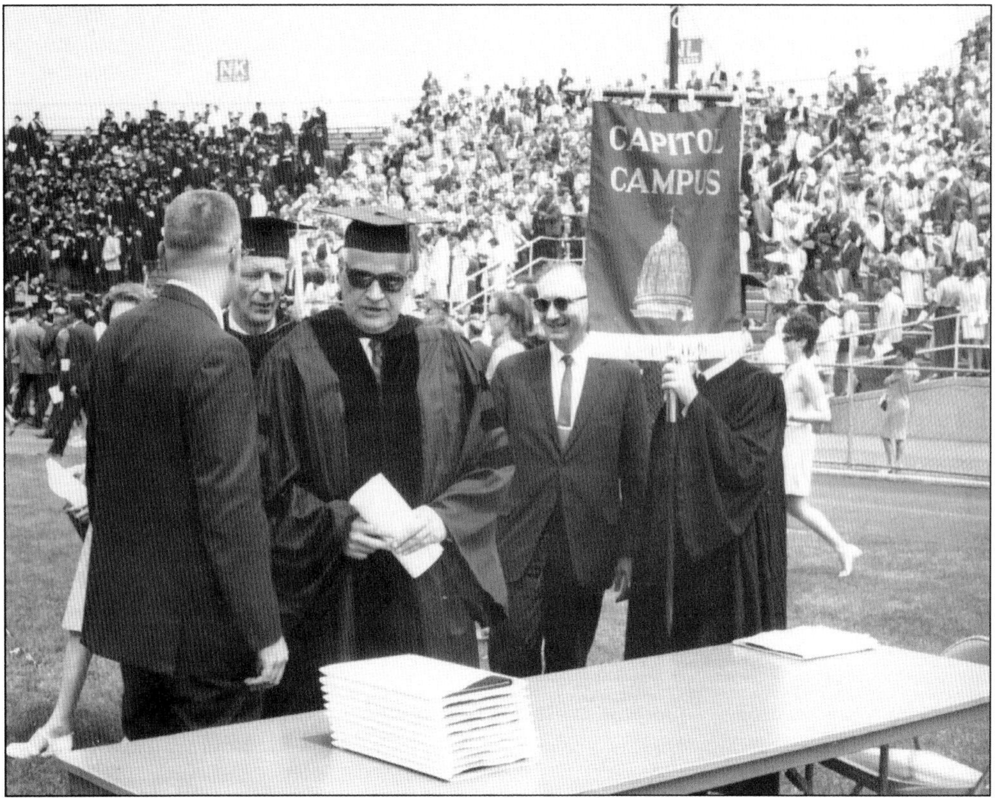

First Commencement Ceremony, 1968. In June 1968, twelve of the original 18 undergraduate students from Capitol Campus travelled to the campus in State College to receive their diplomas—the first ones awarded to graduates of the Capitol Campus. The commencement ceremony was held in Penn State's Beaver Stadium, which opened in 1960. In attendance (as shown in the above image) were Capitol Campus' administrators and faculty Dr. Stanley Miller (left), Dr. Richard Heindel (center), and director Coleman Herpel. Hidden from view (but holding the Capitol Campus commencement banner at right) is one of Capitol Campus' first graduates, David R. Powell. The photograph below, taken after the commencement ceremony, features Powell (left), Dr. Heindel (center), and Dr. Miller (right) standing in the field at Beaver Stadium with the football scoreboard visible in the distance.

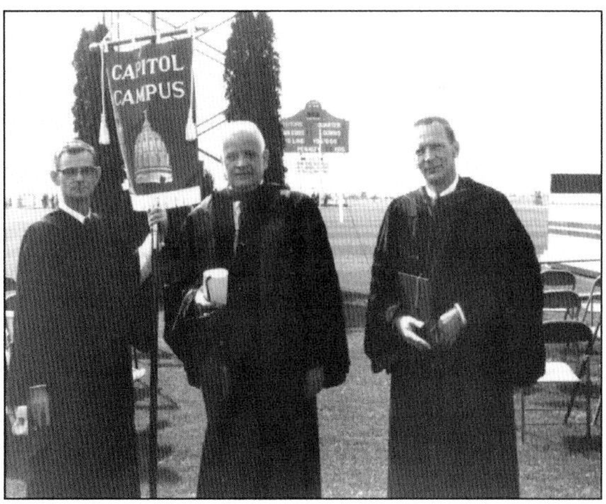

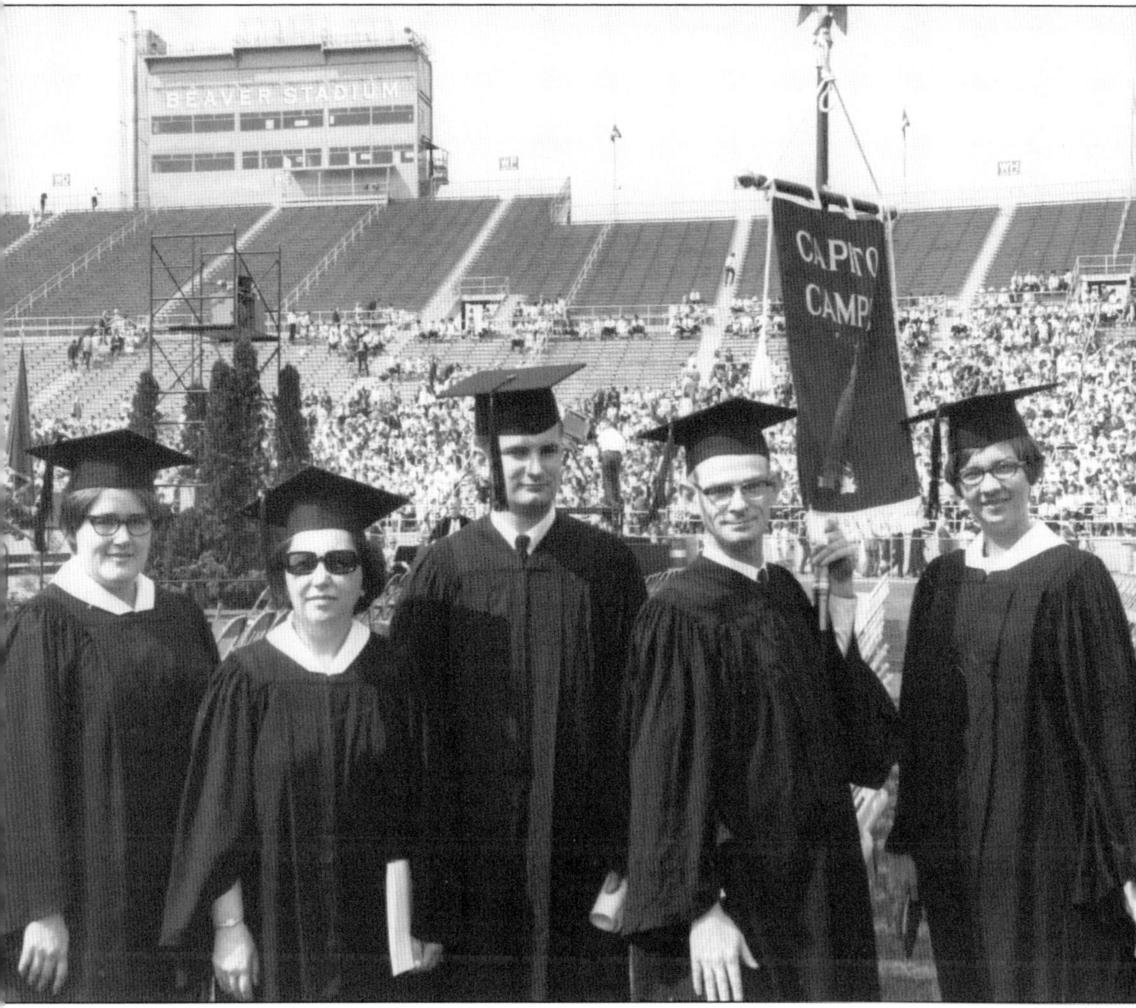

Capitol Campus Graduates, 1968. This significant group photograph in Beaver Stadium features five of the twelve Capitol Campus undergraduate students who received their diplomas during the 1968 Penn State Commencement exercises. Pictured are, from left to right, Rozan C. Brown, Lorna B. Rudisill, Paul Allen Shirk, David R. Powell, and Marie R. Furjanic.

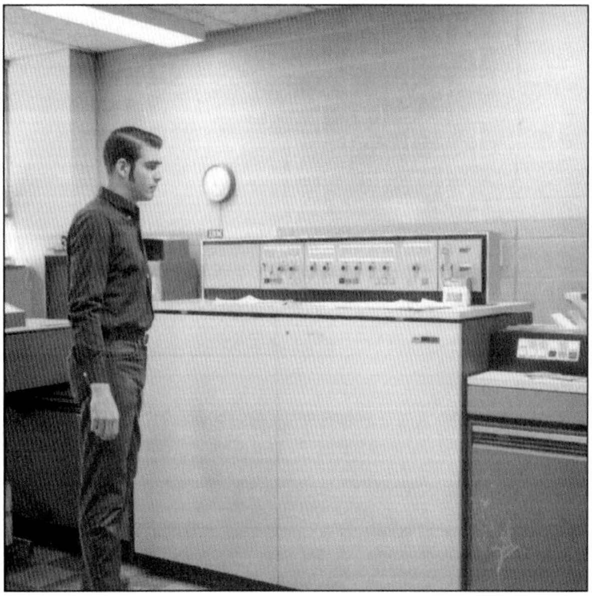

COMPUTER CENTER, 1968. Although students at the Harrisburg campus did not have computers in their everyday classrooms, this photograph provides a unique perspective on how large computing equipment was in the late 1960s. Note the enormous size of the IBM system/360 all-in-one mainframe computer in comparison to the student standing next to it.

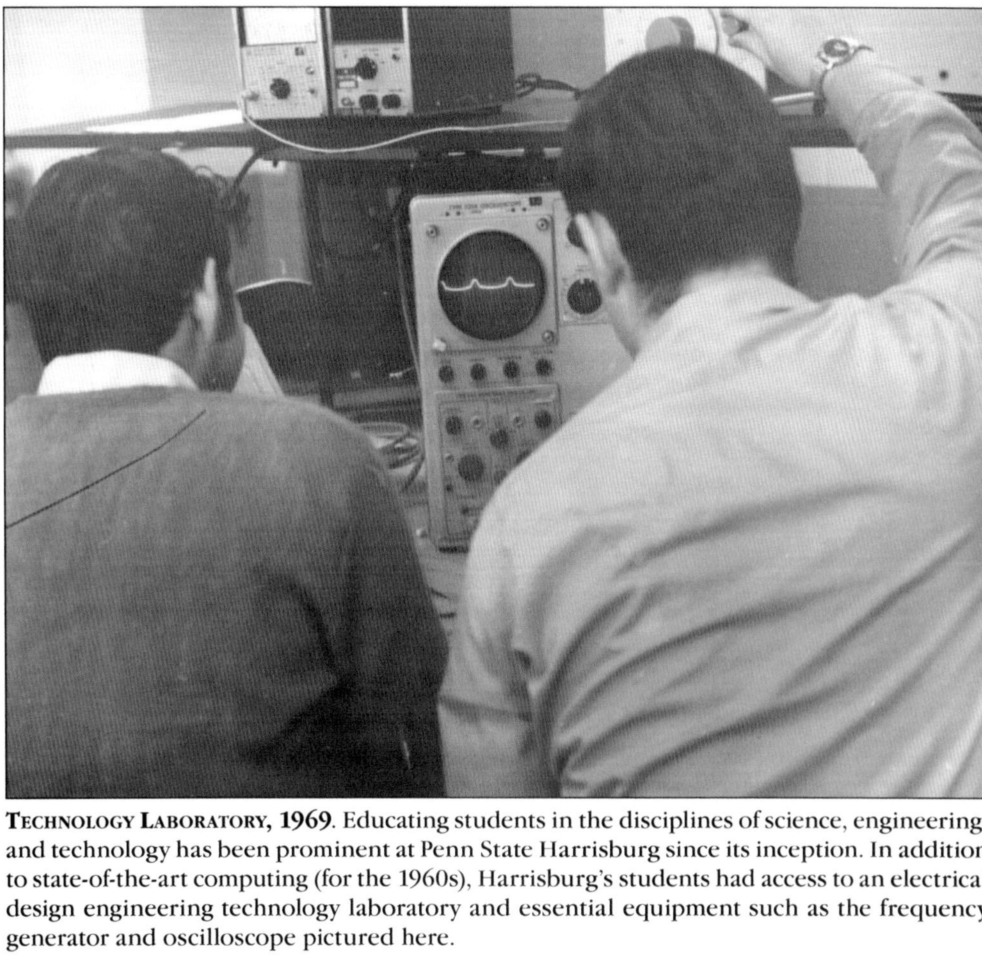

TECHNOLOGY LABORATORY, 1969. Educating students in the disciplines of science, engineering, and technology has been prominent at Penn State Harrisburg since its inception. In addition to state-of-the-art computing (for the 1960s), Harrisburg's students had access to an electrical design engineering technology laboratory and essential equipment such as the frequency generator and oscilloscope pictured here.

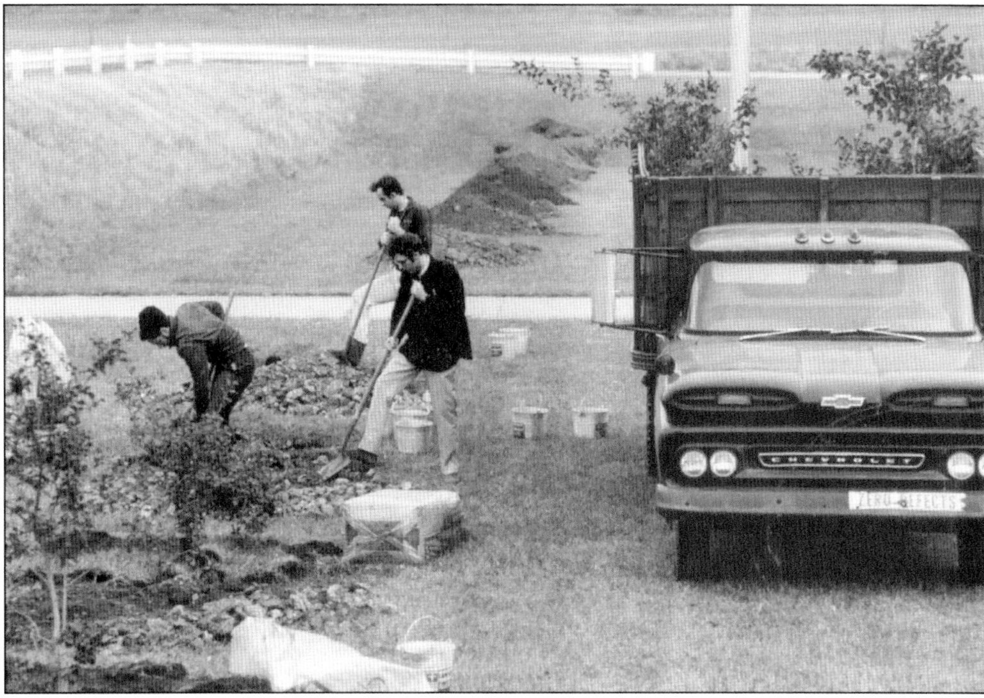

CAMPUS BEAUTIFICATION, 1969. After acquiring the Olmsted Air Force Base in 1966, the Capitol Campus gradually made improvements to the facilities and grounds. Prior to the official celebration of Earth Day throughout the United States in 1970, students at the Capitol Campus endeavored to beautify the campus one tree at a time. This image shows students planting holly trees behind the Olmsted Building in spring 1969.

FIRST COMMENCEMENT AT CAPITOL CAMPUS, 1969. At the end of the third academic year, 1968–1969, the school held its first commencement exercises on campus. The ceremony took place on Friday, June 19, 1969, in front of the Olmsted Building. The school awarded 251 bachelor's degrees, with 55 graduates earning degrees in engineering technology, followed by 68 in business, 68 in social sciences, 55 in elementary education, and 5 in humanities.

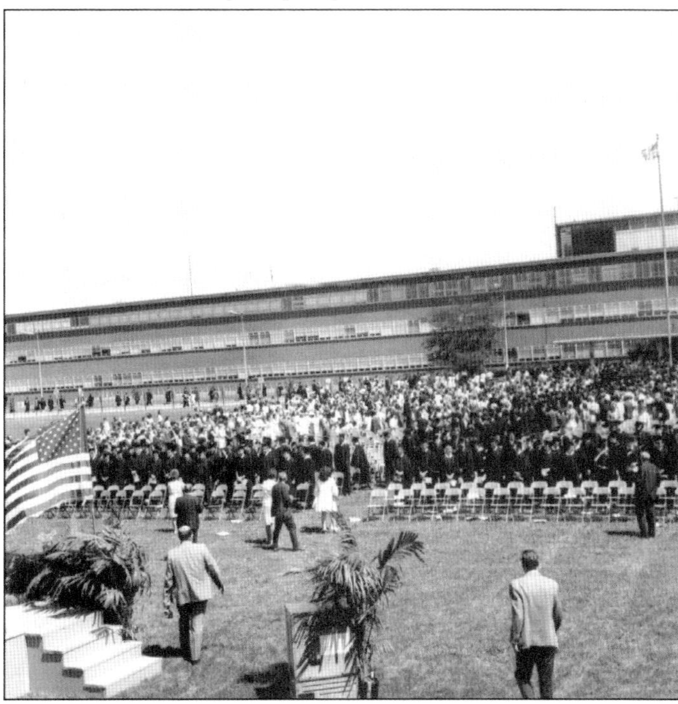

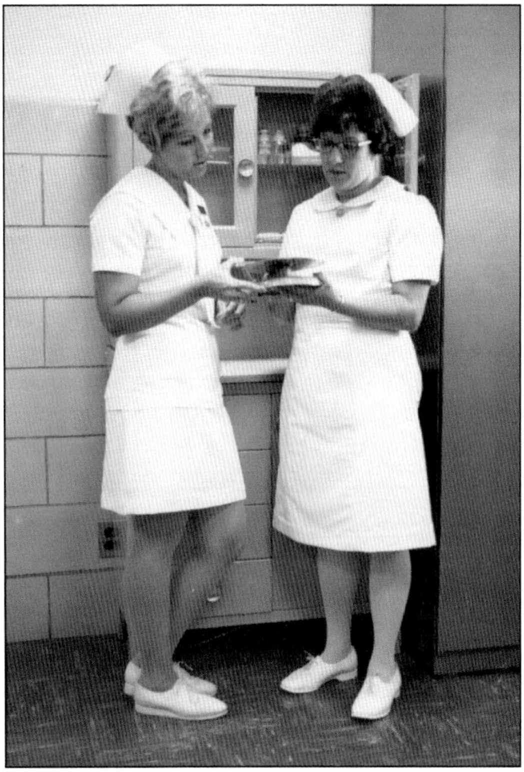

CAPITOL CAMPUS NURSES, 1969. By fall 1969, the fourth academic year at Penn State Harrisburg, Capitol Campus was thriving and bustling with over 1,100 undergraduate students. In order to provide important services for a growing community of students, the first student health services center opened in the Olmsted Building. Pictured here are nurses Charlotte McElroth (left) and Eleanor Long (right).

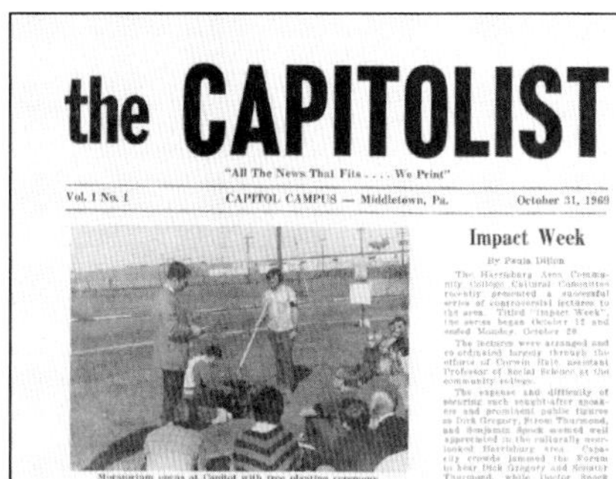

the CAPITOLIST

"All The News That Fits . . . . We Print"

Vol. 1 No. 1 — CAPITOL CAMPUS — Middletown, Pa. — October 31, 1969

Moratorium opens at Capitol with tree planting ceremony.

Campus Participates in Moratorium

Impact Week

By Paula Dillon

Do You Want to Vote?

XGI's In Action

FIRST ISSUE OF THE *CAPITOLIST*, 1969. During the first three academic years (1966–1969) at Capitol Campus, communication among students, faculty, and administrators was facilitated by the student newspaper, which was published inconsistently under the names *Angst*, *Vox*, and the *Capitol Cap*. However, a formal effort to produce a student newspaper began on October 31, 1969, when the first issue of the *Capitolist* was published.

Three

Thriving in Turbulent Times

1970–1979

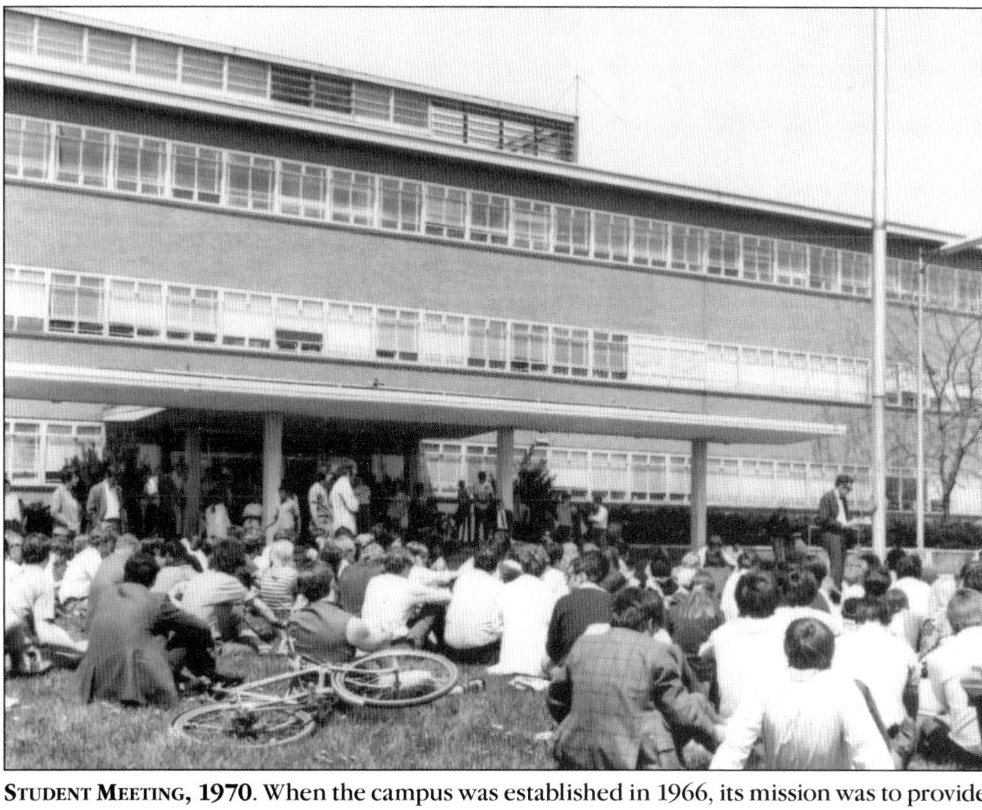

Student Meeting, 1970. When the campus was established in 1966, its mission was to provide innovative and interdisciplinary programs as a unique undergraduate and graduate center. As a result, juniors, seniors, and graduate students would regularly interact with each other, as illustrated in this photograph of a student meeting held during spring 1970 on the lawn in front of the Olmsted Building.

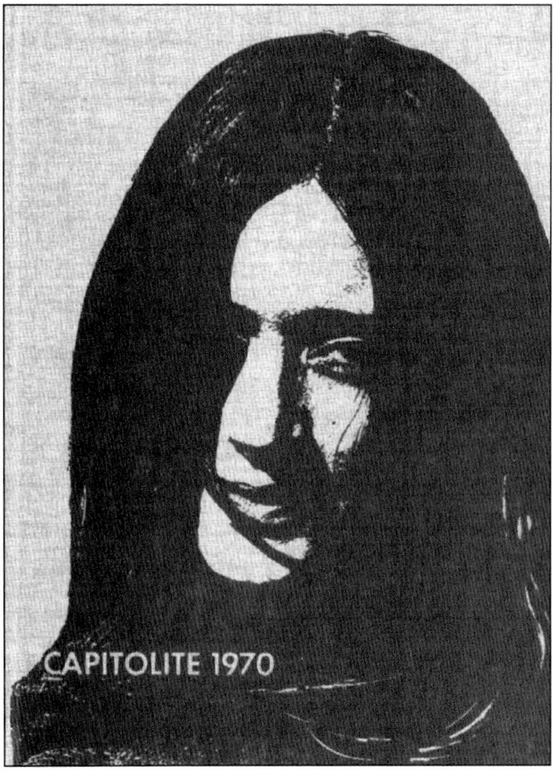

EARLY *CAPITOLITE* YEARBOOK, 1970. The student yearbook at Capitol Campus, known initially as the *Capitolite* and later in 1986–1987 as the *Capitalite*, when the school changed its name, was published from 1968 through 1995 and survives as a record of students' academic and social activities. The image of a female student that graces the cover of this 1970 yearbook is iconic for the "Me" decade, which included numerous social changes inspired by the hippie and feminist movements.

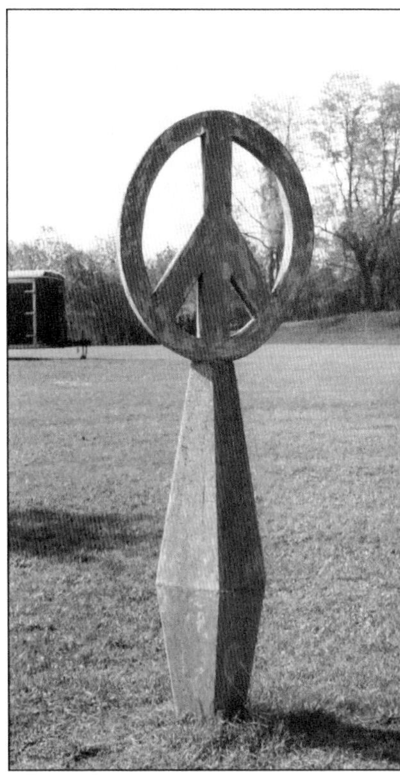

***PEACE SYMBOL MONUMENT*, C. 1970–1971.** Designed in 1970 by the "Capitol Campus Six," a group of water resources students at the Capitol Campus, and made of concrete donated by Pennsy Supply, Inc., of Harrisburg, the *Peace Symbol Monument* originally stood behind the Olmsted Building. It is now located near the Engineering Technology Laboratory on campus. The monument, a student plea for peace during the Vietnam War, stands 85 inches tall.

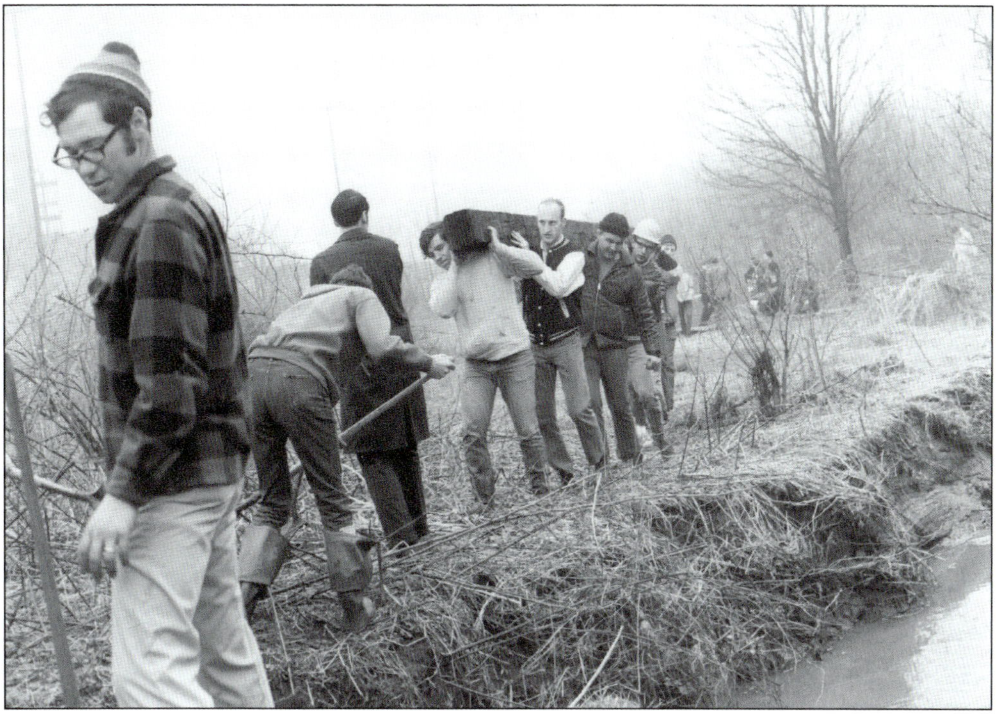

FERTILITY DAY AND *NITTANY LION SHRINE*, 1970. On April 21, 1970, before the first official Earth Day, students gathered to beautify the campus. However, they called it "Fertility Day." The above photograph shows students removing an old railroad tie on the school's grounds. Professors permitted students to miss classes if they participated. The Class of 1970 and Penn State president Dr. Eric A. Walker gifted the Capitol Campus' first *Nittany Lion Shrine* (below), a miniature replica of the famous Heinz Warneke sculpture in State College. Located in the lobby of the Olmsted Building, its placard reads: "This statue memorializes the mountain lions which roamed the hills around Nittany Valley before the University was founded there in 1855. At Capitol it symbolizes the continuation of an honored tradition of the University and the young strength of the student body."

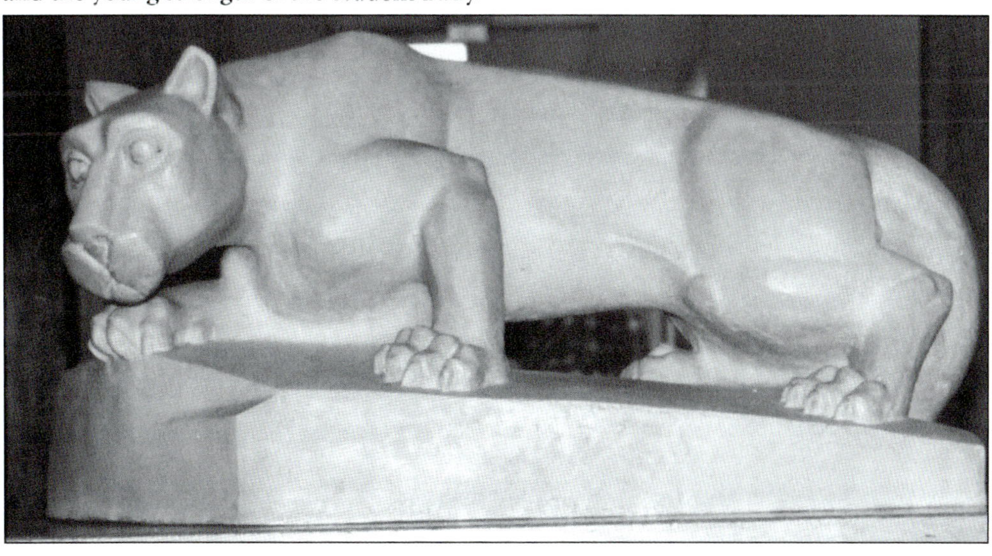

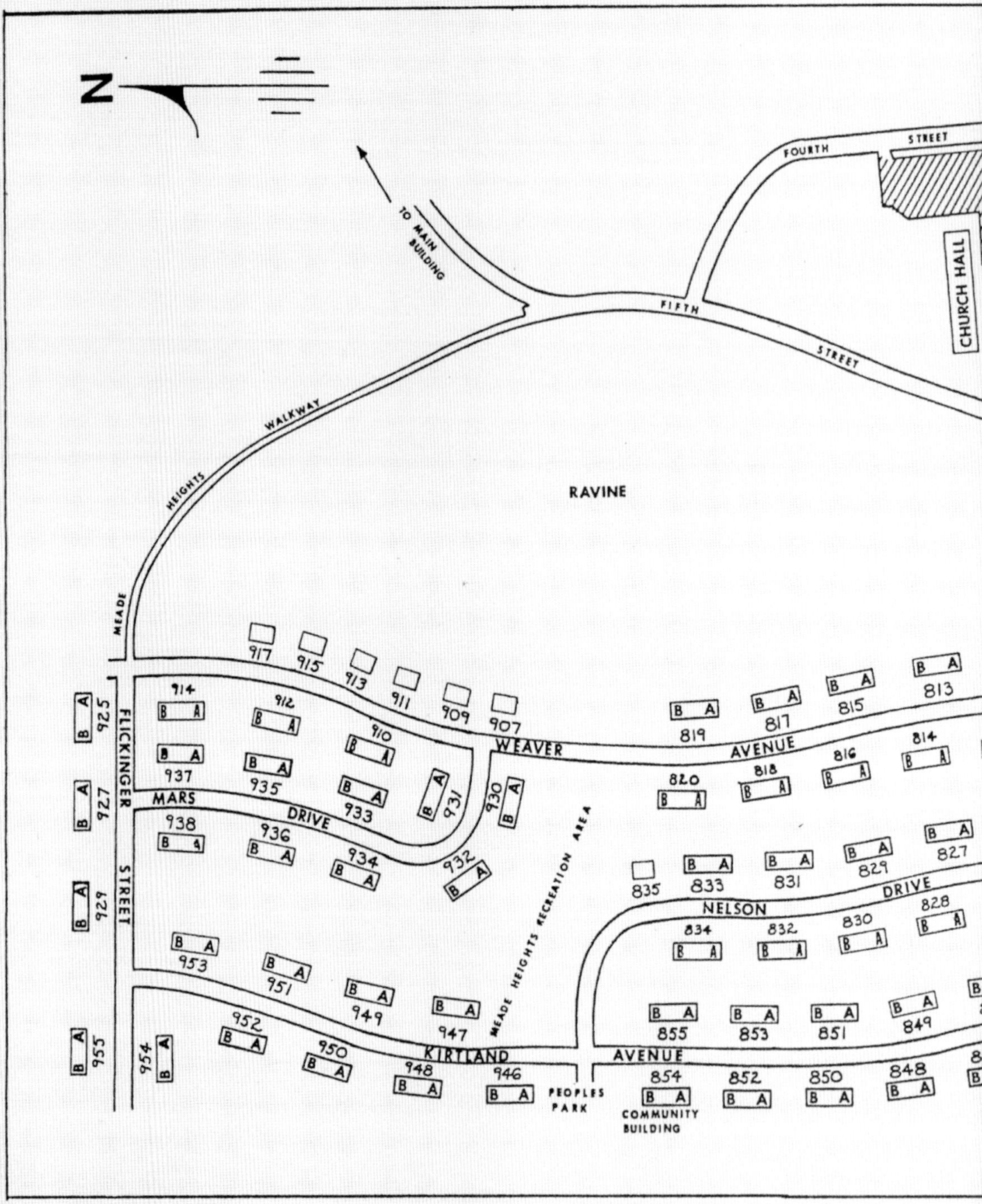
N
TO MAIN BUILDING
FOURTH STREET
CHURCH HALL
FIFTH STREET
HEIGHTS WALKWAY
MEADE
RAVINE
917
915
913
911
909
907
914
912
910
925
FLICKINGER STREET
937
935
933
931
930
WEAVER AVENUE
819
817
815
813
820
818
816
814
927
MARS DRIVE
938
936
934
932
929
MEADE HEIGHTS RECREATION AREA
835
833
831
829
827
NELSON DRIVE
834
832
830
828
953
951
949
947
855
853
851
849
955
954
952
950
948
946
KIRTLAND AVENUE
854
852
850
848
PEOPLES PARK
COMMUNITY BUILDING

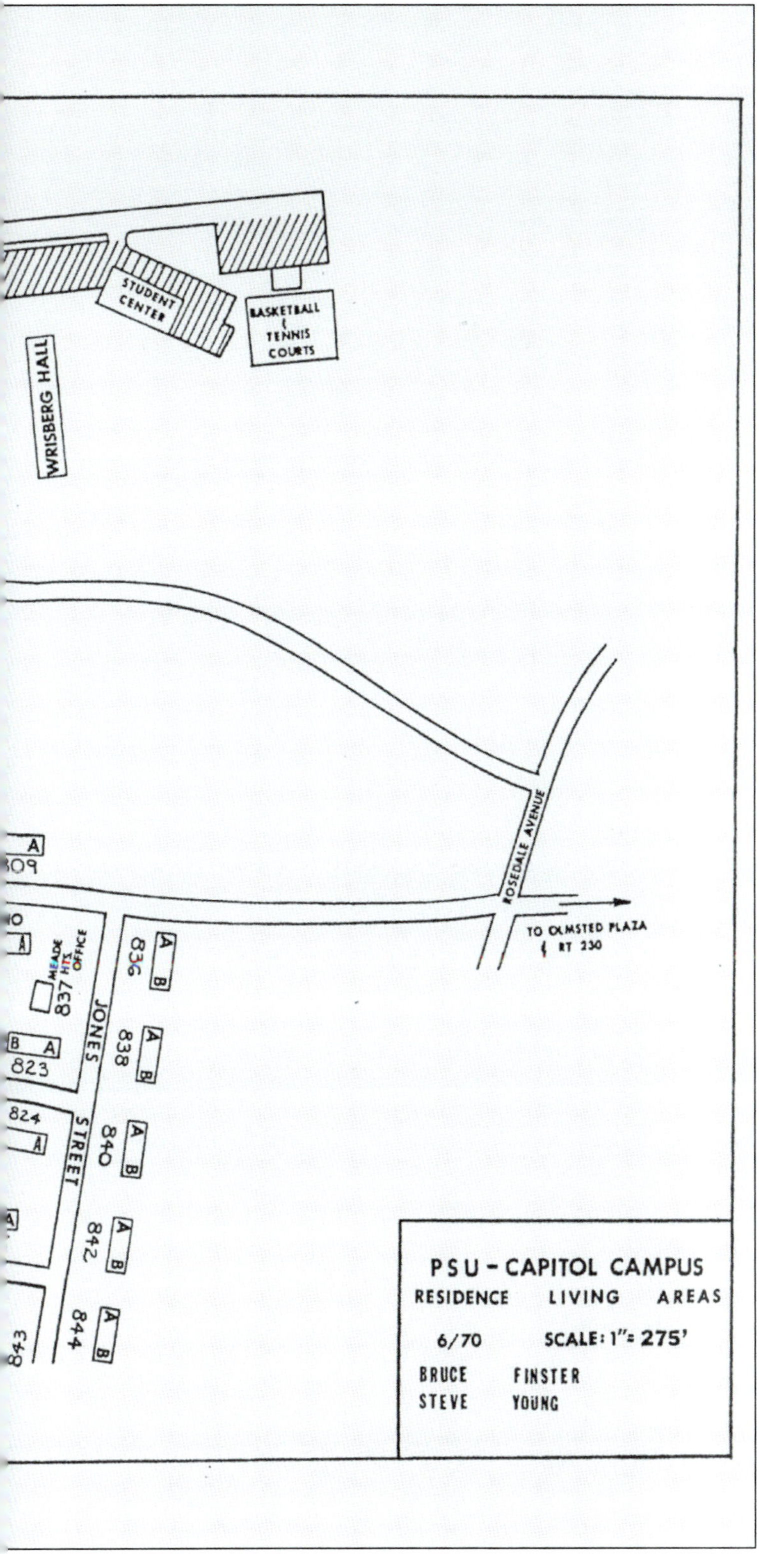

Map of Meade Heights, 1970. When the University purchased the former Olmsted Air Force Base in 1966, the acquisition of land and buildings did not include the Meade Heights housing complex. Instead, the west region of campus was acquired from the US Department of Defense on November 26, 1968, for $1,175,000 and included 40 acres with 140 family housing units. The purchase of Meade Heights increased the size of the campus from 177.5 to 217.5 acres with a total of 90 buildings. In this June 1970 map of Meade Heights, the lasting influence of the Olmsted Air Force Base is evident. Roads in the complex were named after officers, such as Mars Drive, named in honor of Col. James A. Mars, commanding officer from 1919 to 1920, when the base was called the Aviation General Supply Depot.

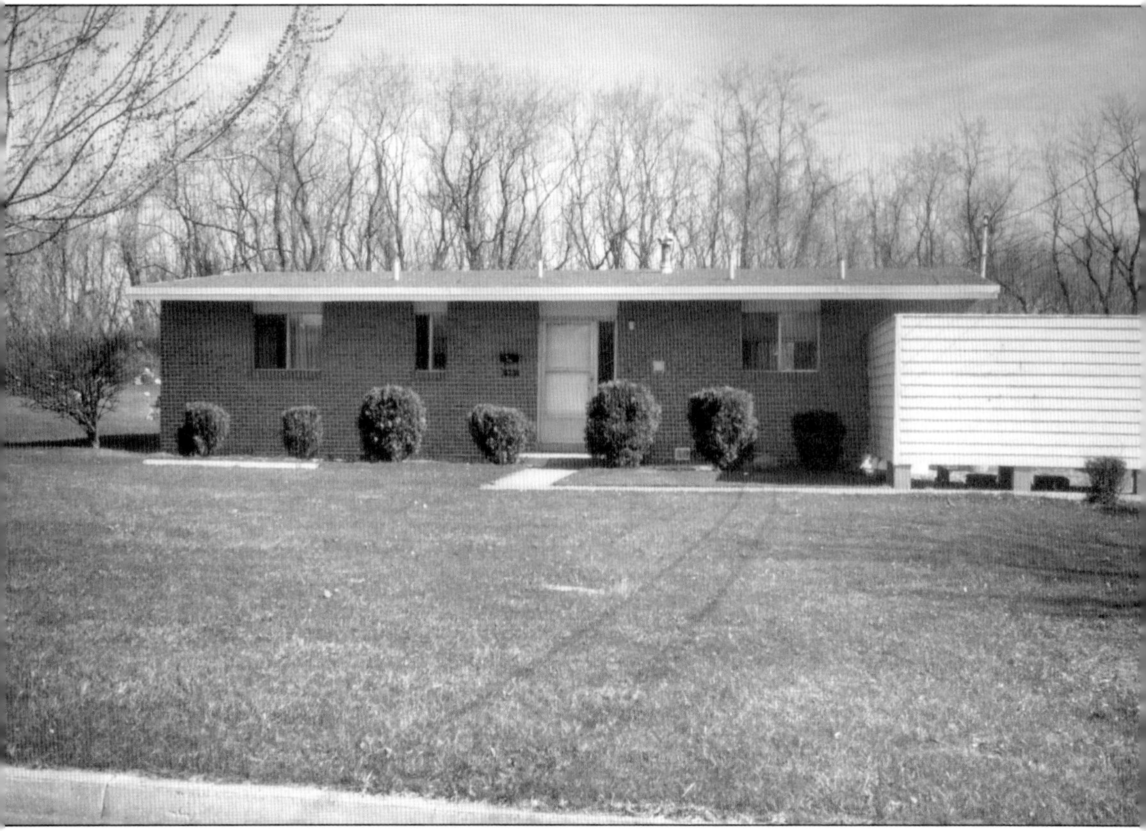

HOUSING IN MEADE HEIGHTS, C. 1970–1975. Although Meade Heights was built by the US Air Force between 1958 and 1960, students at Capitol Campus did not live there until 1970, when a board of governors was created to assist with the complex's day-to-day management. It was a unique "learning-living environment," with some houses occupied by students while others were home to faculty and their families. This photograph shows a typical duplex, ranch-style house. Each side of the house (A and B) was large enough for four people and featured a floor plan with three bedrooms, one bathroom, a kitchen, and a common living area. Two noteworthy elements of each house were the lack of insulation and the sliding patio doors, housing details considered undesirable in Pennsylvania, especially during the cold winter months. A long-standing legend states that the design plans for Meade Heights were intended for a warmer climate and accidentally switched with those for the Homestead Air Force Base, located in Homestead, Florida, which was destroyed in 1992 by Hurricane Andrew and rebuilt in 1994.

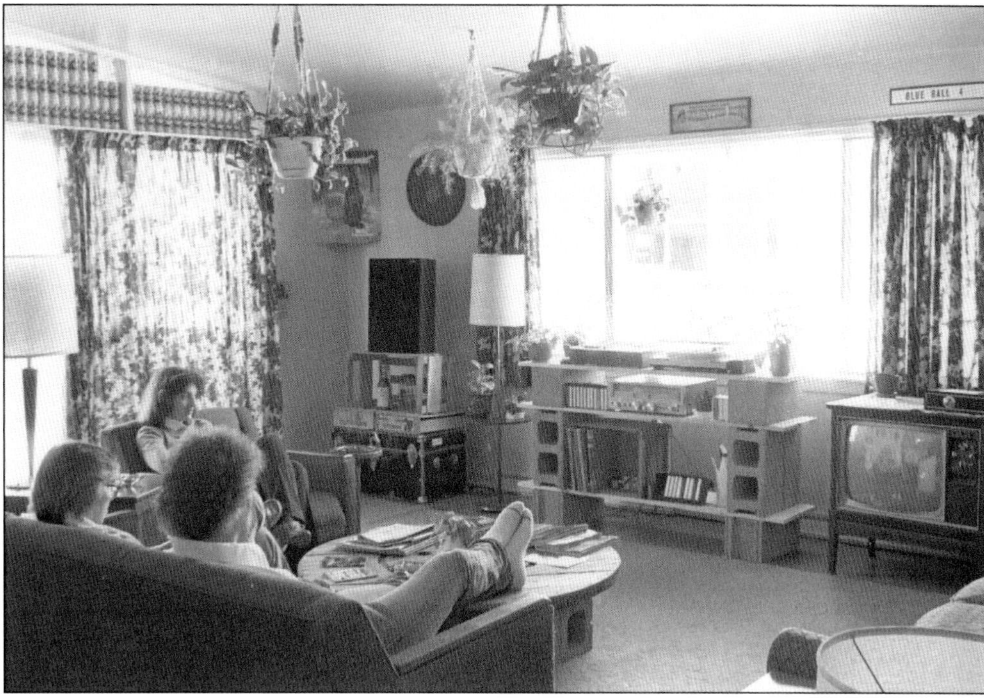

Student Life in Meade Heights, c. 1970–1975. With a student body comprised of juniors, seniors, and graduate students during the 1970s, the average age of a Capitol Campus student was 26. Meade Heights was a popular option for housing, as many students balanced work and family obligations and the demands of pursuing a graduate degree. This lifestyle was most prevalent in the Meade Heights neighborhood, sometimes called "The Heights," where studying and weekend social activities were pursued with equal intensity. In this view of a common living area (above), several students are relaxing and watching television. The makeshift cinder-block shelving, hanging indoor plants, large stereo equipment, patterned curtains, and beer cans stacked above the windows (at upper left) are iconic for the 1970s. The photograph below features a classic Volkswagen Beetle and depicts a student gathering on the lawn.

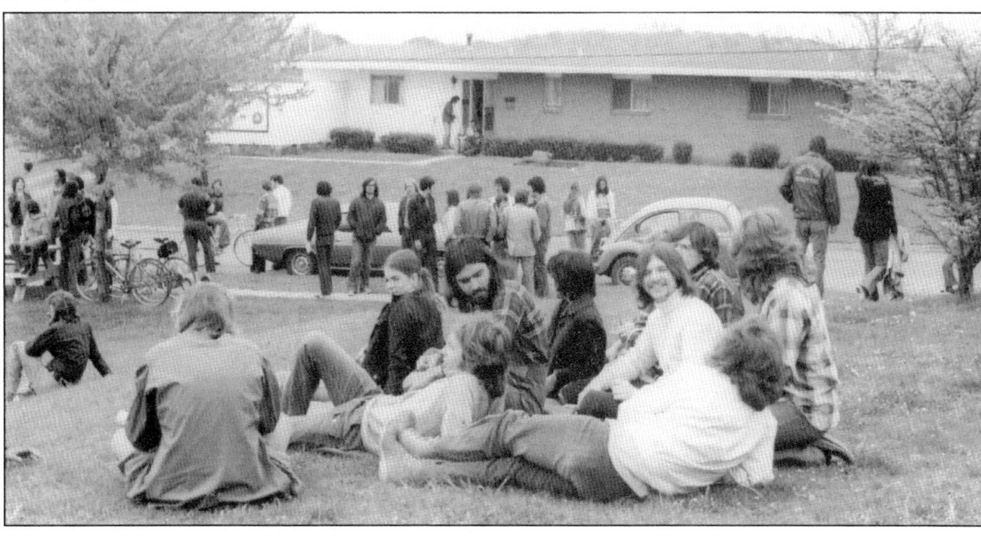

the CAPITOLIST

"All The News That Fits . . . . We Print"

Vol. 3, No. 1 — CAPITOL CAMPUS - MIDDLETOWN, PA. — Wednesday, May 26, 1971

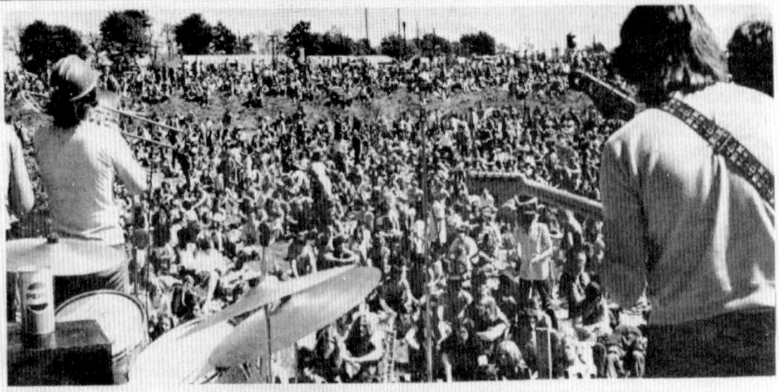

HARRISBURG ROCK FESTIVAL—Sunshine, Music, and Goodpeople combined to make Sunday a beautiful day!!

On Behalf of the Campus and Community,
The Capitolist Wishes to thank:

Good People Productions

Howie Weitz — *Don Lewis*
Mike Beckner — *Mike Bauer*

Head Shop
Student Marshalls
Concession People
Announcers
Sound Technicians
Light Show People
Student Affairs
The Jesus People
Social Committee
Jim Paul, Russ Rorbaugh & Co

Big City Music Band
Locust Grove
Molly McGuires
Straight Lace
Organ Grinders
Hard Times

Shades Of Doubt
Willow Mill Park
September Morn
Shanghai
Emmie Lou Harris
Annie Ferrino

and the beautiful, beautiful Audience!

Thanks To Goodpeople Productions and the Harrisburg Rock Festival,
Capitol Campus finally may be getting it together.

HARRISBURG ROCK FESTIVAL, 1971. For most of the 1970s, students at the Capitol Campus organized a rock festival every spring in May. This tradition, which usually took place on a Sunday in front of the Olmsted Building, is one of the most celebrated events in the school's 50-year history. The student organizers, who called themselves "Good People Productions," aimed to provide a day of free music and fun because, as student and cochairman of the event, Howie Weitz, stated, "Music does bring people together." The May 26, 1971, issue of the student newspaper, the *Capitolist*, highlights the crowd of 15,000 that gathered on Sunday, May 16, 1971, for the first rock festival on campus. (Another festival was planned in 1970, but the event was hindered by bad weather.) Among the 12 performers featured that day, Emmylou Harris was the only one to receive national acclaim. Although the band Three Dog Night was supposedly going to play at the 1971 Harrisburg Rock Festival, which likely boosted attendance, the band's $2,000 performance fee was cost prohibitive.

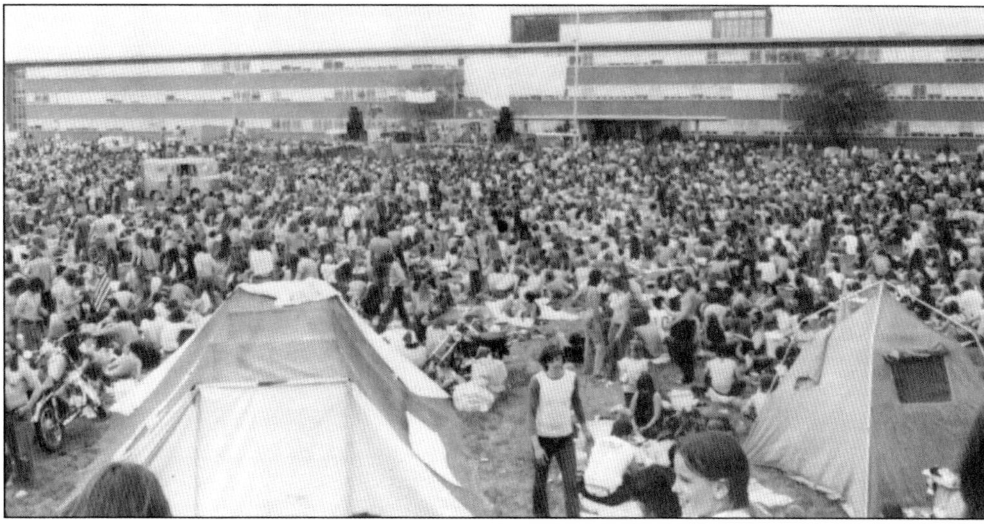

Harrisburg Rock Festival II, 1972. The second annual Harrisburg Rock Festival was held on Sunday, May 21, 1972, again in front of the Olmsted Building. Twelve hours of free music were provided to a crowd in excess of 25,000, which led to locals giving the event its informal name, "Little Woodstock." Bands from central Pennsylvania, as well as Philadelphia and Washington, DC, took the stage as Capitol Campus students, faculty, and residents from surrounding communities put up tents (above) to enjoy the festival. The poster (right) for the event features the ankh symbol (top right) of eternal life that was used by Good People Productions on T-shirts and other promotional materials. Large spring concerts on campus came to an end in fall 1978, when university administrators cited concerns about drug, alcohol, noise, and crowd-control problems.

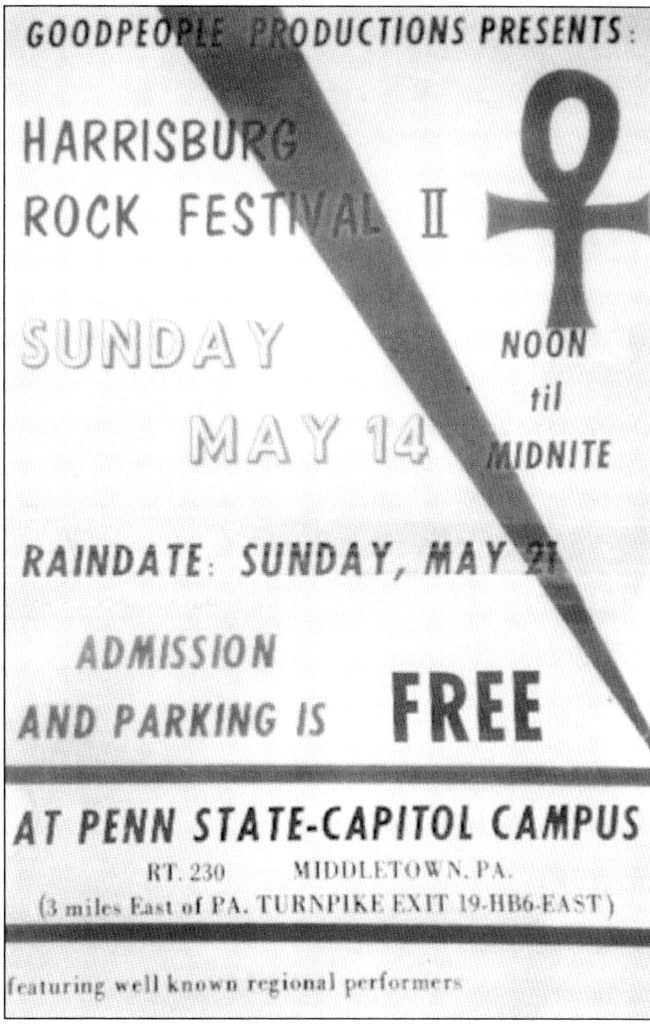

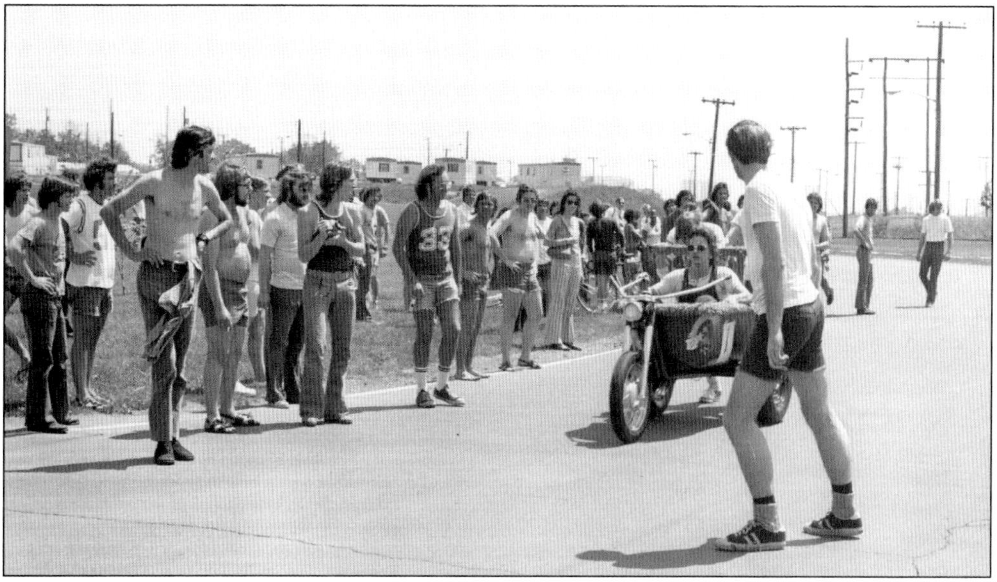

First Bathtub Race, 1972. On Wednesday, May 24, 1972, at 1:00 p.m., the first annual Bathtub Race was held on the west side of campus near the Student Center (now the Childcare Center) next to Wrisberg Hall. The race, organized by members of the student organization PSPE (Pennsylvania Society of Professional Engineers), featured five teams of students gathered for a 3.25-mile endurance test of homemade racing bathtubs. The race lasted for over 18 minutes.

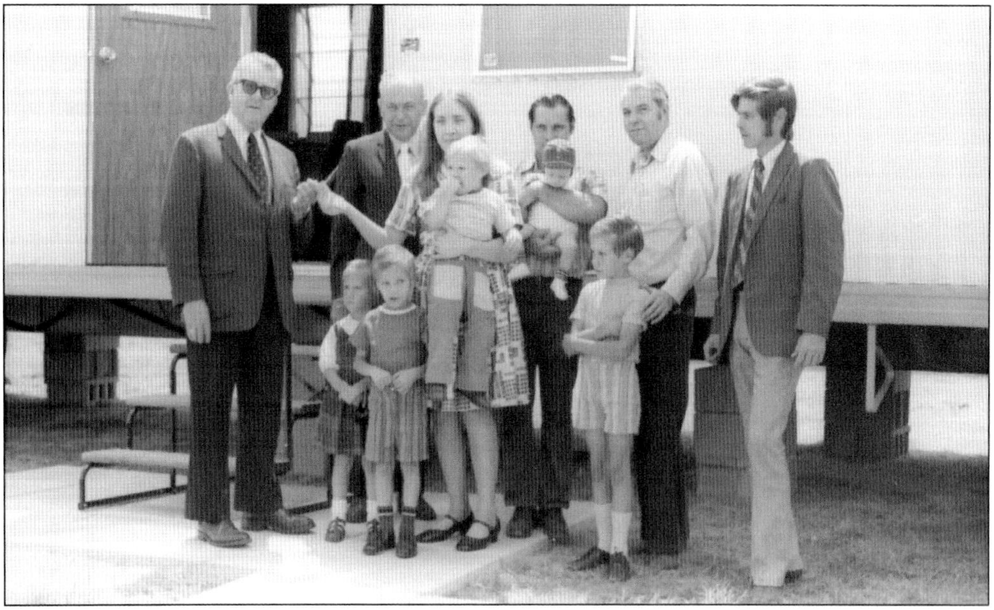

Hurricane Agnes, 1972. In June 1972, Hurricane Agnes caused disastrous flooding across Pennsylvania. The Capitol Campus responded by providing food, shelter, and supplies to over 1,000 people. When 100 local families were displaced by the flood, the school built "Capitol Campus Village" (pictured), with trailers in front of the Olmsted Building providing temporary housing. Formal graduation exercises were cancelled, but creative students held their own unofficial graduation ceremony that became known as the "Rump Commencement."

Provost Dr. Robert E. McDermott, 1972. After Director Coleman Herpel retired in June 1972 with over 40 years of service to Penn State University, Dr. McDermott was named the first provost of Capitol Campus. Although Dr. McDermott was a professor of regional planning and forestry at Penn State, he is best remembered for increasing the size of the student body. During his leadership, from 1972 to 1978, student enrollment rose from 1,500 to 2,618.

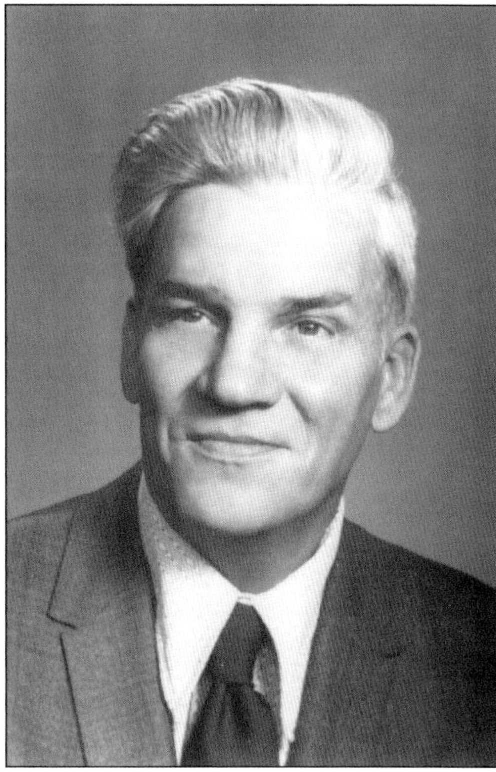

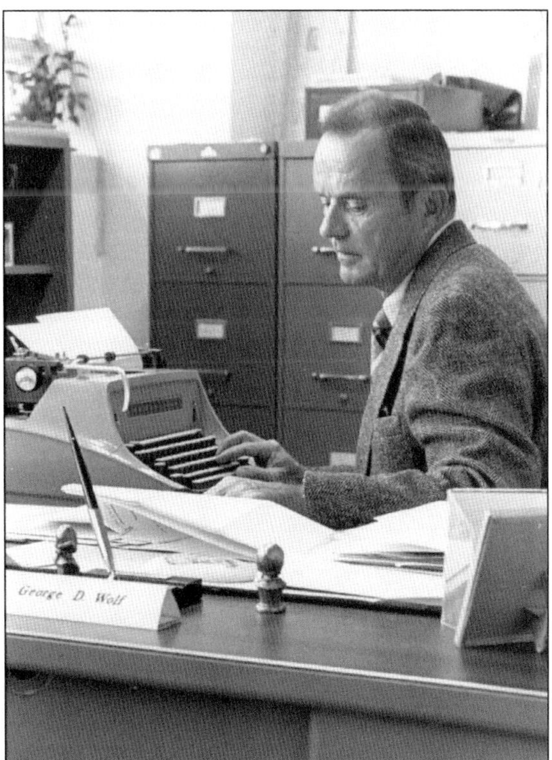

Dr. George Wolf, Dean of Faculty, c. 1973–1974. Academic programs were originally distributed across departments. However, Dr. Richard Heindel organized them into three divisions: Engineering and Technology; Administration, Business, and Regional Planning; and Humanities, Social Sciences, and Education. Dr. Wolf served as division head for Humanities, Social Sciences, and Education from 1971 to 1973. When Dr. Heindel returned to teaching in 1973, Dr. Wolf was appointed dean of faculty.

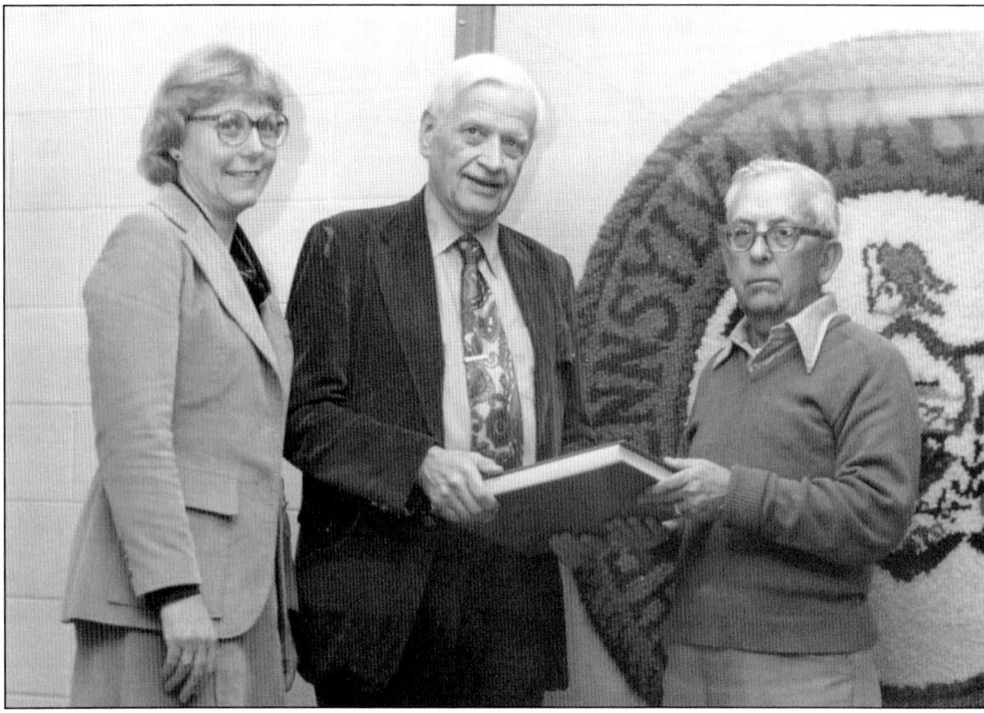

Dr. Richard Heindel and Dr. Emerson Jacob, c. 1975. Before retiring in 1977, Dr. Heindel donated some of his papers and books to the Capitol Campus library, which was then located in the Olmsted Building. Pictured here are Cecile McAree (left), wife of the late Dr. James G. McAree; Dr. Heindel (center); and Dr. Emerson Jacob (right), the first Penn State Harrisburg librarian, who served the campus from 1971 to 1979.

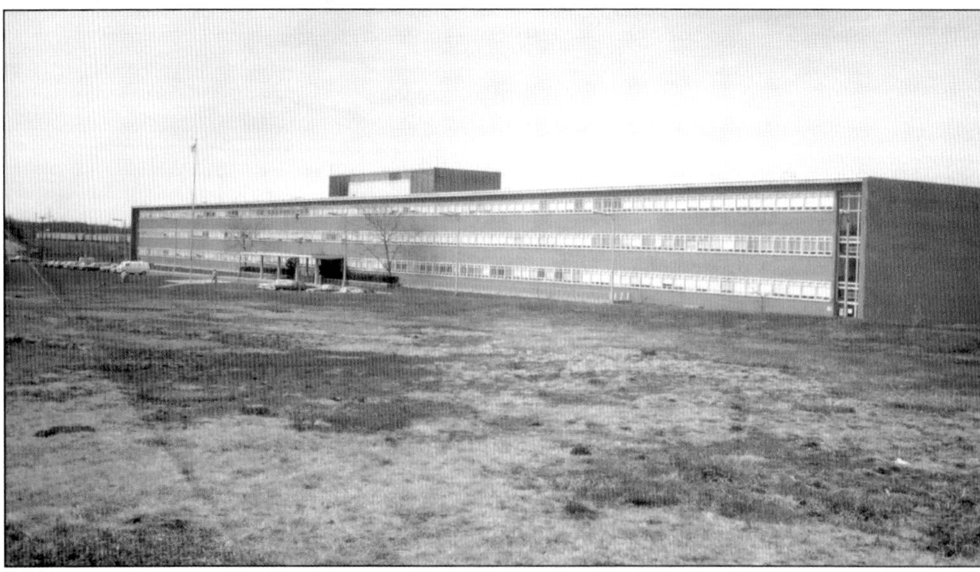

Olmsted Building, 1974–1975. In this striking photograph of the Olmsted Building from the mid-1970s, the stark and industrialized architecture of the former Olmsted Air Force Base is highlighted. Also evident are the lack of trees or landscaping and the negative impact that the 1972 flood, caused by Hurricane Agnes, had upon the campus' grounds.

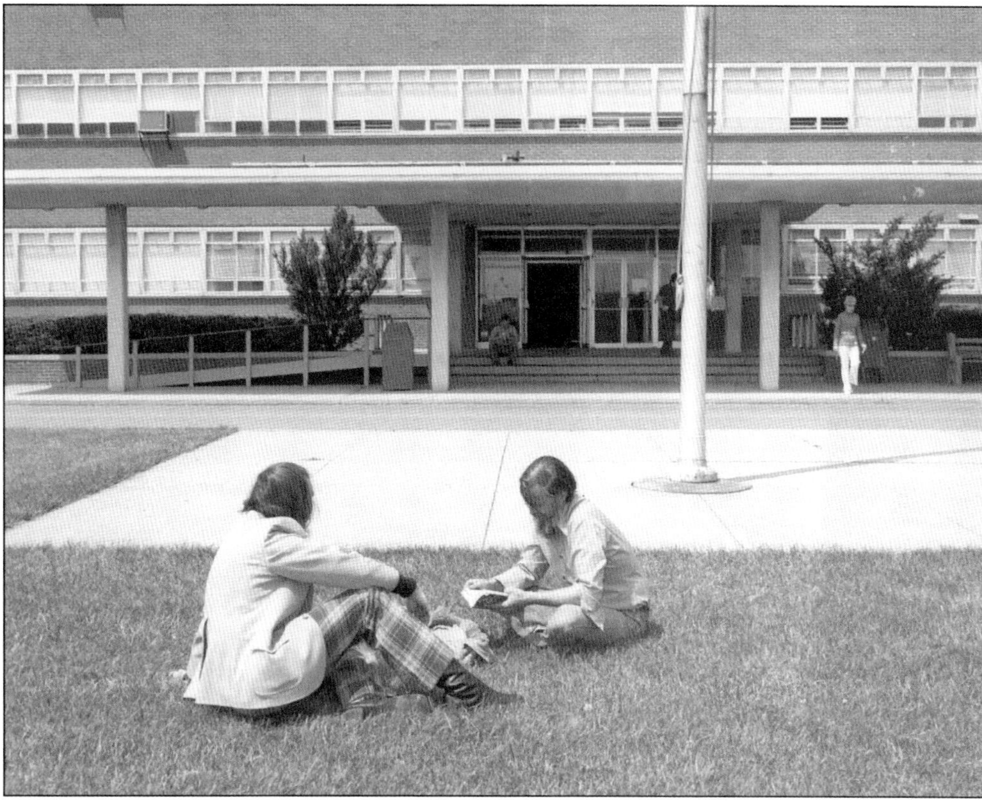

Olmsted Lawn, 1974. The Olmsted Building was—and still is—the hub of activity on campus and housed the school's administrative services, classrooms, faculty offices, food, and student services in the 1970s. Students often gathered to relax or study in front of Olmsted. By fall 1974, the Capitol Campus boasted 2,143 students and a faculty of 128 full-time professors.

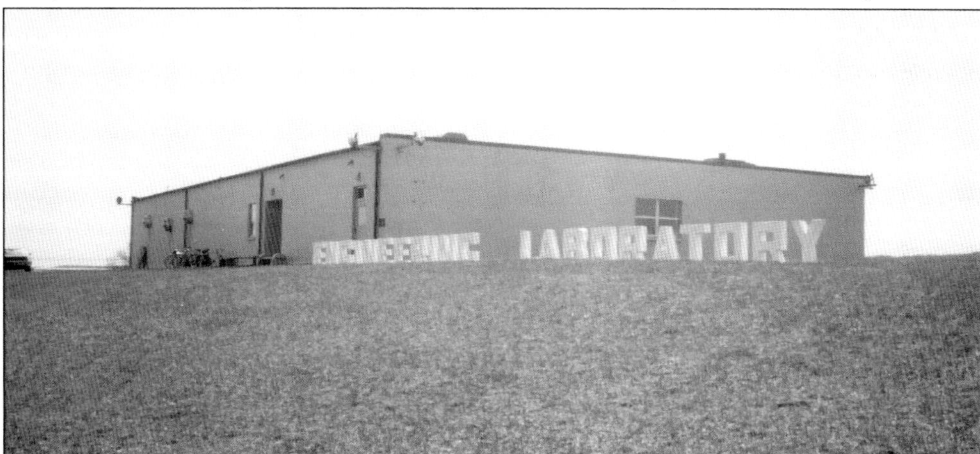

Engineering Laboratory, c. 1975. Located on a hill near the main entrance to campus, the Engineering Laboratory was heavily used by the science and technology faculty and students. The building was formerly used as an instrument lab on the Olmsted Air Force Base. The large, white letters that spell out "Engineering Laboratory" on the hill no longer exist, but the building still stands.

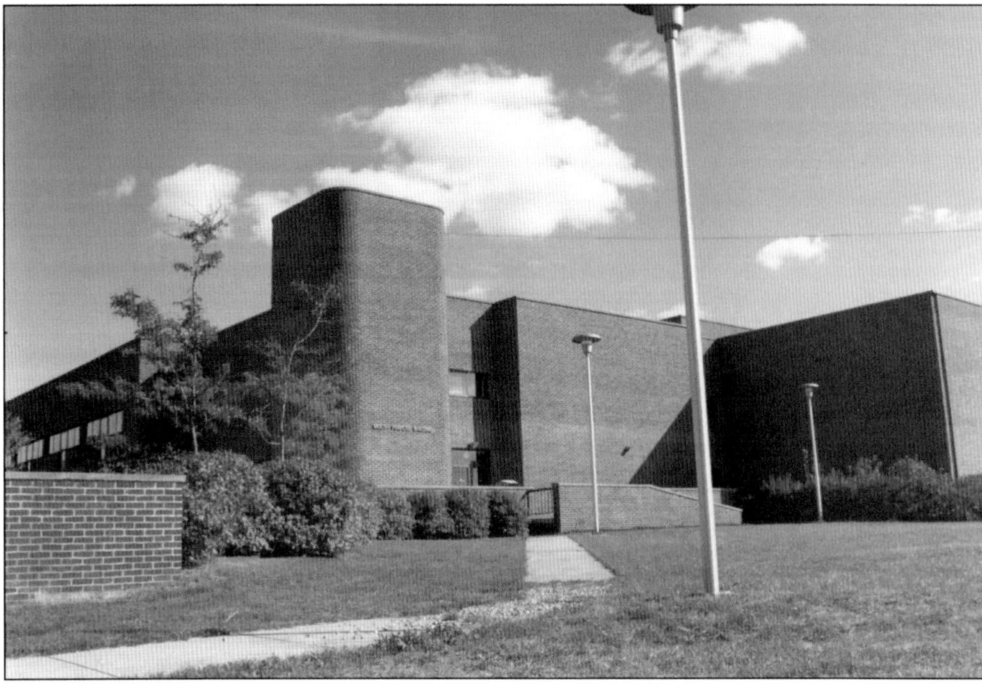

Multi-Purpose Building, 1977. With student enrollments reaching 2,500 by fall 1975, and student recreational needs growing as well, on October 19, 1977, after two years of construction and at a cost of $2 million, the Capitol Campus dedicated a new facility—the Multi-Purpose Building. Subsequently renamed the Capitol Union Building (CUB), it still provides athletic facilities, classrooms, conference rooms, office space, and areas for recreational and cultural programming.

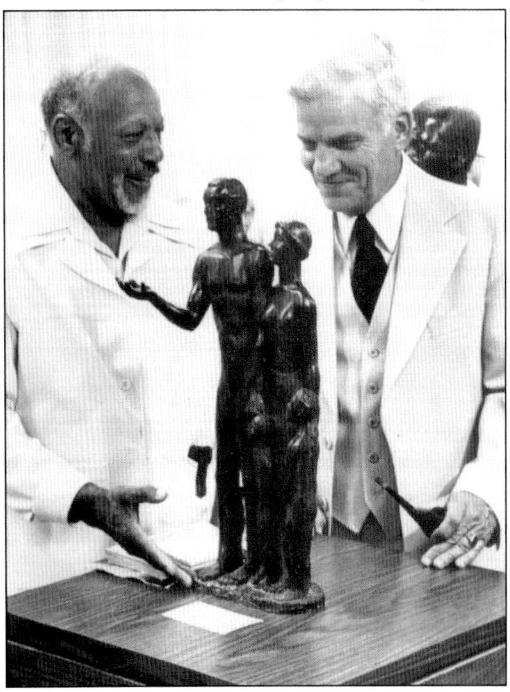

Professor C. Oliver LaGrone, c. 1977. This photograph captures former Capitol Campus lecturer in art education and African American history, Professor LaGrone (left), with Provost Robert E. McDermott. LaGrone served as Penn State University's Artist-in-Residence in 1975. This image shows him presenting his sculpture, *Family*, to Provost McDermott. LaGrone was an acclaimed sculptor, poet, teacher, and humanitarian who had a profound impact upon the Capitol Campus community.

Dr. Charles Townley, 1979. On September 1, 1979, Dr. Townley was appointed the first head librarian of the Heindel Memorial Library, named for the first dean of faculty, Dr. Richard H. Heindel. The library was located on the first floor in the east wing of the Olmsted Building (now Stacks Market) from 1966 until 1999. Dr. Townley served as head librarian from 1979 to 1990.

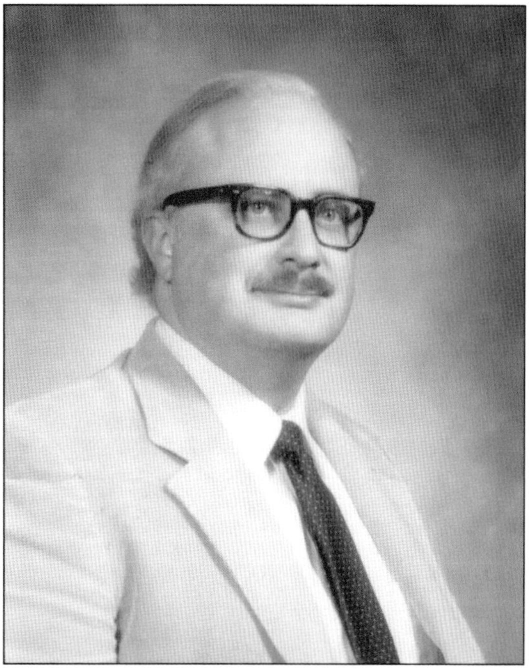

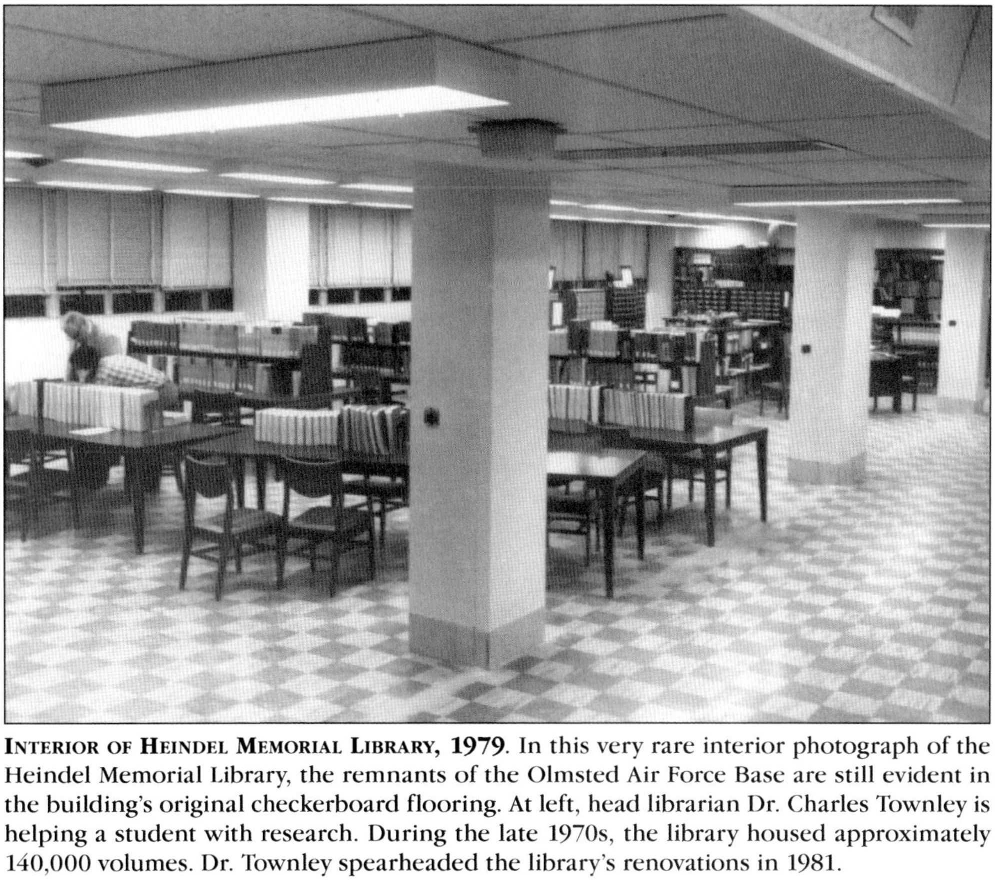

Interior of Heindel Memorial Library, 1979. In this very rare interior photograph of the Heindel Memorial Library, the remnants of the Olmsted Air Force Base are still evident in the building's original checkerboard flooring. At left, head librarian Dr. Charles Townley is helping a student with research. During the late 1970s, the library housed approximately 140,000 volumes. Dr. Townley spearheaded the library's renovations in 1981.

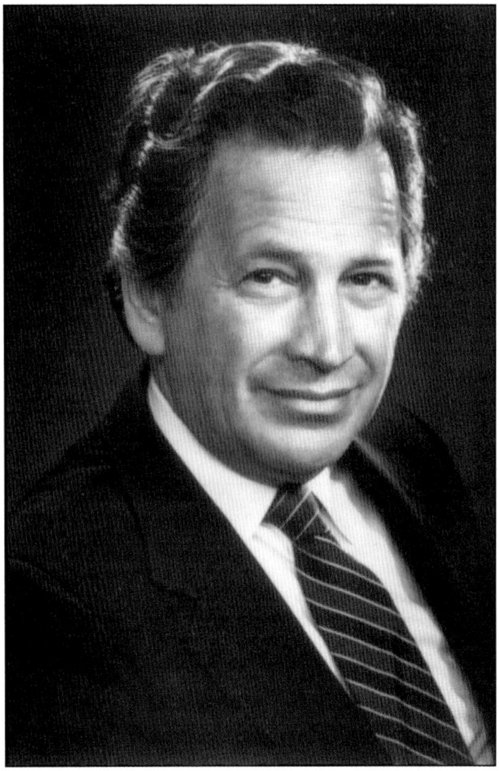

PROVOST AND DEAN THEODORE L. GROSS, 1979. After Provost Robert McDermott and Dr. George Wolf, dean of faculty, both resigned from their positions in 1978, the school appointed Dr. Theodore L. Gross as the new provost and dean of Capitol Campus on February 1, 1979. During his tenure, from 1979 to 1983, Dr. Gross organized the first Board of Advisors for the campus, reactivated the Capitol Campus Alumni Society, and was instrumental in raising funds to name the campus library after Dr. Richard H. Heindel.

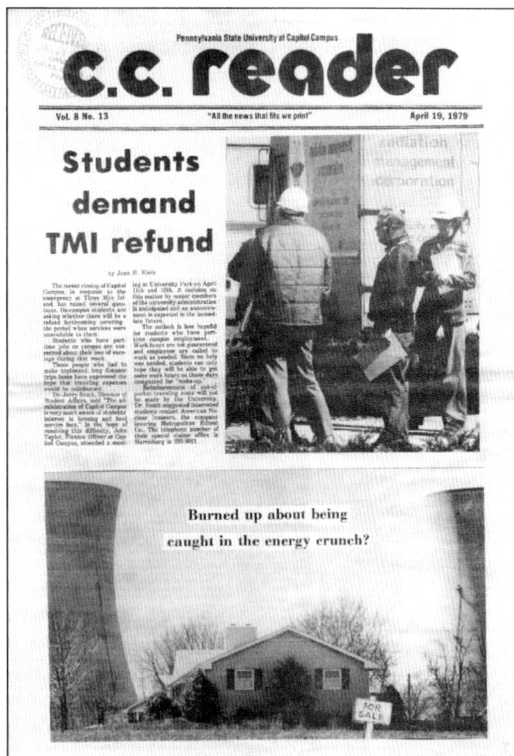

Pennsylvania State University at Capitol Campus

c.c. reader

Vol. 8 No. 13 | "All the news that fits we print" | April 19, 1979

Students demand TMI refund

by Joan B. Klein

The recent closing of Capitol Campus, in response to the emergency at Three Mile Island, has raised several questions. On-campus students are asking whether there will be a refund forthcoming covering the period when services were unavailable to them.

Students who have part-time jobs on campus are concerned about their loss of earnings during that week.

Those people who had to make unplanned, long distance trips home have expressed the hope that traveling expenses would be reimbursed.

Dr. Jerry South, Director of Student Affairs, said "The administration of Capitol Campus is very much aware of students interest in housing and food service fees." In the hope of resolving this difficulty, John Taylor, Finance Officer at Capitol Campus, attended a meeting at University Park on April 11th and 12th. A decision on this matter by senior members of the university administration is anticipated and an announcement is expected in the immediate future.

The outlook is less hopeful for students who have part-time campus employment. Work hours are not guaranteed and employees are called to work as needed. Since no help was needed, students can only hope they will be able to get some work hours on those days designated for "make-up."

Reimbursement of out-of-pocket traveling costs will not be made by the University. Dr. South suggested interested students contact American Nuclear Insurers, the company insuring Metropolitan Edison Co. The telephone number of their special claims office in Harrisburg is 233-9021

Burned up about being caught in the energy crunch?

FOR SALE

STUDENTS DEMAND TMI REFUND, 1979. During the 1970s, the Capitol Campus thrived despite the turbulent events of the decade, including the Vietnam War and the flood of 1972. The most significant crisis for students at the Capitol Campus was the March 1979 accident at Three Mile Island (TMI), located just five miles from campus. This issue of the student newspaper, *C.C. Reader*, poignantly illustrates students' perspectives on the accident.

Four

Transforming from Campus to College

1980–1989

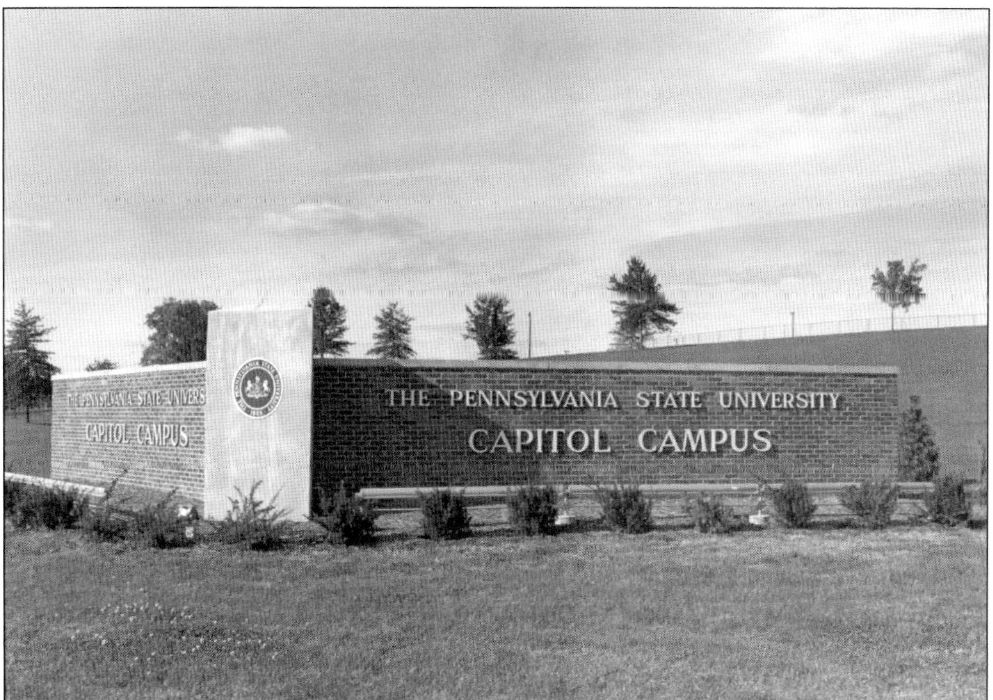

New Campus Entrance Sign, c. 1980–1981. At the dawn of the new decade, the Capitol Campus was positioned for change. Six new academic divisions were established in 1980: Behavioral Sciences and Education; Business Administration; the Heindel Library; Humanities; Public Affairs; and Science, Engineering, and Technology. In 1981, a phone-a-thon—the first one held by the school—raised $9,000 to pay for a new brick sign at the campus' Route 230 entrance.

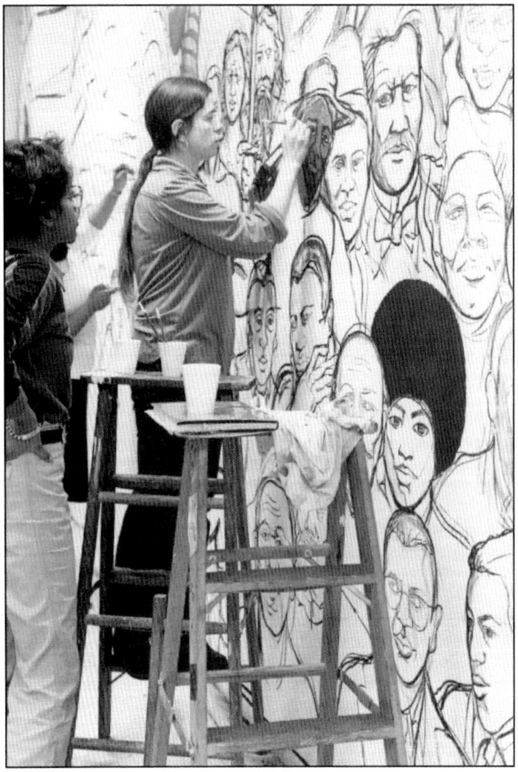

BLACK CULTURAL ARTS CENTER, 1980. By 1980, the campus included 126 faculty and 2,450 students. Under the direction of Provost and Dean Theodore Gross, the school implemented an institutional beautification program focused on recruiting more students and improving public relations. The Black Cultural Arts Center and its new mural (pictured) were part of these initiatives. Located in Room W-132 in the west wing of the Olmsted Building, the mural depicts important figures of African American history.

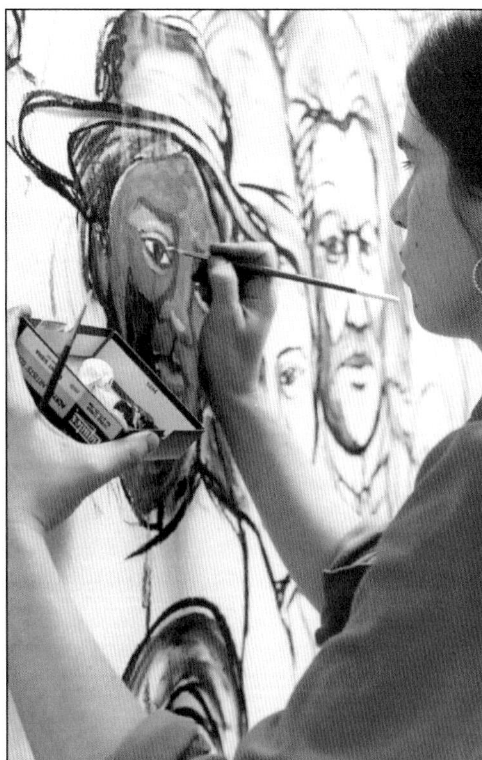

MURAL OF AFRICAN AMERICAN HISTORY, 1979–1980. Painted by nationally known Harrisburg muralist Toni Truesdale, the mural is a chronological history of notable African Americans, such as Muhammad Ali, Louis Armstrong, and Dr. Martin Luther King Jr. The mural was completed in summer 1980. In September 1998, the name of the Black Cultural Arts Center was changed to the Oliver LaGrone Cultural Arts Center in honor of Professor Oliver LaGrone, who died in 1995.

Capitolite, **1980**. Juniors, seniors, and graduate students at the Capitol Campus continued to produce a student yearbook throughout the 1970s and 1980s. Unlike the student newspaper, the yearbook had no significant changes to its title over the years. It remained the *Capitolite* until 1986 and changed to the *Capitalite* in 1987 when the school changed its name. The yearbook still serves as a valuable historical record of places, events, students' activities, and perspectives at Capitol College.

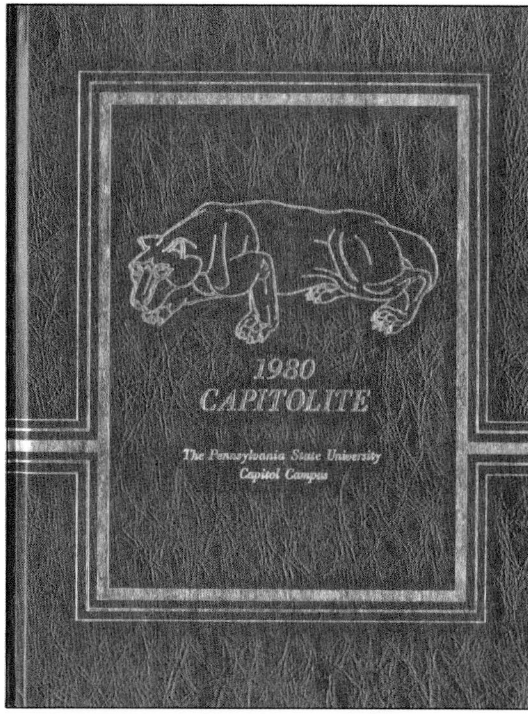

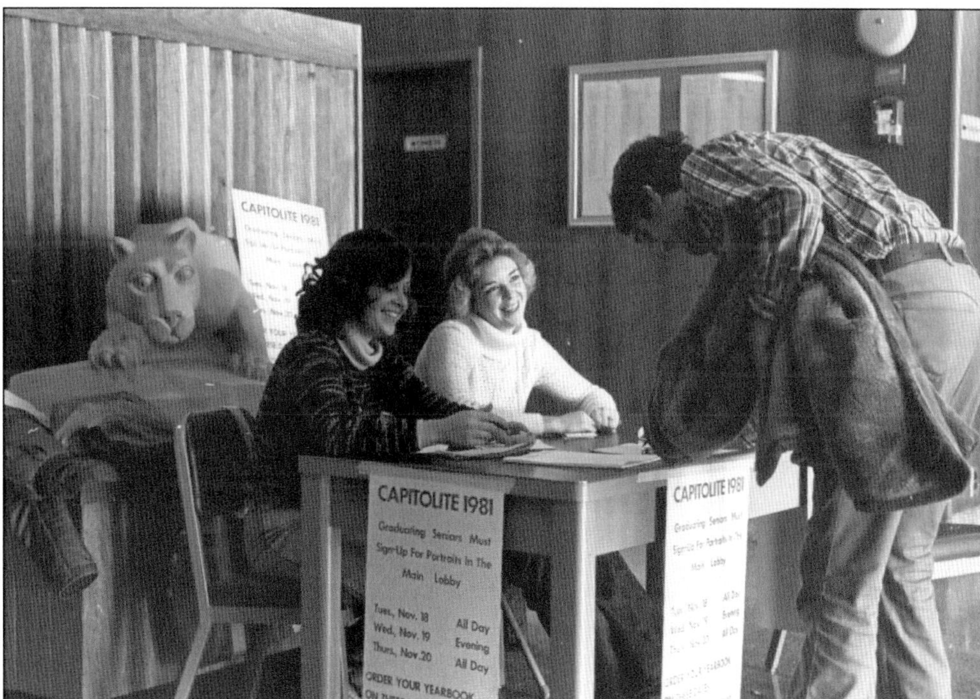

Capitolite Staff, 1981. This photograph shows volunteers from the 1981 *Capitolite* staff and offers a glimpse inside the main lobby of the Olmsted Building on campus. The *Nittany Lion Shrine*, which has graced the Olmsted lobby since 1970, is visible in the background at left.

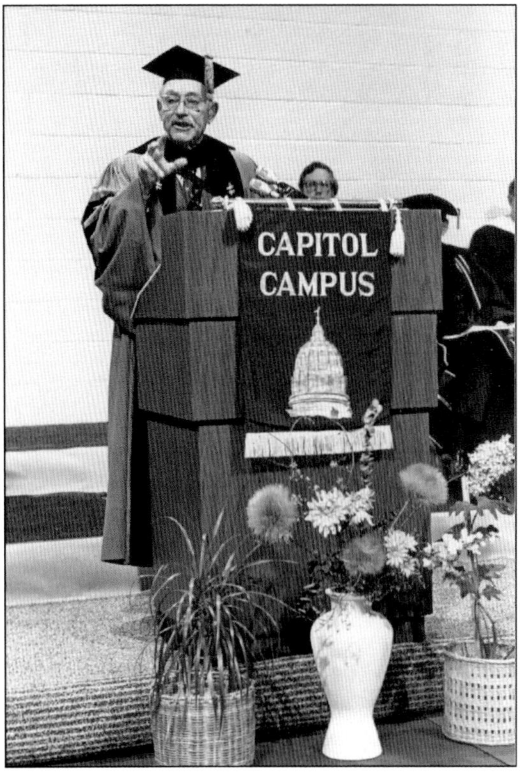

Fifteenth Anniversary Celebration, 1981. The beginning of the 1980s also marked a milestone for the Capitol Campus: the celebration of the school's first 15 years. An invitation-only event was held to mark the occasion on Wednesday, November 11, 1981. The celebration took place in the gym of the Multi-Purpose Building on campus and included a procession of special guests and guest speakers. One of the esteemed speakers during the convocation was Dr. Eric A. Walker (left), president emeritus of Penn State University. Pictured below are, from left to right, Provost and Dean Theodore L. Gross; Dr. John W. Oswald, president of Penn State University; Dr. Walker; and the Honorable William W. Scranton, governor of Pennsylvania from 1963 to 1967, who was instrumental in establishing the Capitol Campus in 1966.

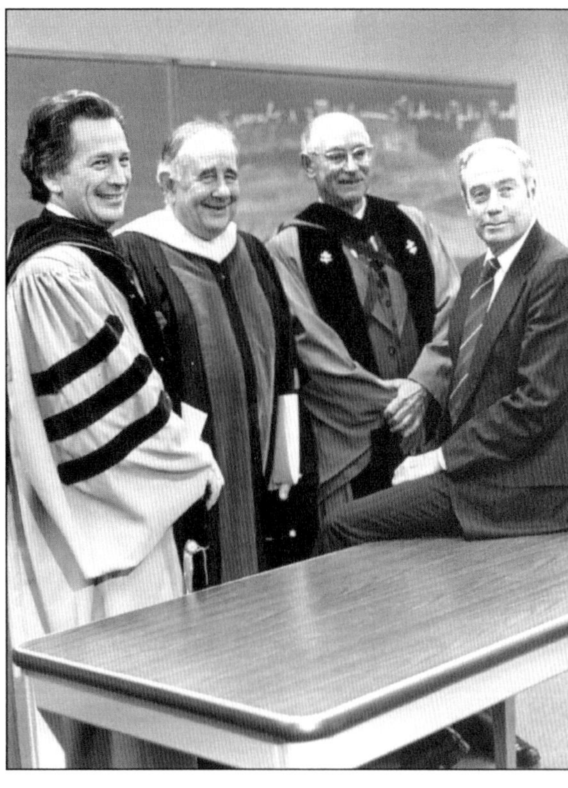

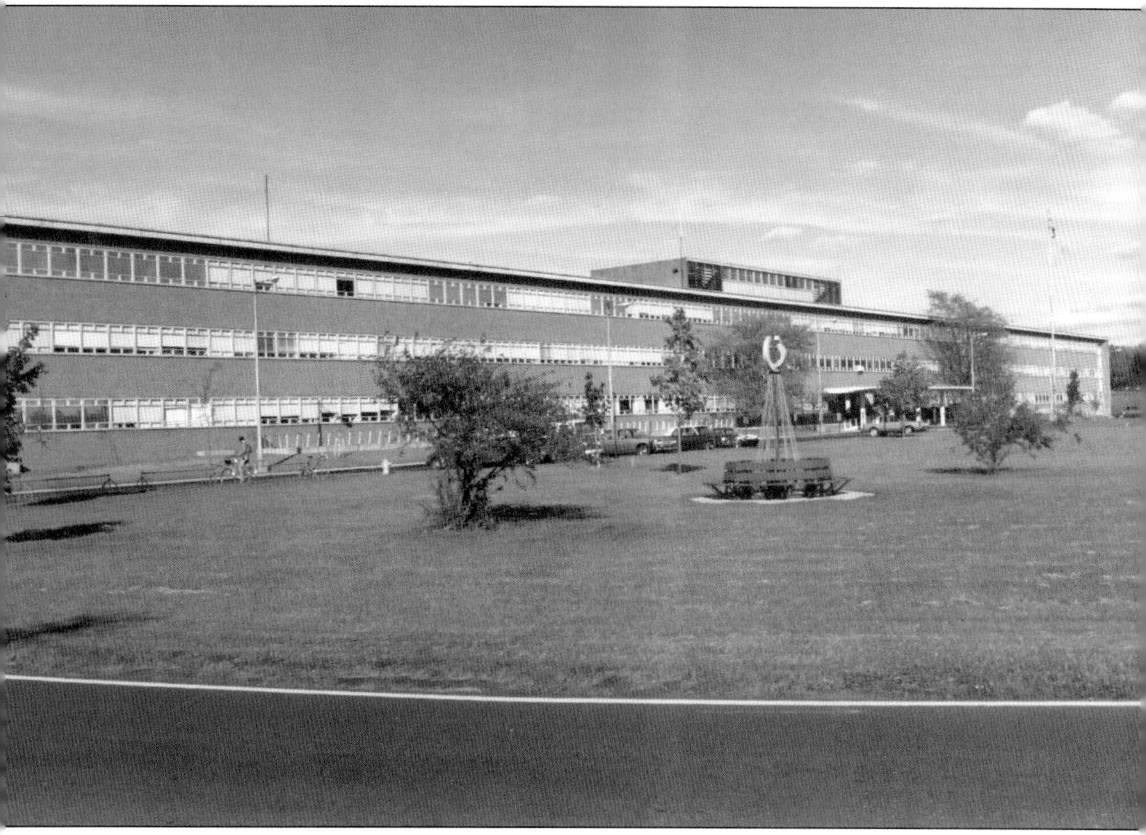

***Capitol Campus Sculpture*, c. 1981**. This image of the Olmsted Building shows it looking much different from when it served as the headquarters for the Olmsted Air Force Base in the 1960s. After the US Air Force held its last retreat in front of Olmsted on August 28, 1966, the building remained. However, throughout the late 1970s and 1980s, gradual improvements to the campus were made with landscaping and aesthetic elements such as the *C.C. Sculpture* (*Capitol Campus Sculpture*), visible near the center of the photograph. The bench and sculpture were designed in 1977 and constructed in May 1978 by Mechanical Design Engineering Technology (MDET) students Mat Brnik, Bill Gallagher, Robert Suchebich, and Dan Weigel. The sculpture originally featured a 10-foot pole topped by two red letter "Cs" (for "Capitol Campus") and surrounded by a hexagonal bench. The school funded its construction at a cost of $1,000. The sculpture still stands on the lawn in front of the Olmsted Building. In summer 2015, members of the student organization PSPEC (Penn State Professional Engineers and Contractors) refurbished this campus landmark and repainted the letter "Cs" blue.

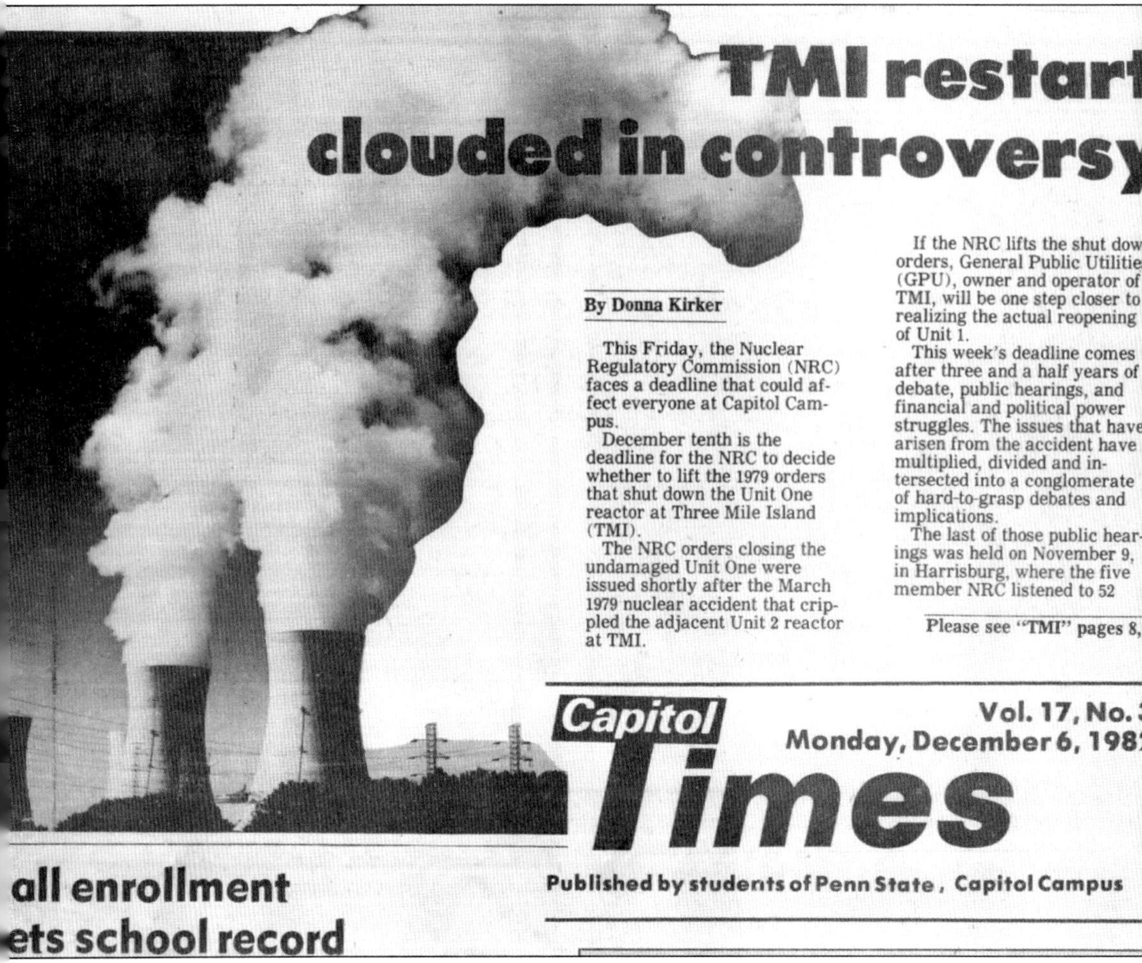

TMI restart clouded in controversy

By Donna Kirker

This Friday, the Nuclear Regulatory Commission (NRC) faces a deadline that could affect everyone at Capitol Campus.

December tenth is the deadline for the NRC to decide whether to lift the 1979 orders that shut down the Unit One reactor at Three Mile Island (TMI).

The NRC orders closing the undamaged Unit One were issued shortly after the March 1979 nuclear accident that crippled the adjacent Unit 2 reactor at TMI.

If the NRC lifts the shut down orders, General Public Utilities (GPU), owner and operator of TMI, will be one step closer to realizing the actual reopening of Unit 1.

This week's deadline comes after three and a half years of debate, public hearings, and financial and political power struggles. The issues that have arisen from the accident have multiplied, divided and intersected into a conglomerate of hard-to-grasp debates and implications.

The last of those public hearings was held on November 9, in Harrisburg, where the five member NRC listened to 52

Please see "TMI" pages 8,

Capitol Times

Vol. 17, No.

Monday, December 6, 198

Published by students of Penn State, Capitol Campus

all enrollment
ets school record

TMI Restart, the *Capitol Times*, 1982. In 1982, the student newspaper changed its title from the *Capitol Campus Reader* to the *Capitol Times*. This issue from December 6, 1982, not only illustrates a continued interest in Three Mile Island, but also highlights record enrollment at the campus. For the first time in the school's history, fall undergraduate enrollment totaled 1,813. Nearly half of all new students transferred from other Penn State campuses.

MEN'S BASKETBALL TEAM, c. 1980–1983. Athletics have always been an important part of the Penn State University tradition and college life at Capitol Campus. Although few historical images of the early athletics program still exist, the school has offered sports activities to students since 1967. One year after the campus opened, Paul J. Reichwein, the head of physical education, created a formal athletics program that included six intramural sports (flag football, basketball, volleyball, softball, bowling, and table tennis) as well as six instructional sports (archery, golf, tennis, badminton, weight training, and modern dance). Also, beginning in 1967, the basketball and volleyball teams competed in an inter-Commonwealth Campus league against local colleges. These photographs capture the men's basketball team, known as the Lions, in the early 1980s.

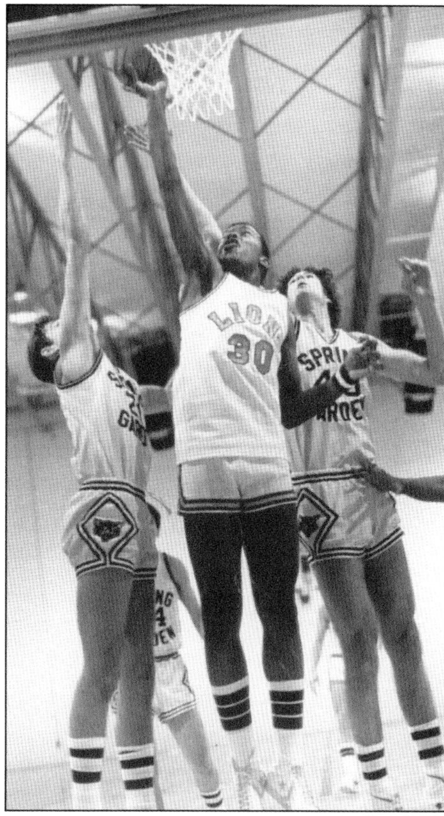

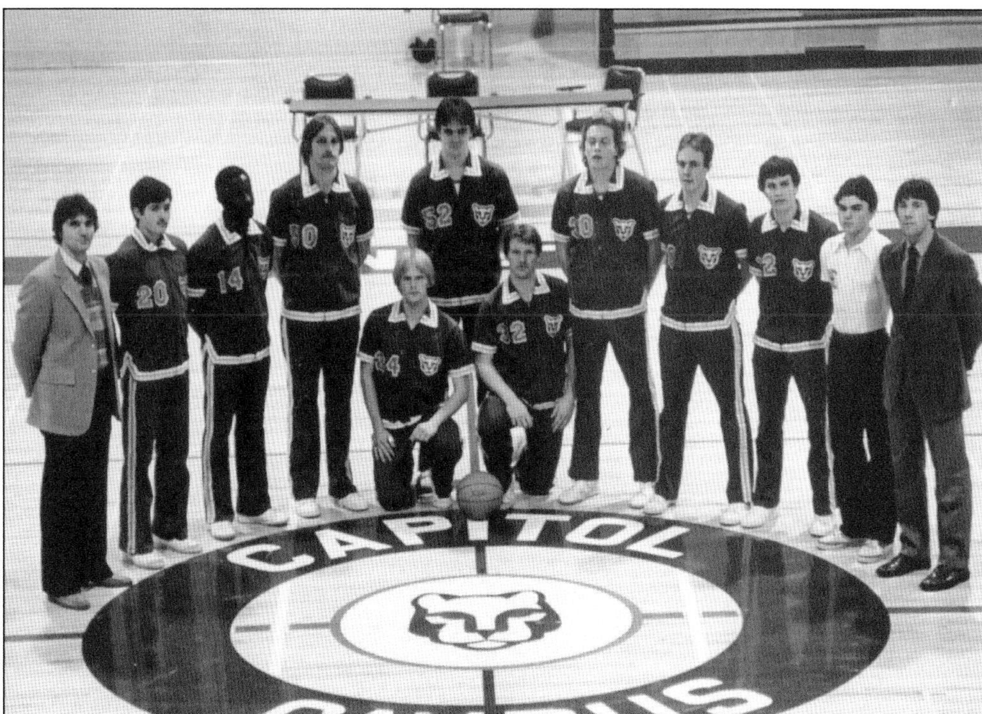

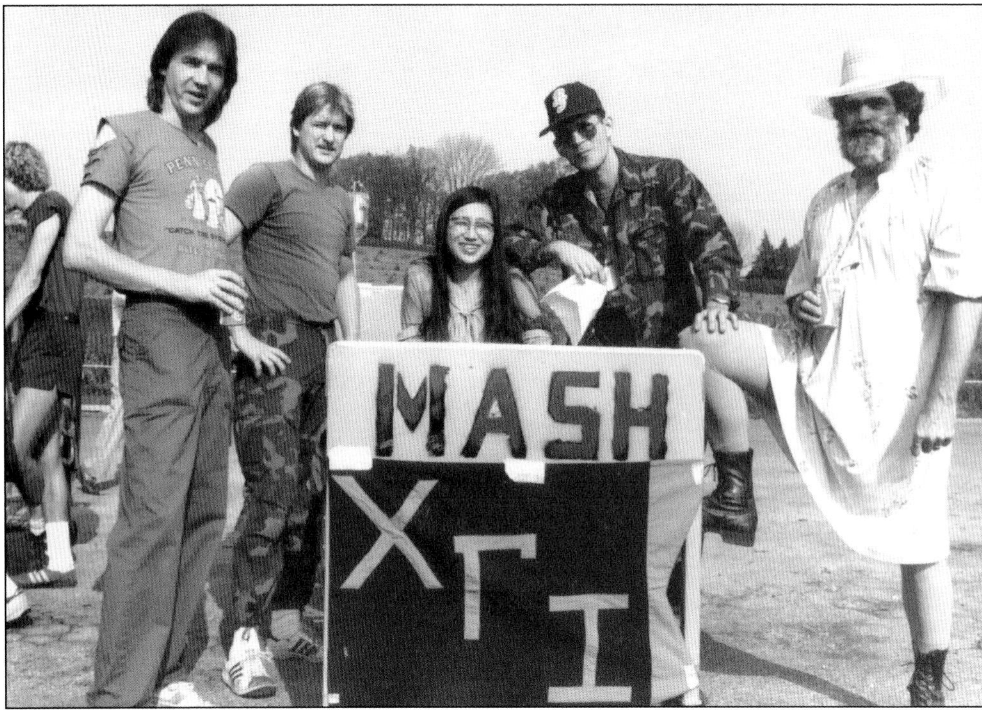

Chi Gamma Iota Fraternity, c. 1983. The oldest student organization on campus is the Chi Gamma Iota Veteran's Fraternity, or XGI, which supports student veterans in their transition from military to civilian life. Chartered on March 4, 1968, XGI has a long history of sponsoring campus blood drives as well as participating in the annual Bathtub Race and Veteran's Day celebrations. This photograph shows XGI members enjoying a campus event.

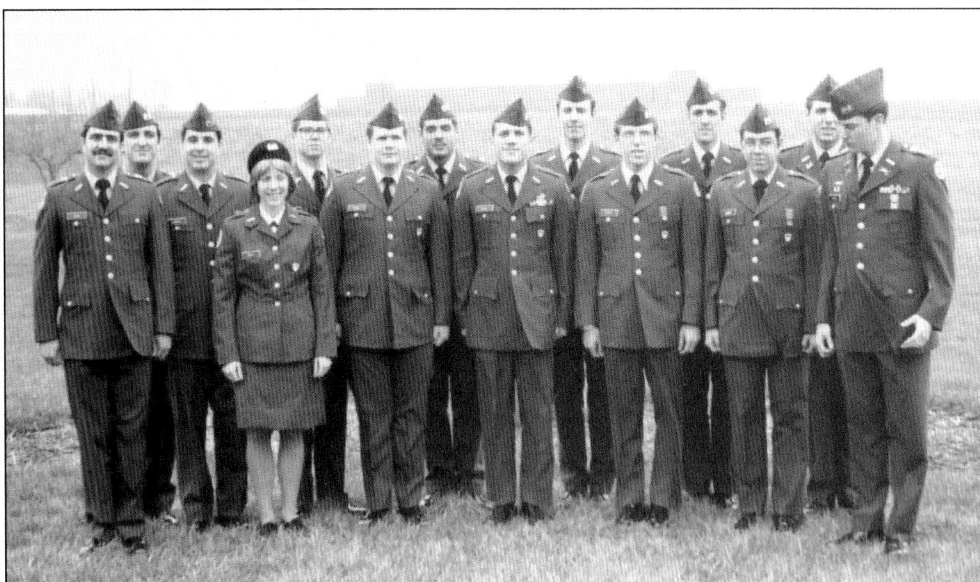

Army ROTC, 1983. The military connection to the Capitol Campus is evidenced in the history and strength of the XGI student organization as well as in the popularity and presence of the Army ROTC (Reserve Officers' Training Corps) during the 1980s.

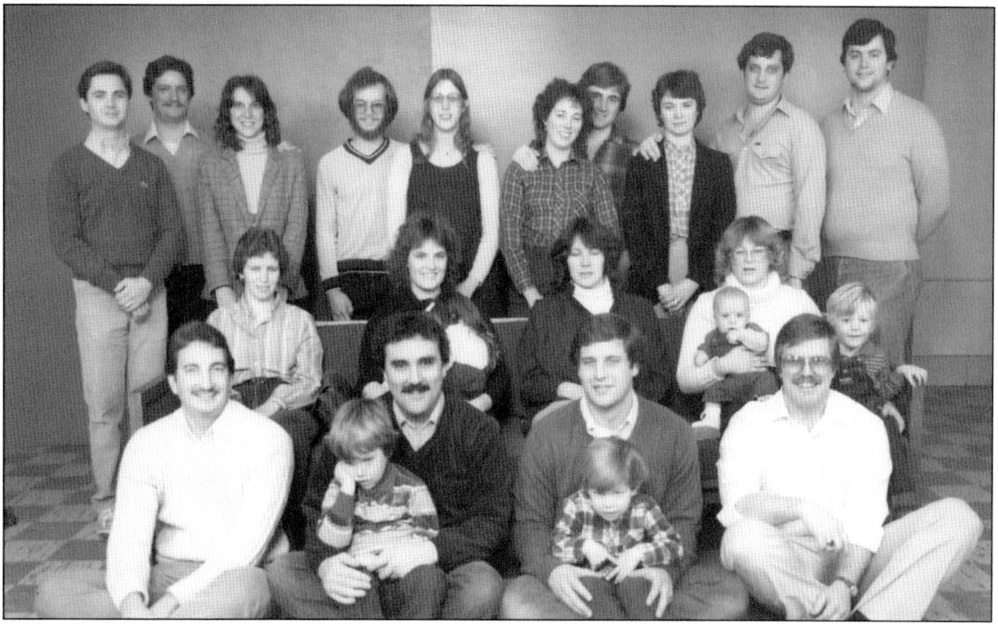

MARRIED STUDENT UNION, 1983. One of the unique strengths of the Capitol Campus has always been its successful combination of upper division undergraduate and graduate programs and students. Not surprisingly, the campus has always been home to married students and their families. The Married Student Union (MSU) is a student organization chartered in spring 1976. It continued to exist into the late 1980s.

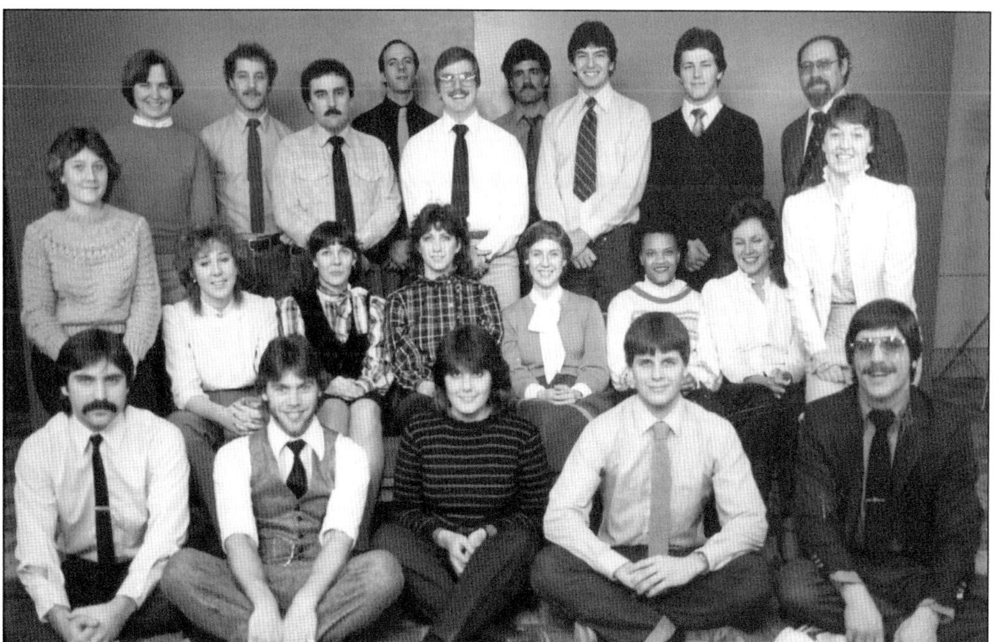

STUDENT GOVERNMENT ASSOCIATION, 1983. The Student Government Association (SGA) is one of the oldest student groups on campus, established in 1967. SGA serves as the governing body for the student population at Capitol Campus. Pictured here are members of the 1983 SGA. It is still an active and vital student group that contributes to the betterment of student life.

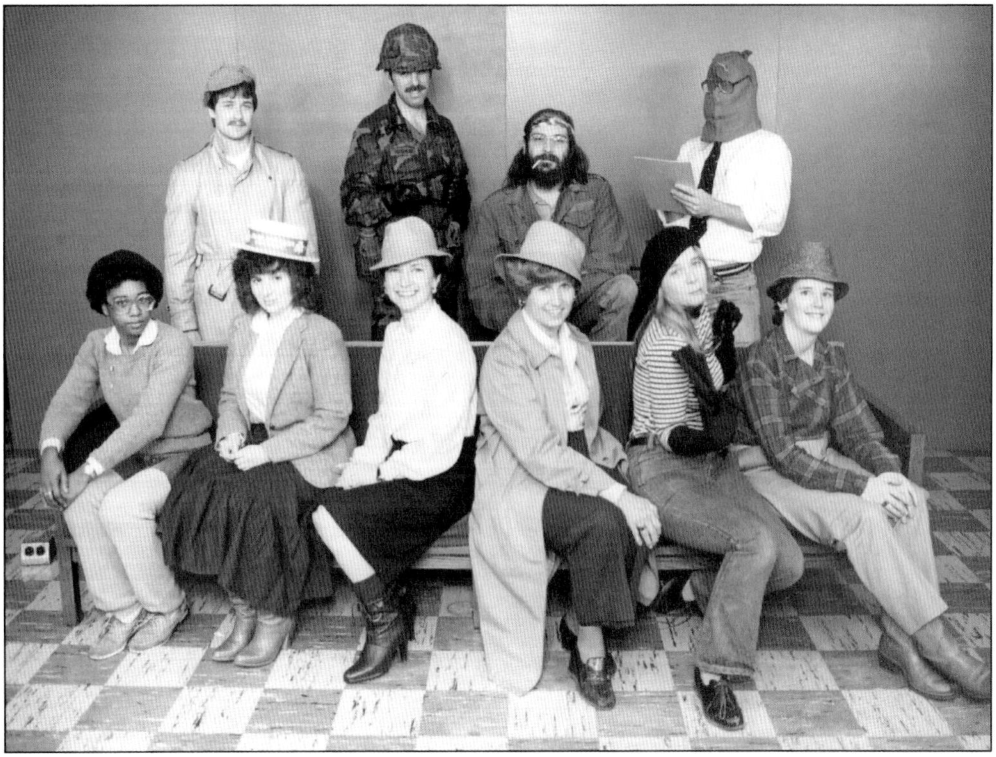

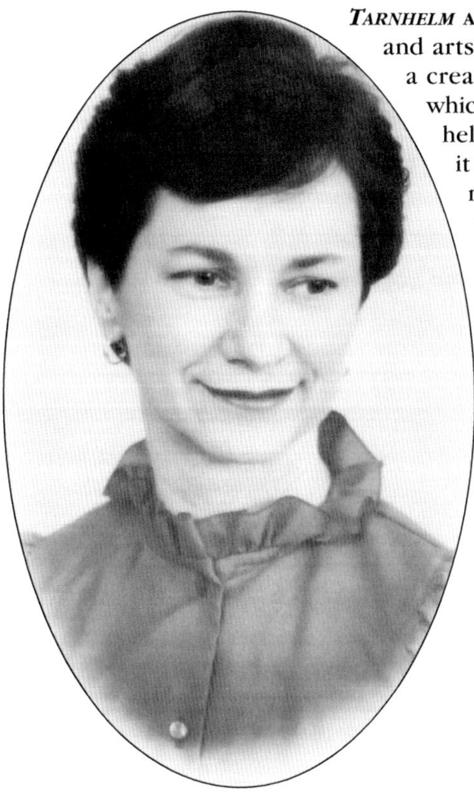

Tarnhelm* and Dr. Theodora Graham, 1983.** The literary and arts magazine, *Tarnhelm*, provided students with a creative outlet beginning in fall 1971. *Tarnhelm*, which owes its name to the German word for "winged helmet," was published annually until 2008, when it became ***From the Fallout Shelter. The 1983 members of the *Tarnhelm* staff are pictured above with their faculty advisor, Dr. Graham, seated third from the left in the front row. Dr. Graham (left), professor of English and humanities, came to the Capitol Campus in 1971 and not only served as the *Tarnhelm* faculty advisor since its inception, but also started the student club and publication. She retired from Penn State Harrisburg in May 1999.

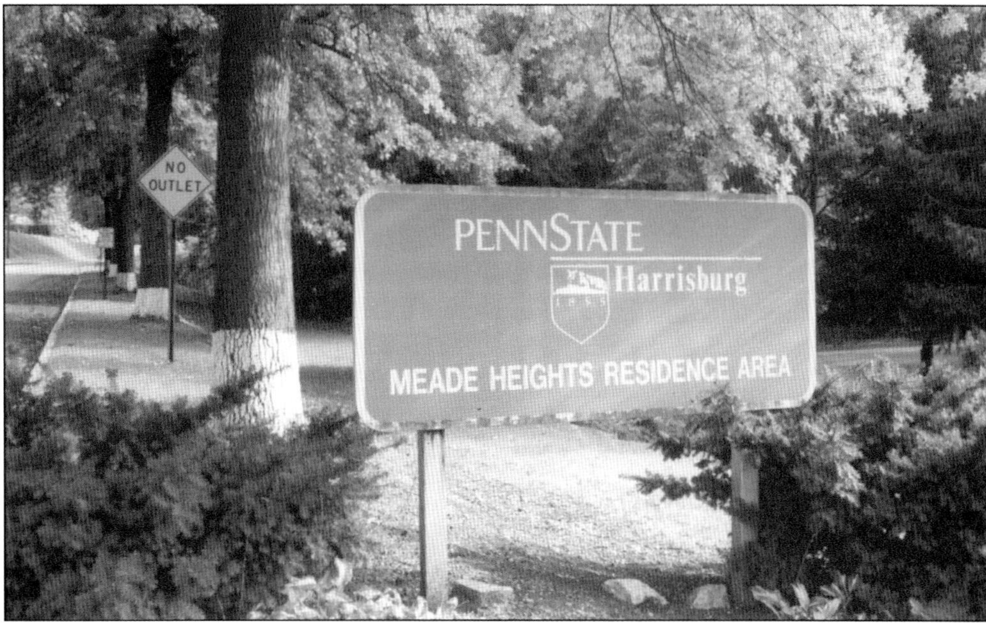

MEADE HEIGHTS SIGN, C. 1980S. In the 1980s, students' options for on-campus housing were limited to Church and Wrisberg Halls, Meade Heights, and the University Apartments. This Meade Heights sign stood in the neighborhood during the 1980s, when it was still a popular residential choice for students.

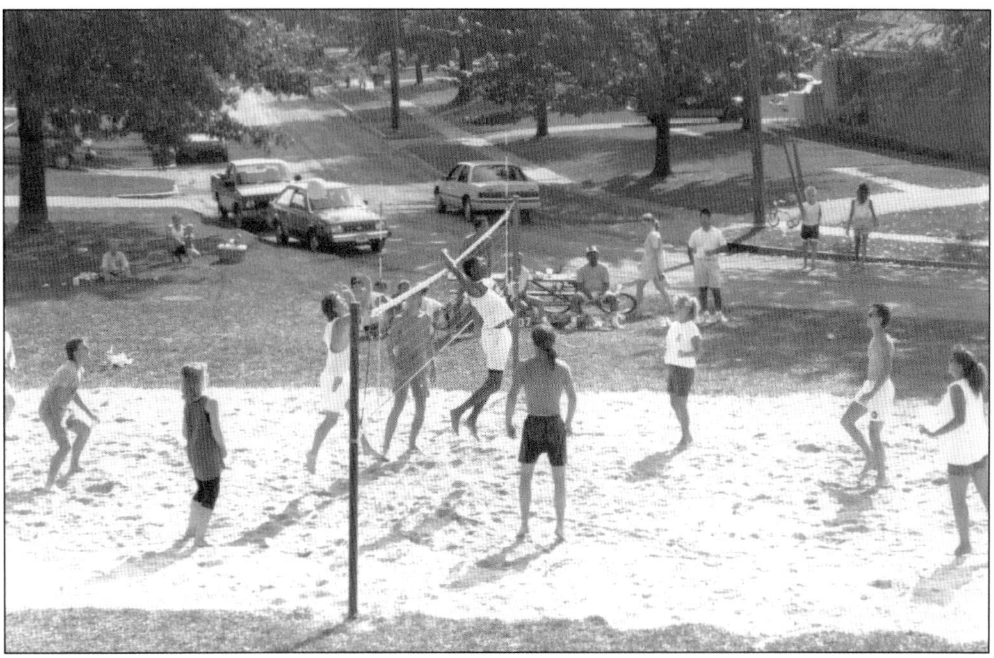

MEADE HEIGHTS RECREATION, C. 1980S. The Meade Heights housing complex offered students several options for outdoor recreation, including a volleyball court with sand, People's Park (near the intersection of Kirtland Avenue and Nelson Drive), and a large open area between Mars Drive and Nelson Drive. A laundry facility, affectionately known as "Suds City," was also available for student use in Meade Heights.

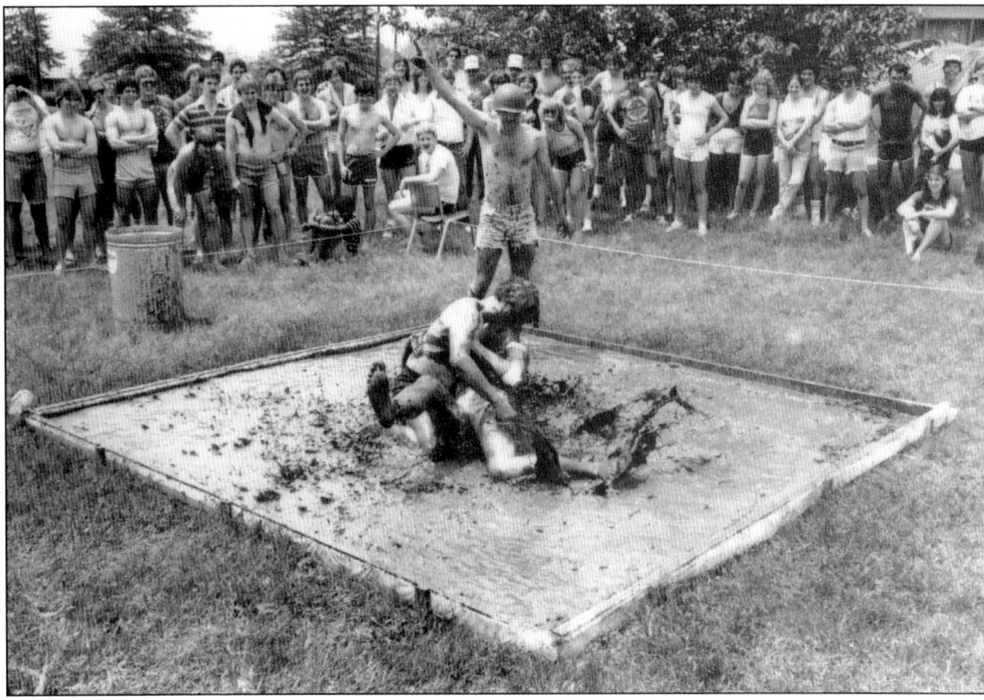

Rites of Spring, c. 1980s. Toward the end of the spring semester, in May 1973, students at Capitol Campus started a new tradition called the Rites of Spring. It started as a festival to unite everyone in the community—students from the dormitories and "The Heights," and even commuters. Rites of Spring was held in People's Park in Meade Heights and included events such as a free picnic, bonfire, road rally, and games like a three-legged race and a sack race. The tradition has evolved over the years and featured mud wrestling and riding on the Slip-N-Slide in the Meade Heights recreational area, as shown in these photographs from Rites of Spring in the 1980s.

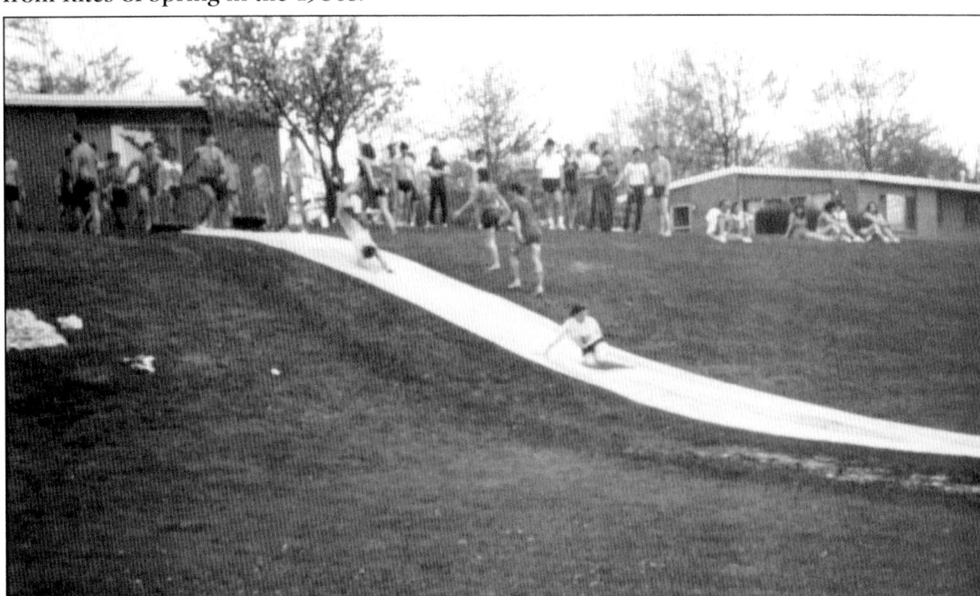

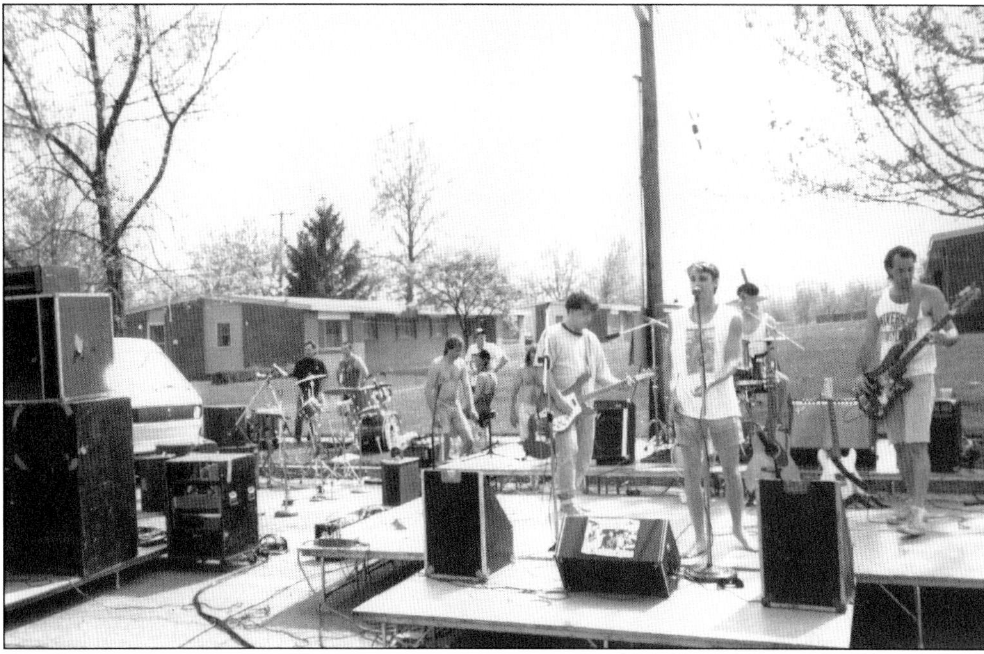

Spring Concert, c. 1980s. Another Rites of Spring tradition, which can trace its origins back to the Harrisburg Rock Festivals of the 1970s, is the spring music concert. Pictured here is a small concert in the Meade Heights residential neighborhood.

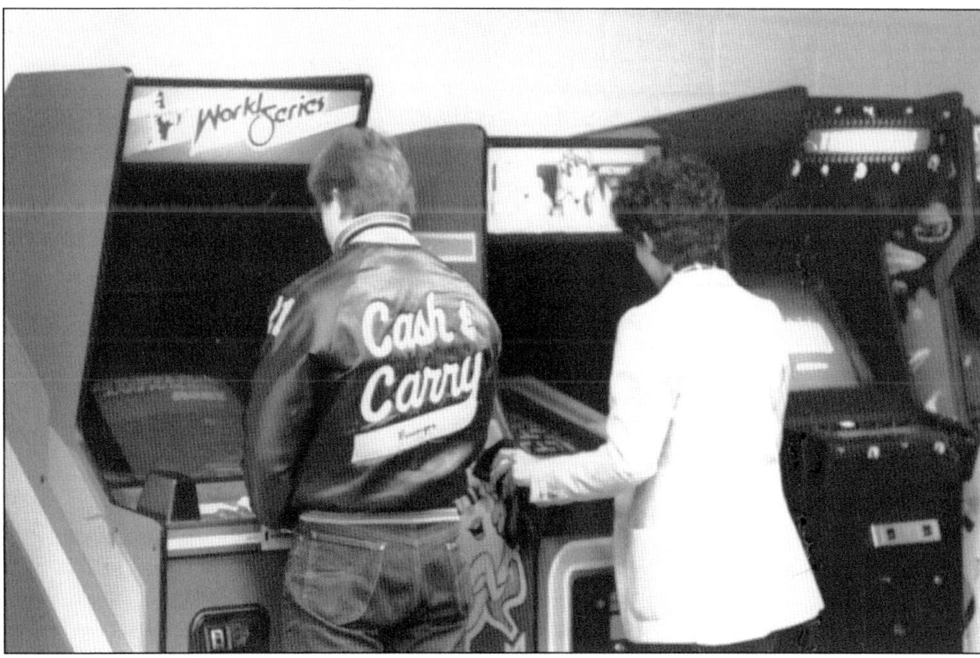

Campus Game Room, c. 1980s. The video game mania of the 1980s was present at the Capitol Campus. Students retreated to the game room in the cafeteria, known as "Vendorville" until the early 1980s and as "The Lion's Den" after 1981. The student cafeteria, which was located in the basement of the Olmsted Building, had a game room complete with pinball machines and upright video games such as Ms. Pac-Man.

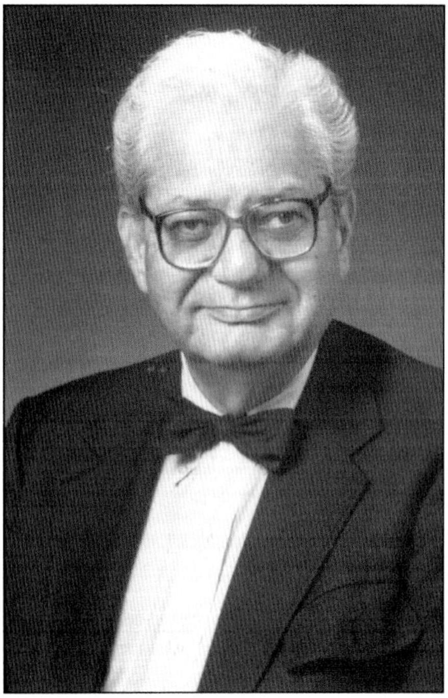

Institute of State and Regional Affairs, c. 1980s. Established in 1973, the Institute of State and Regional Affairs (ISRA) facilitates Penn State University's public service and applied research mission. ISRA was led by Dr. Irving Hand (pictured), director and professor of state and regional planning at the Capitol Campus for over 20 years until his retirement in 1993.

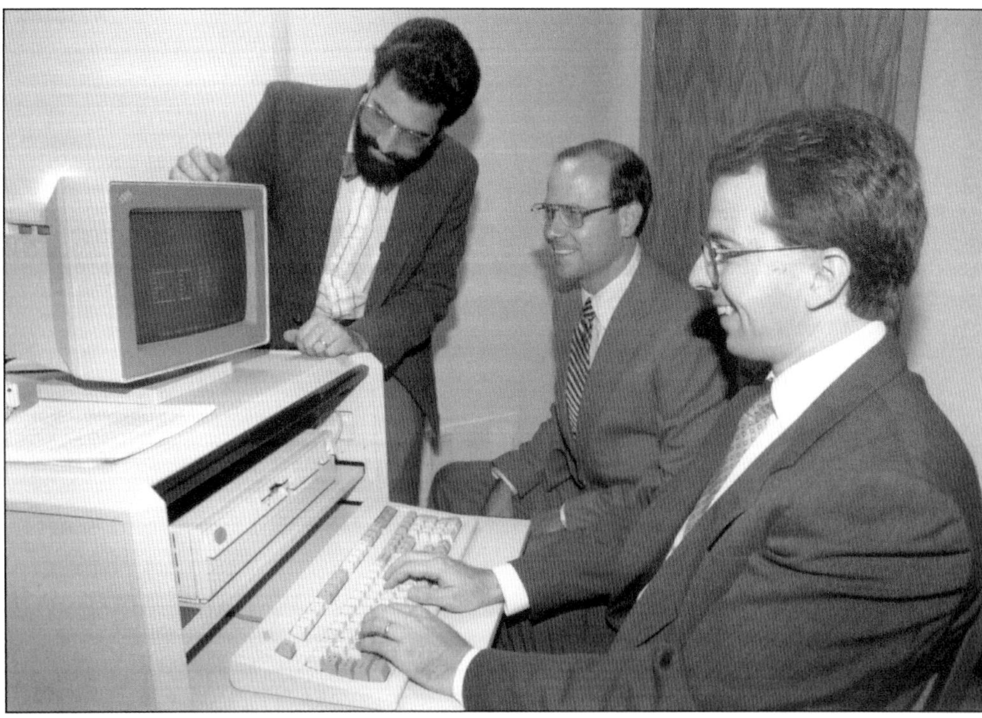

Pennsylvania State Data Center, c. 1982–1983. Created in November 1981 by an executive order of Pennsylvania governor Dick Thornburgh, the Pennsylvania State Data Center (PaSDC) is the Commonwealth of Pennsylvania's official source for population and economic statistics. This early photograph of staff at the PaSDC includes Michael Behney (left, now director of the Institute of State and Regional Affairs), Paul Hallacher (center), and Kevin Geist.

New SET Building, 1983–1984. The photograph at right captures the groundbreaking ceremony held on June 29, 1983, for the new Science, Engineering, and Technology (SET) Building at the Capitol Campus. It was the first new building constructed completely for academic purposes. Present for the ceremony were, from left to right, Ralph E. Peters, chairman of the Penn State Capitol Campus Board of Advisors; Lt. Gov. William W. Scranton III; Dr. Theodore L. Gross, provost and dean of the Capitol Campus; and Walter J. Conti, president of the Penn State University Board of Trustees. The largest gift supporting the new building came from Capitol Campus' 1973 alumnus John O. Vartan, CEO and chairman of the Harrisburg-based engineering firm Associated American Engineers, Inc. The photograph below shows the completed $2-million SET Building after it was dedicated in 1984.

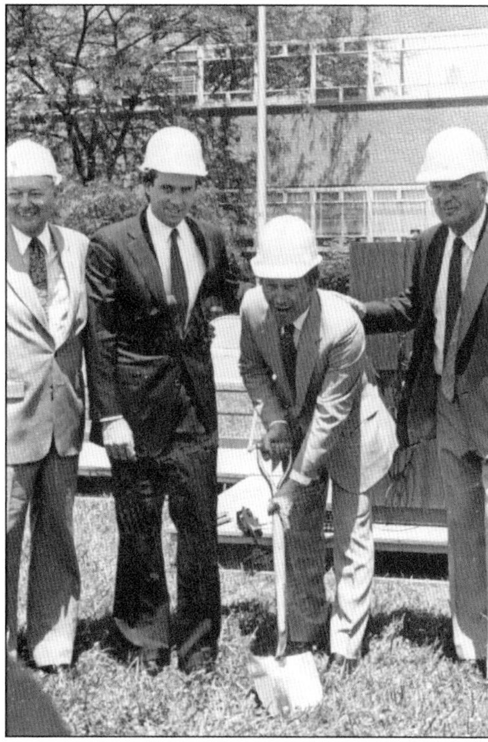

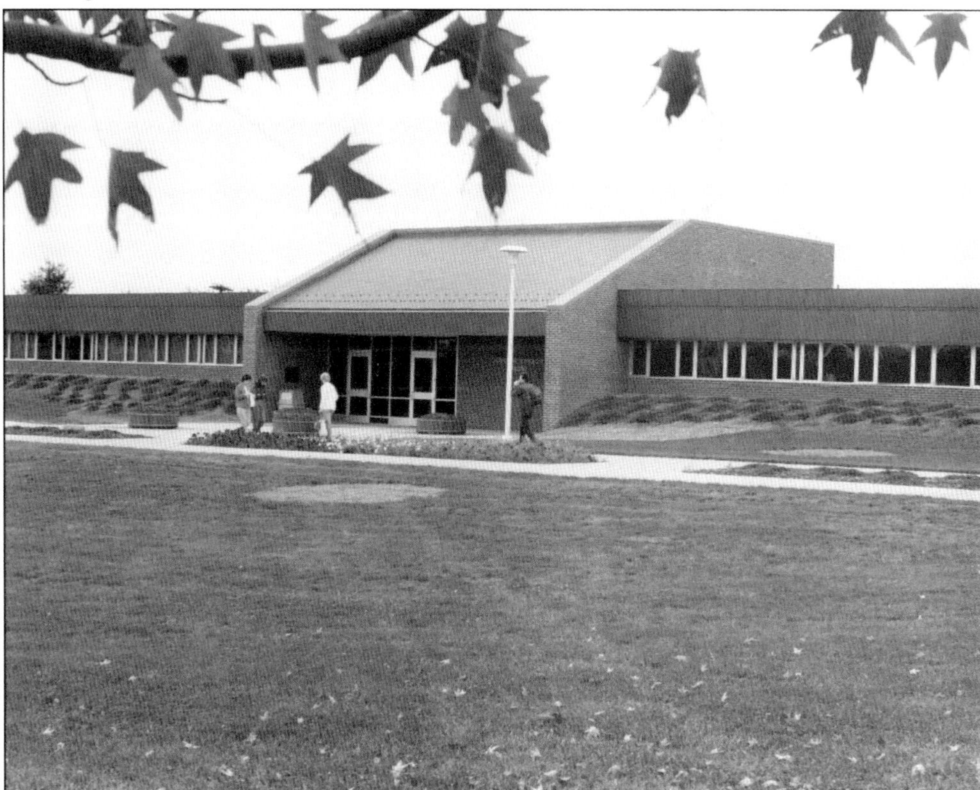

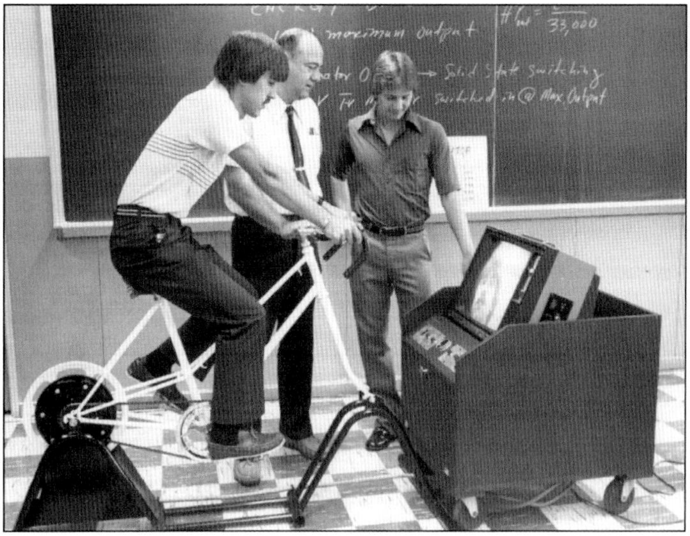

ELECTRICITY-GENERATING BICYCLE, 1983. Two Capitol Campus students in mechanical design engineering technology created an "energy cycle" as their senior project. The bicycle demonstrated how much human effort would be required to generate a small amount of electric power. Pictured here are Greg Sloditskie (on the bike); Edward Trunk, associate professor of engineering (center); and Judd Woeifel.

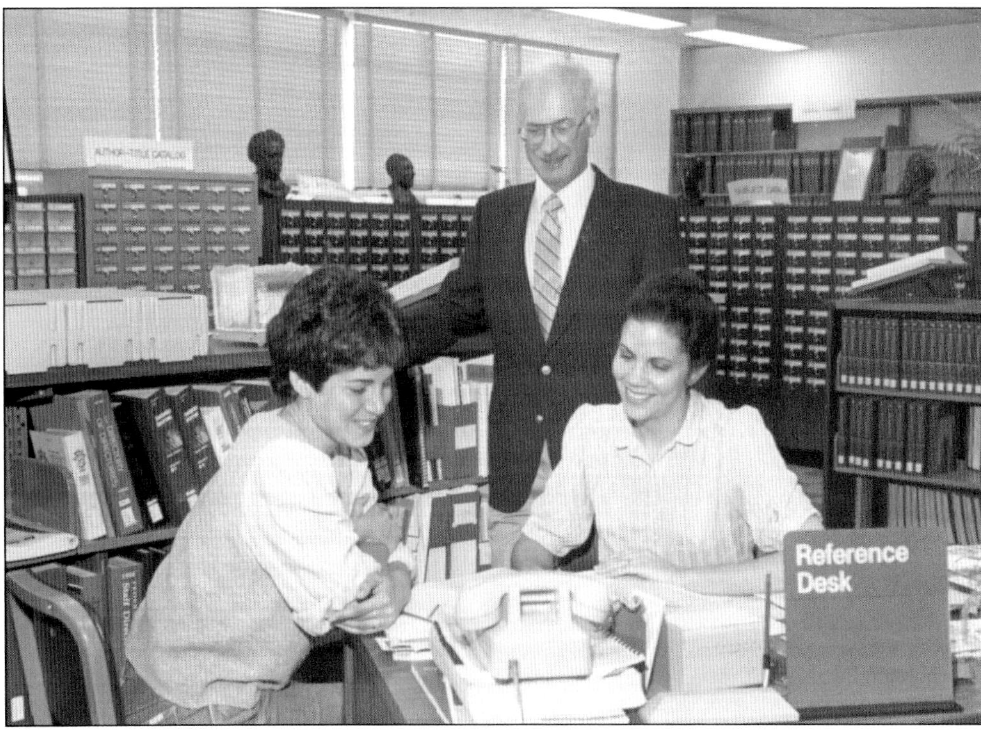

HEINDEL LIBRARY STAFF, 1983–1984. After the Heindel Memorial Library was renovated in 1981, it had new study areas for students as well as 20 percent more shelving space to accommodate up to 185,000 volumes. Pictured here at the library's reference desk are, from left to right, an unidentified student; Dr. Charles Townley, head librarian; and Nancy Dewald, assistant reference librarian.

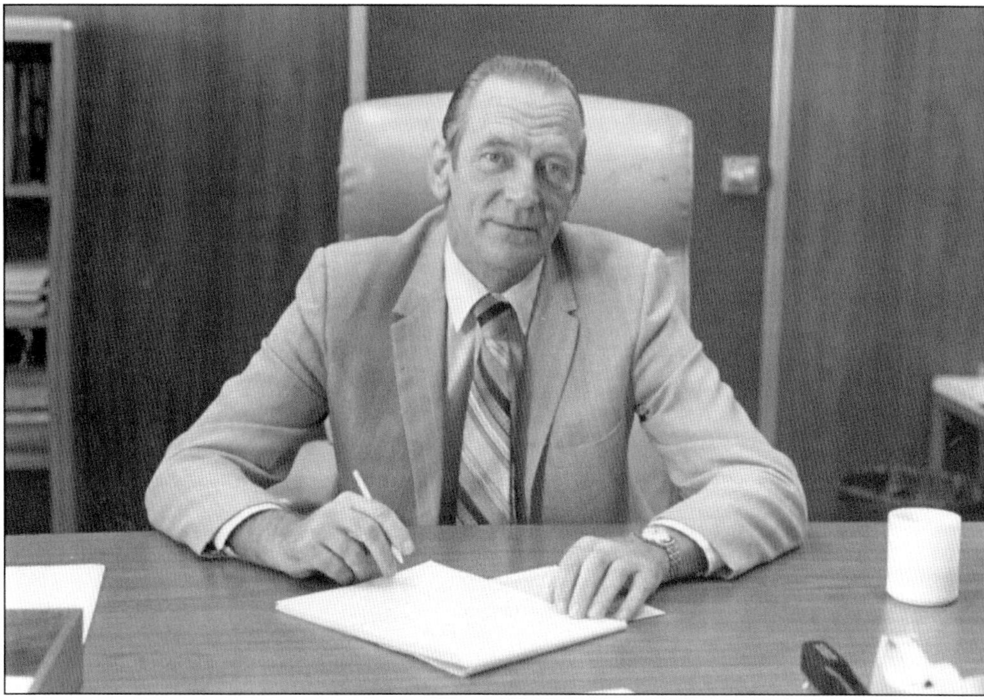

Acting Provost and Dean Stanley H. Miller, 1984. After the departure of Provost and Dean Theodore Gross in July 1983, Dr. Miller was named acting provost and dean of the Capitol Campus. Previously, Dr. Miller served as Capitol Campus' head of the Division of Behavioral Sciences and Education.

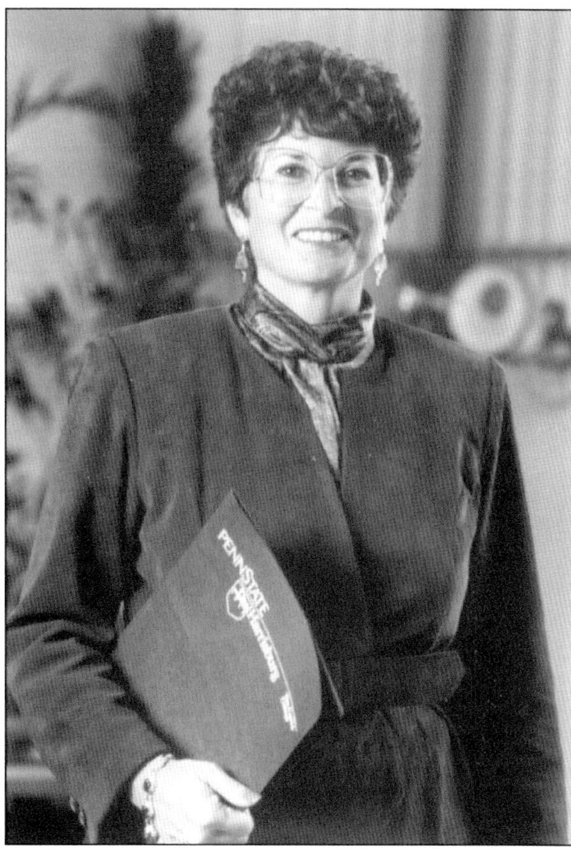

Provost and Dean Ruth Leventhal, c. 1984–1985. The Capitol Campus' fifth leader was Dr. Ruth Leventhal, who served as provost and dean from 1984 to 1994. During her tenure, the campus bookstore was constructed and a PhD program was established in Public Administration. Most importantly, in 1986, the school officially transformed from a campus to a college and changed its name to "Penn State Harrisburg."

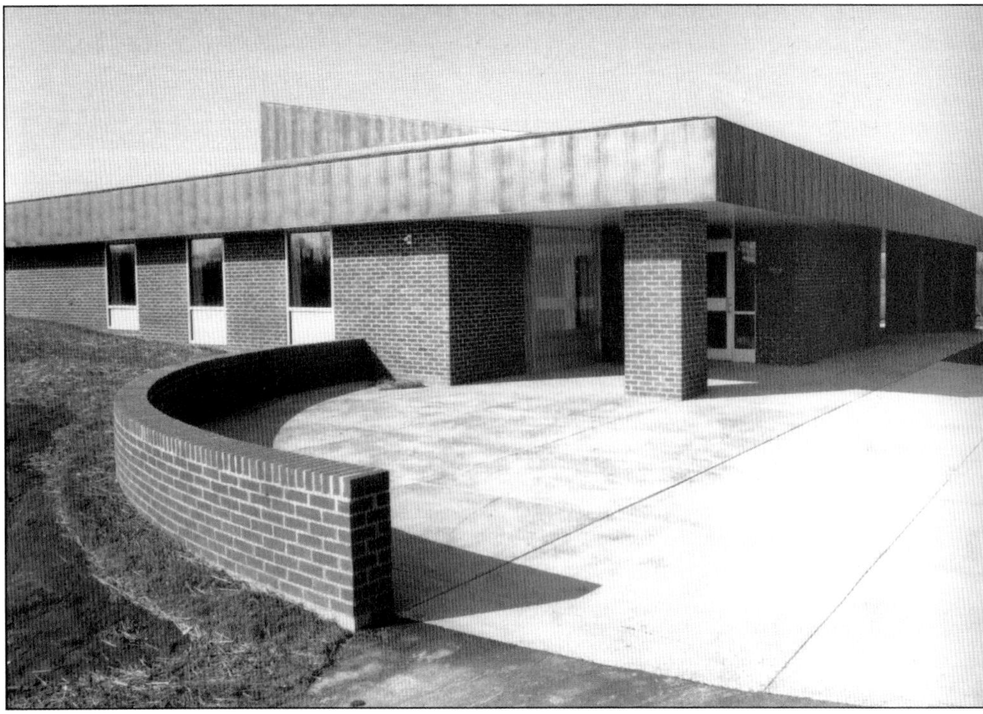

Campus Bookstore, 1985. These photographs capture the exterior and interior of the new campus bookstore constructed near the SET Building on campus and completed in 1985.

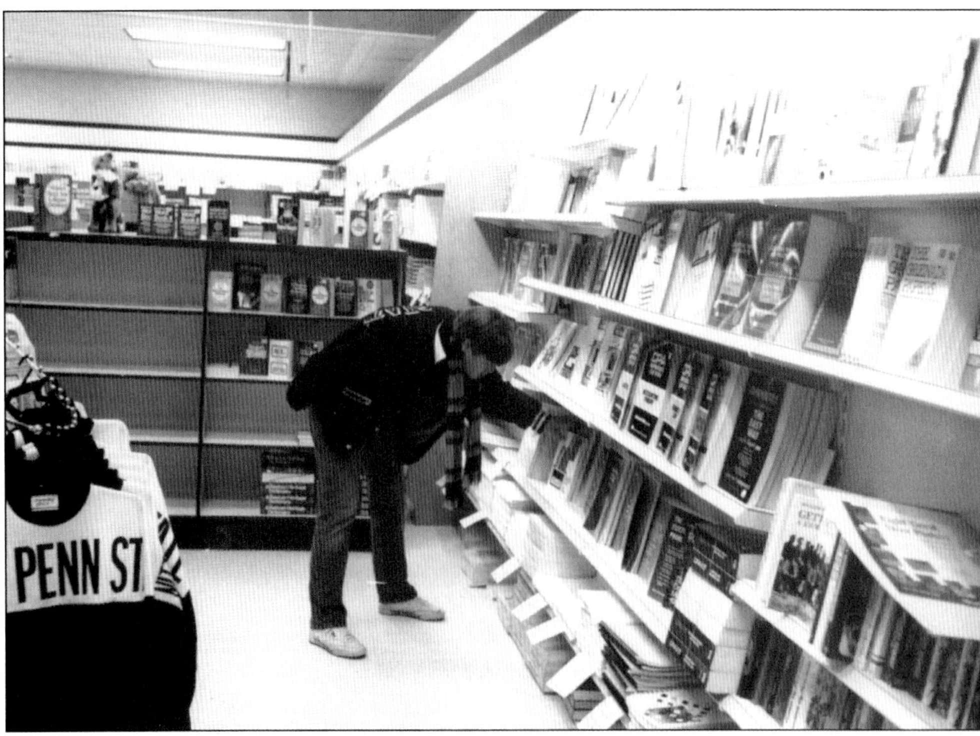

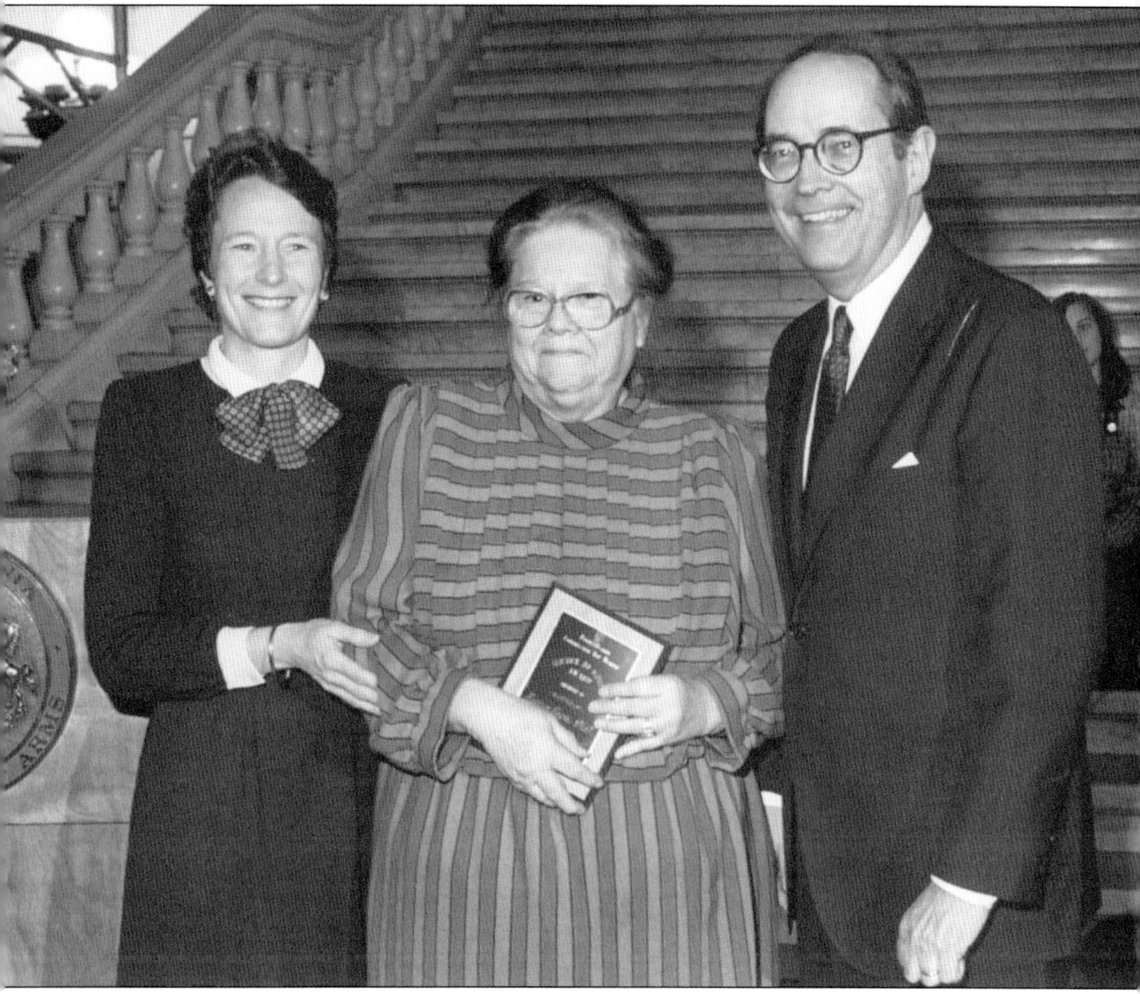

Dr. Kathryn Towns and the Thornburghs, 1986. On March 26, 1986, Penn State Harrisburg's associate dean for research and graduate studies, Dr. Towns (center), was presented the "Service to Women Award" from the Pennsylvania Commission for Women. Dr. Towns received the award from Pennsylvania governor Dick Thornburgh (right) and his wife, Ginny (left). Today, Penn State Harrisburg remembers the commitment that Dr. Towns demonstrated to raising awareness about issues and concerns that impact women with the "Kathryn Towns Award." It is annually given to recognize students, alumni, staff, or faculty who continue Dr. Towns's mission.

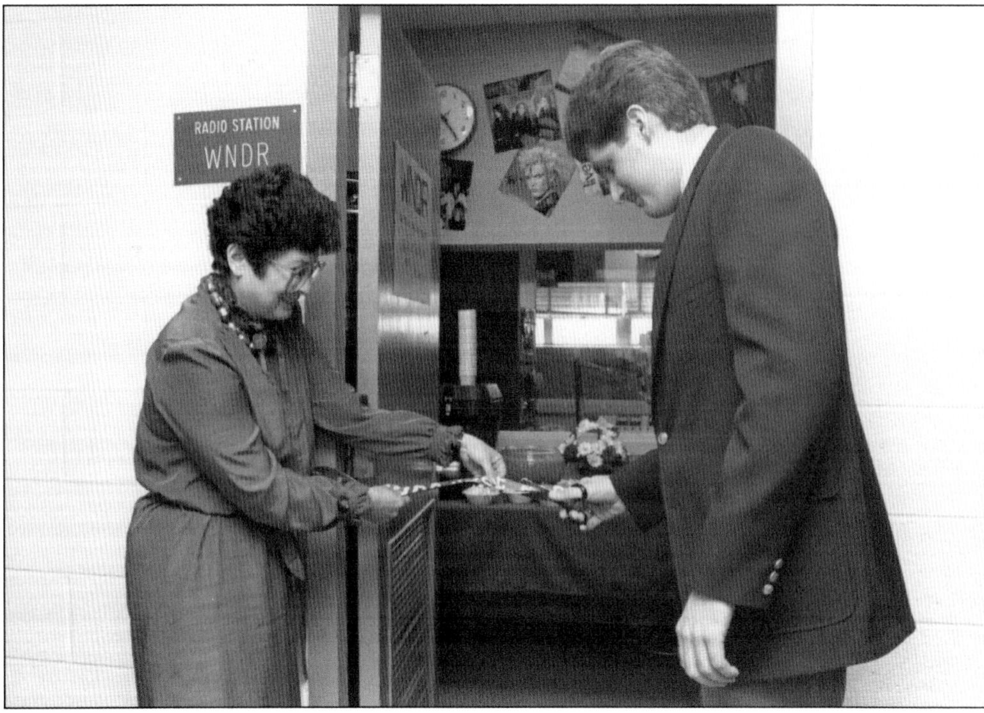

CAMPUS RADIO STATION, 1987. The above photograph documents the dedication of the new campus radio station, WNDR (630 and 1530 AM). The revival of the radio station in spring 1987 was supported by Provost and Dean Ruth Leventhal. It replaced the first campus radio station, WZAP 640 AM, which was created in fall 1969 and operated for 14 hours a day. WZAP featured music in an open format, along with news and community information. Today, the college's radio station is WPSH The Reactor, a reference to the school's proximity to Three Mile Island. The image below captures an unidentified student DJ working inside the radio booth at WNDR in the late 1980s. In keeping with the school's marked transformation to a lively college campus, the Philadelphia-based band Tommy Conwell & the Young Rumblers delighted students with a concert at the Capital Union Building (CUB) on Saturday, October 24, 1987.

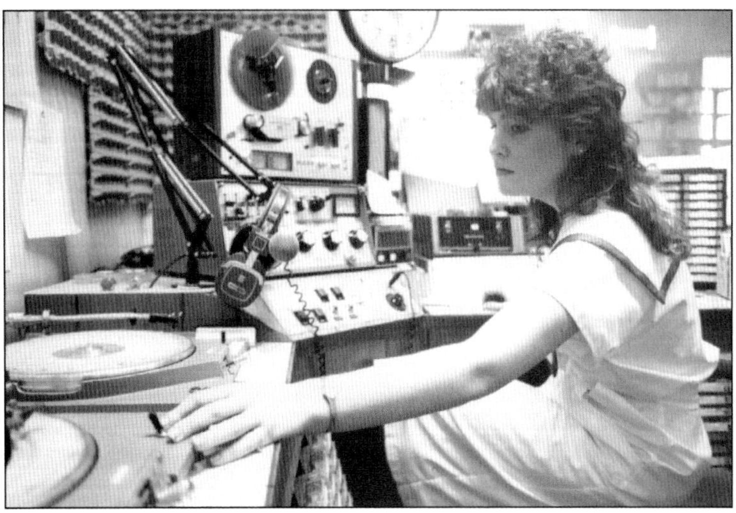

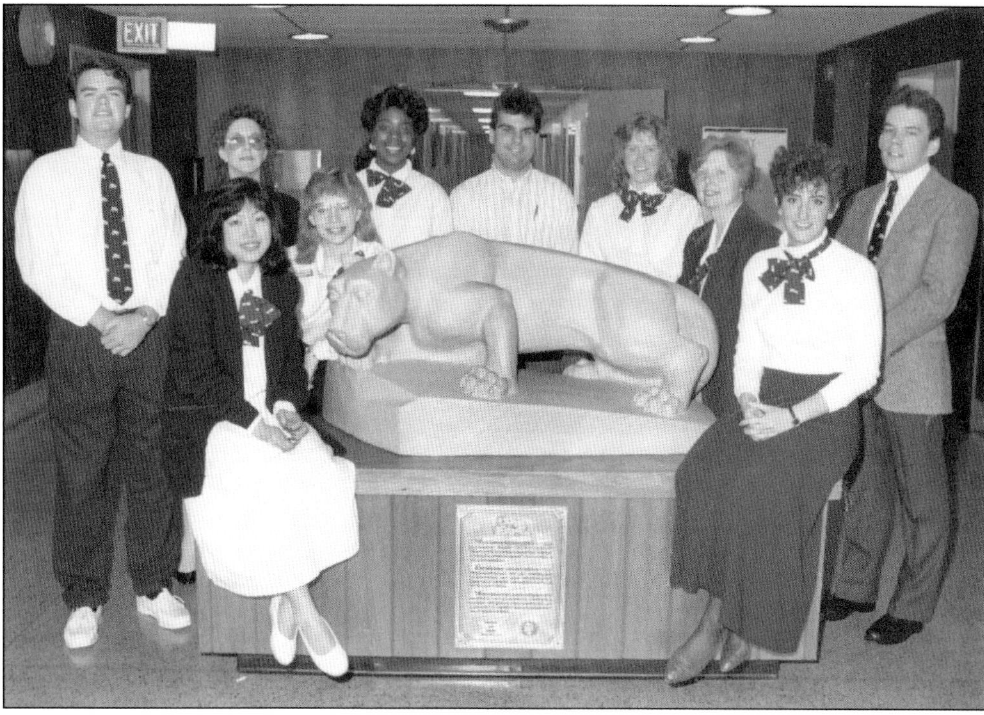

Lion Ambassadors, 1988. The Lion Ambassadors student organization at Penn State Harrisburg fosters pride in the college through various campus activities such as homecoming, Penn State alumni events, campus tours, strengthening university traditions, and working with VIP alumni volunteers. The group of Lion Ambassadors pictured here proudly stand in front of the *Nittany Lion Shrine* in the Olmsted Building.

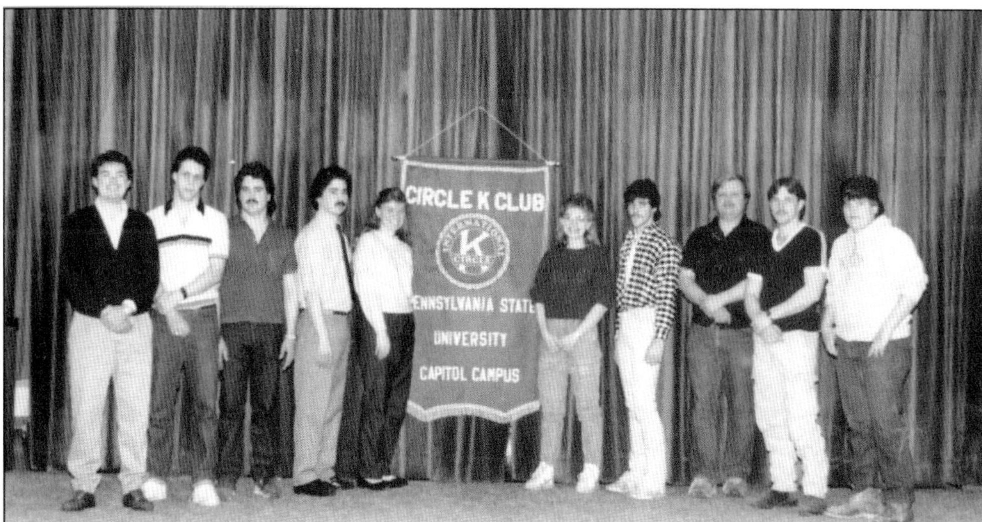

Circle K Club, 1988. The Circle K Club is a community service organization connected to Kiwanis clubs, which focus on service to children. At Penn State Harrisburg, the Circle K Club was active in the late 1980s as well as in the early 2000s. Unfortunately, due to the growing number and variety of organizations available to students on campus, interest in the Circle K Club ended.

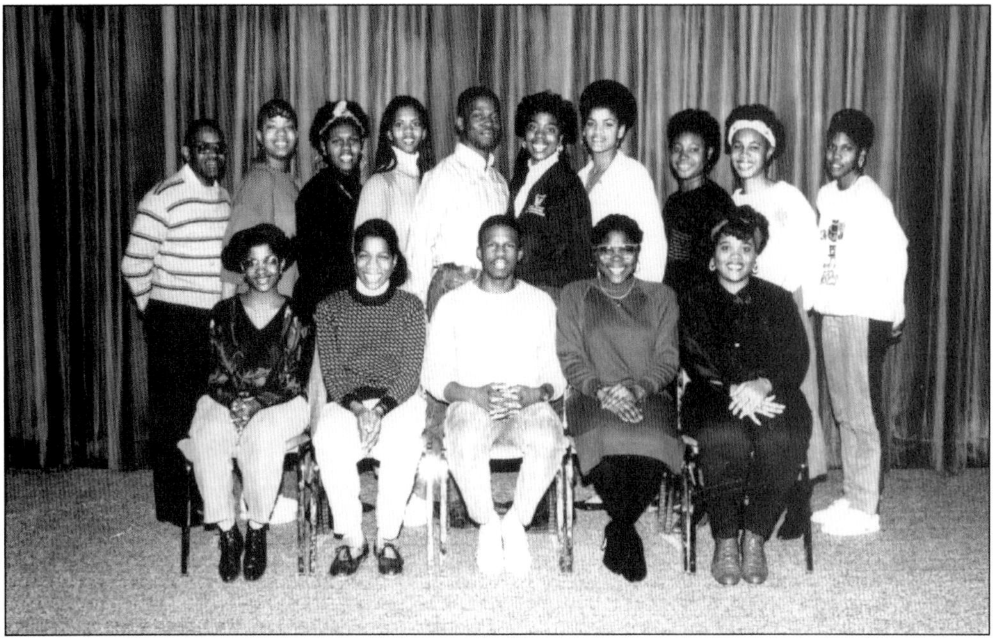

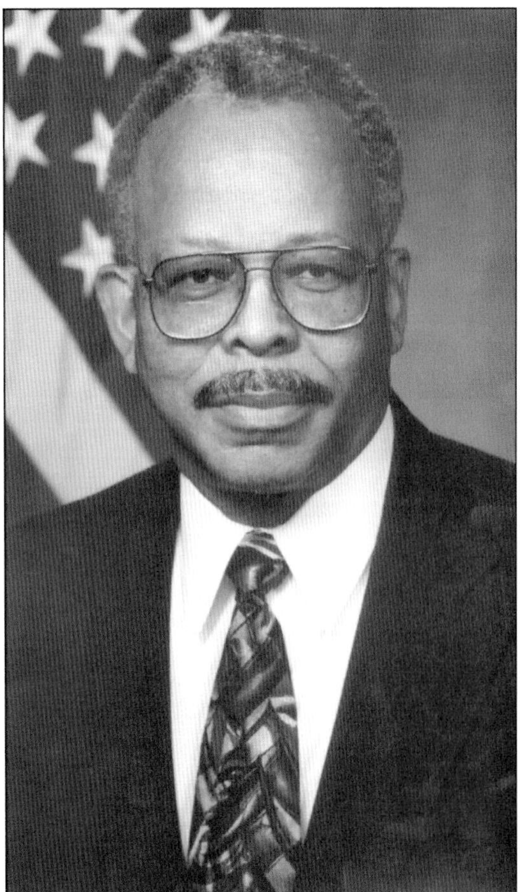

Black Student Union, 1988. The Black Student Union (BSU) was established around 1970 to encourage minority students to enroll at the Capitol Campus. As early as 1973, the BSU organized an annual Black Cultural Arts Festival held during Black History Month in February. BSU was instrumental in establishing the Black Cultural Arts Center on campus, as well as sponsoring numerous events and workshops. It is still an active club today.

Lt. Gen. Emmett Paige Jr., 1988. In 1988, Lt. Gen. Emmett Paige Jr., a 1974 graduate of the Capitol Campus, became the first Capitol Campus recipient of the university's Distinguished Alumni Award. Established in 1951, the award is the highest honor that Penn State bestows upon an outstanding alumna or alumnus. The award recognizes the achievements of outstanding alumni whose lives, professional accomplishments, and community service exemplify the objectives of Penn State.

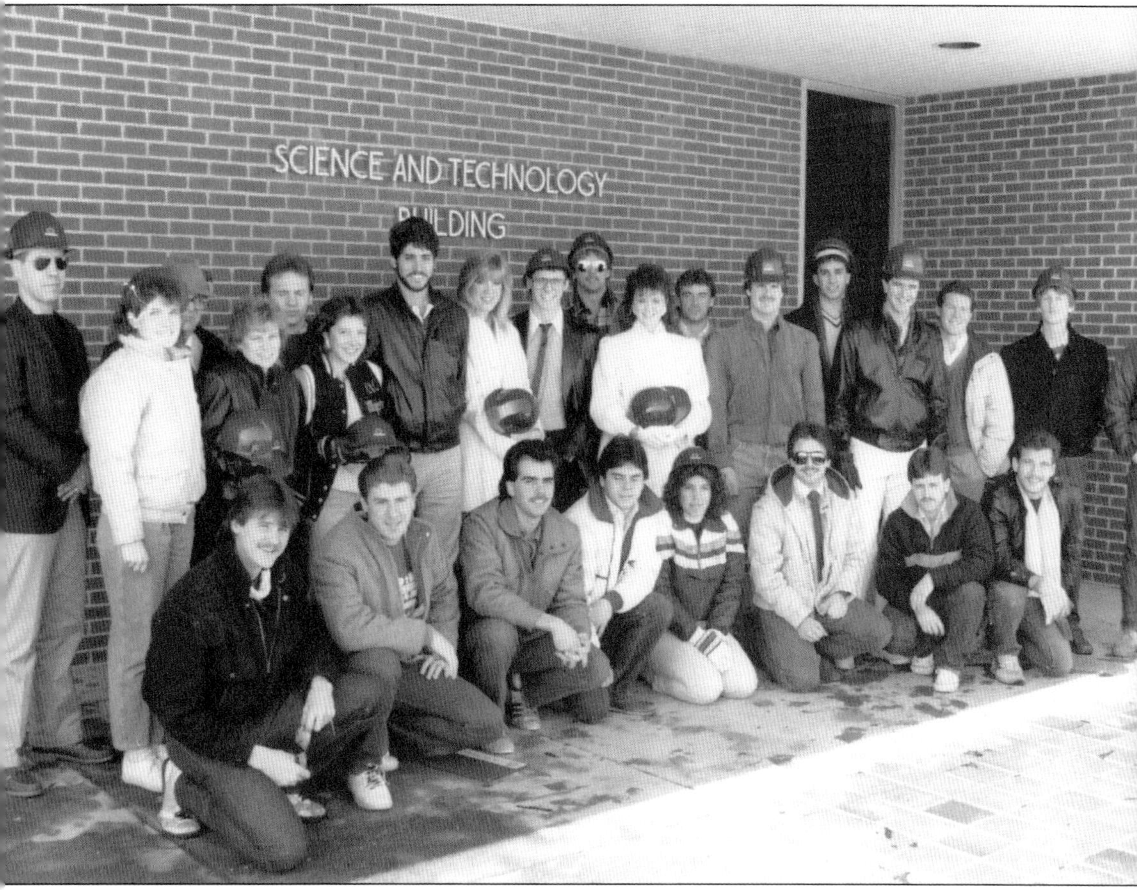

Penn State Professional Engineers and Contractors, c. 1986–1988. The Penn State Professional Engineers and Contractors (PSPEC) student organization is open to all engineering majors at the college and tied to three parent organizations: Pennsylvania Society of Professional Engineers (PSPE), Associated Builders and Contractors (ABC), and Associated General Contractors (AGC). PSPEC has a long and illustrious history at Penn State Harrisburg that dates back to the early years at the school, when the club was the student chapter of the PSPE. As such, PSPEC is closely tied to many of the college's unique traditions, landmarks, and activities. PSPEC organized and sponsored the first bathtub races on campus in 1972 and continues to do so annually. The student group also made a lasting contribution to the campus' facilities by designing and constructing the concrete base that supports Penn State Harrisburg's *Nittany Lion Shrine* in the Vartan Plaza in 2006.

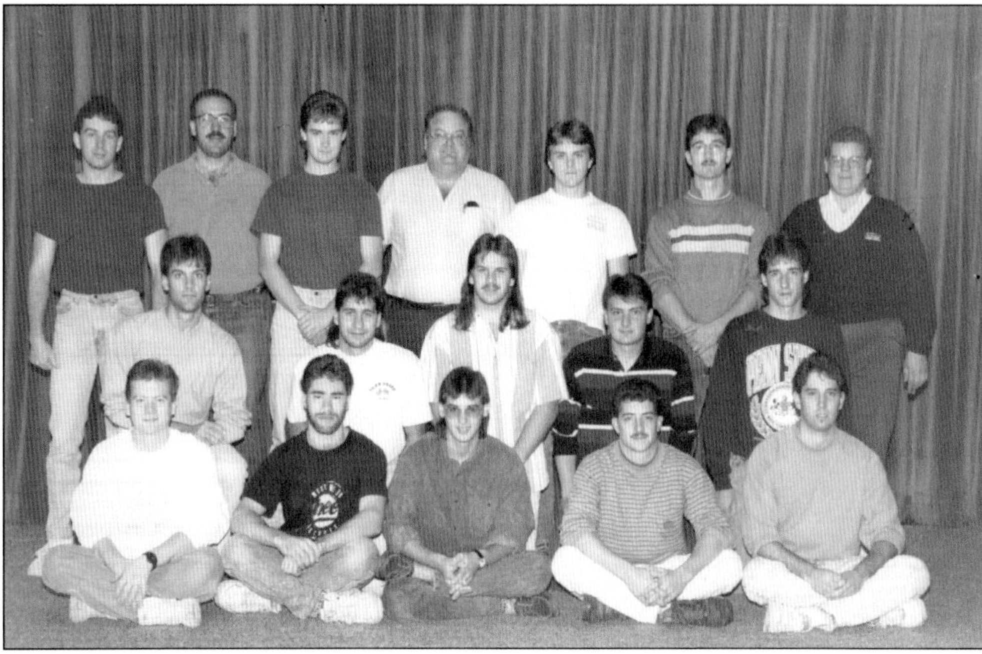

SOCIETY OF AUTOMOTIVE ENGINEERS, C. 1988–1989. With a long history of excellence in science, engineering, and technology programs at Penn State Harrisburg, it is not surprising that the college could sustain more than one student engineering club over the years. Chartered in 1978, the student chapter of the Society of Automotive Engineers (SAE) is an organization for students interested in land, sea, air, and space transportation. Above, the students who gathered for this club photograph in the late 1980s created their own multi-terrain vehicle, a Mini-Baja (pictured below) and entered it into the Mini-Baja East Competition held May 11–13, 1989, at West Virginia State University in Morgantown, West Virginia.

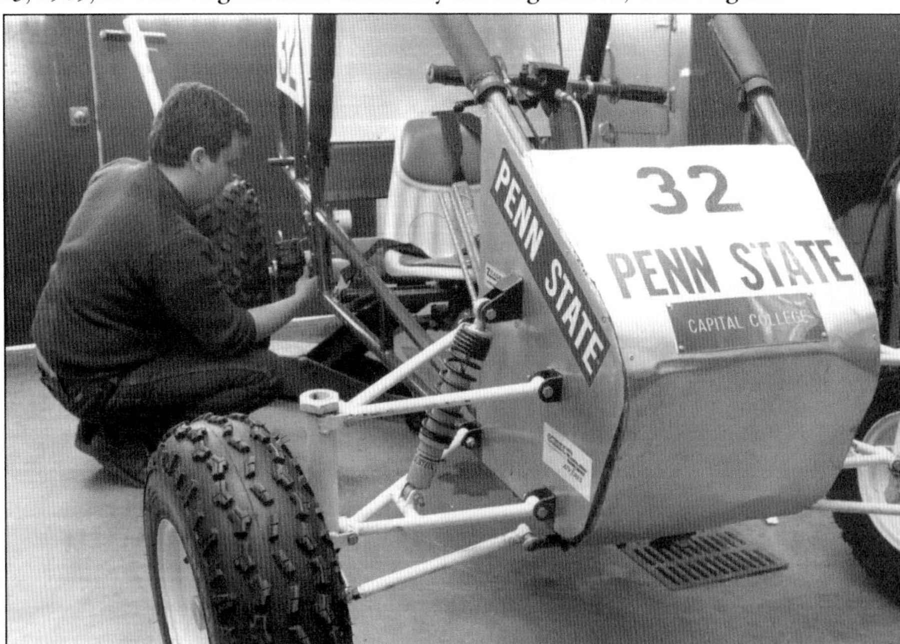

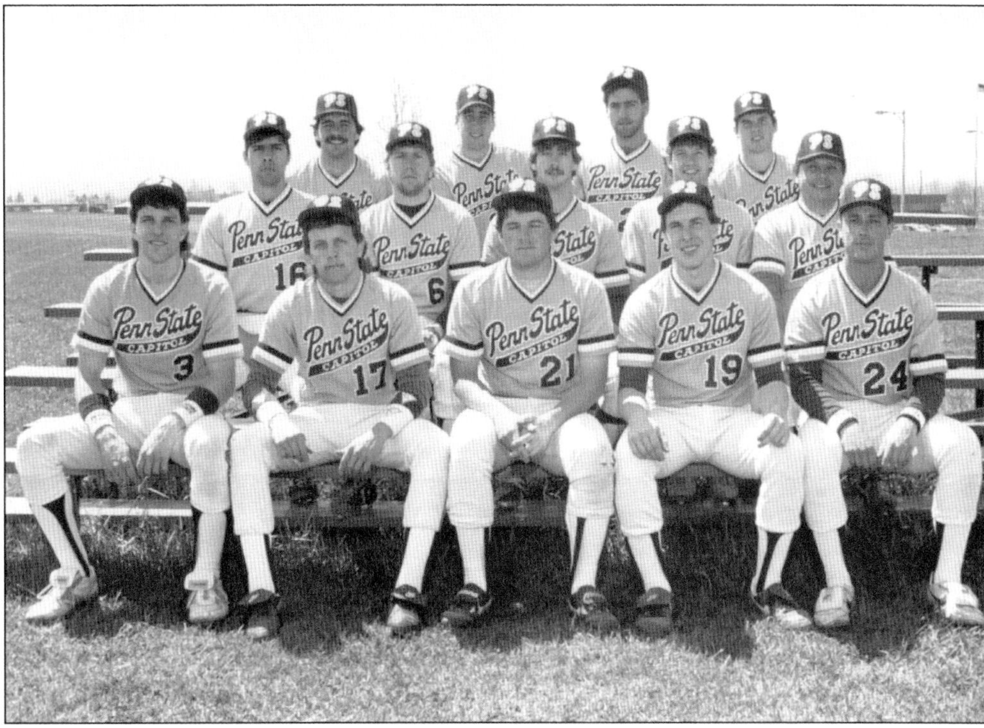

Baseball and Soccer Teams, c. 1985–1988. During the 1980s, Penn State Harrisburg offered students the opportunity to participate in baseball (above), soccer (below), and 20 other intramural sports. Some short-lived but notable intramural sports included walley-ball (volleyball played in a racquetball court), walk-a-mile, bicycle derby, and martial arts.

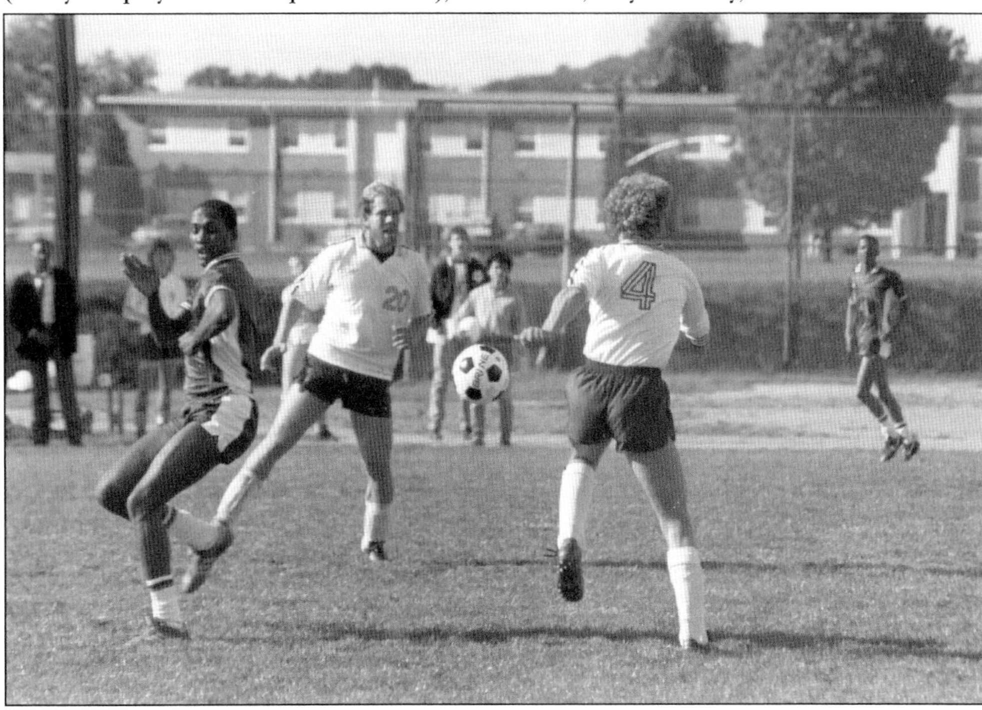

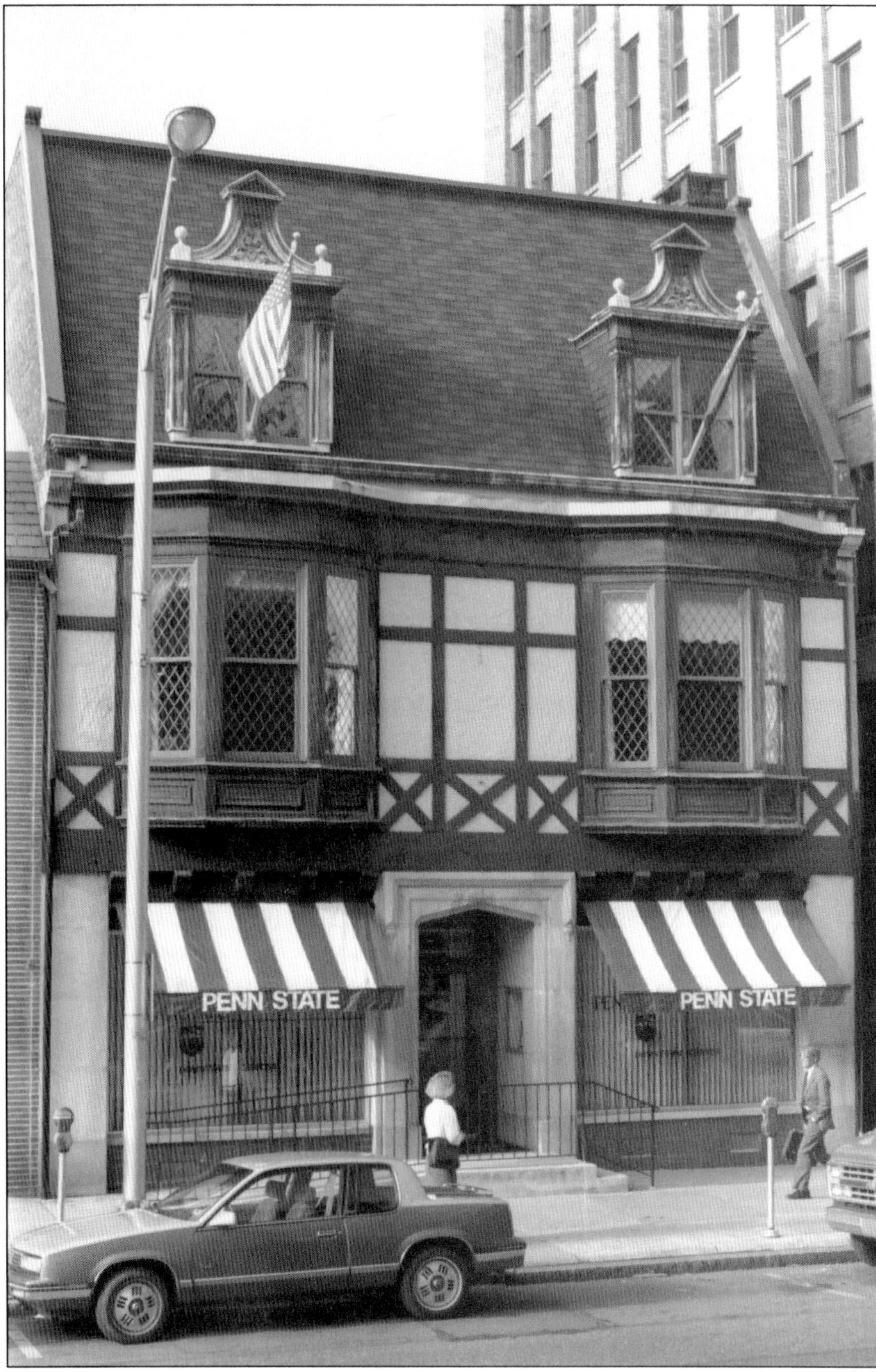

DOWNTOWN CENTER, C. 1988. Located at 234 North Third Street in a historic English-Tudor style building in downtown Harrisburg, the Penn State Downtown Center housed the Penn State Center for Government and Policy Studies. With over 7,000 square feet of space for classrooms and offices, the Downtown Center allowed Penn State Harrisburg, University Park colleges, and Continuing Education to extend services to more people in the greater Harrisburg area. The Downtown Center closed in 2006.

Five

BRANCHING BEYOND MIDDLETOWN 1990–1999

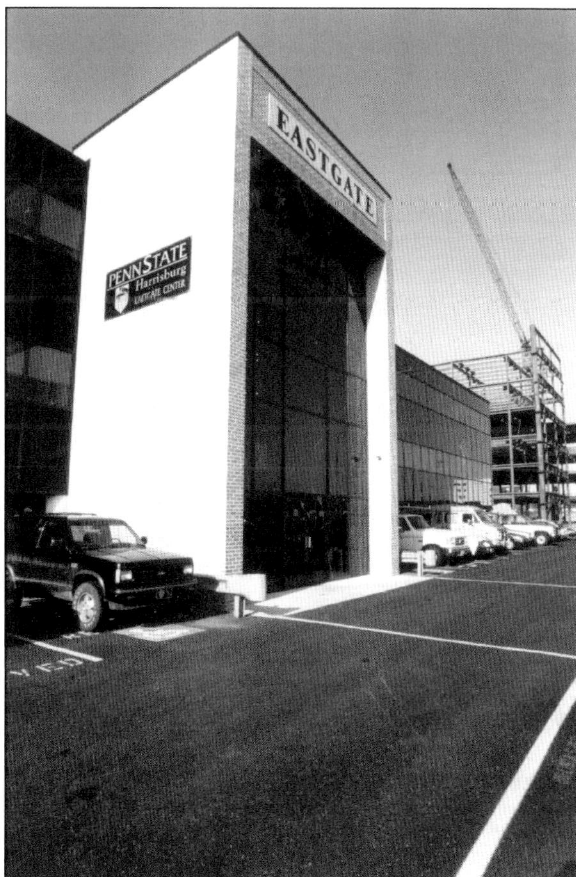

EASTGATE CENTER, C. 1990S. During the 1990s, the college continued to reach beyond the boundaries of Middletown. Three years after the Downtown Center opened, it was overcrowded. The Penn State Harrisburg Eastgate Center, which opened in May 1991, addressed this issue. It was located at 1010 North Seventh Street in downtown Harrisburg and housed a portion of Continuing Education from 1991 to 2012. Continuing Education centralized its offices in June 2012 and is now located on the Penn State Harrisburg campus. The Eastgate Center is owned by the university and houses the south central office of the Ben Franklin Technology Partners of Central and Northern Pennsylvania.

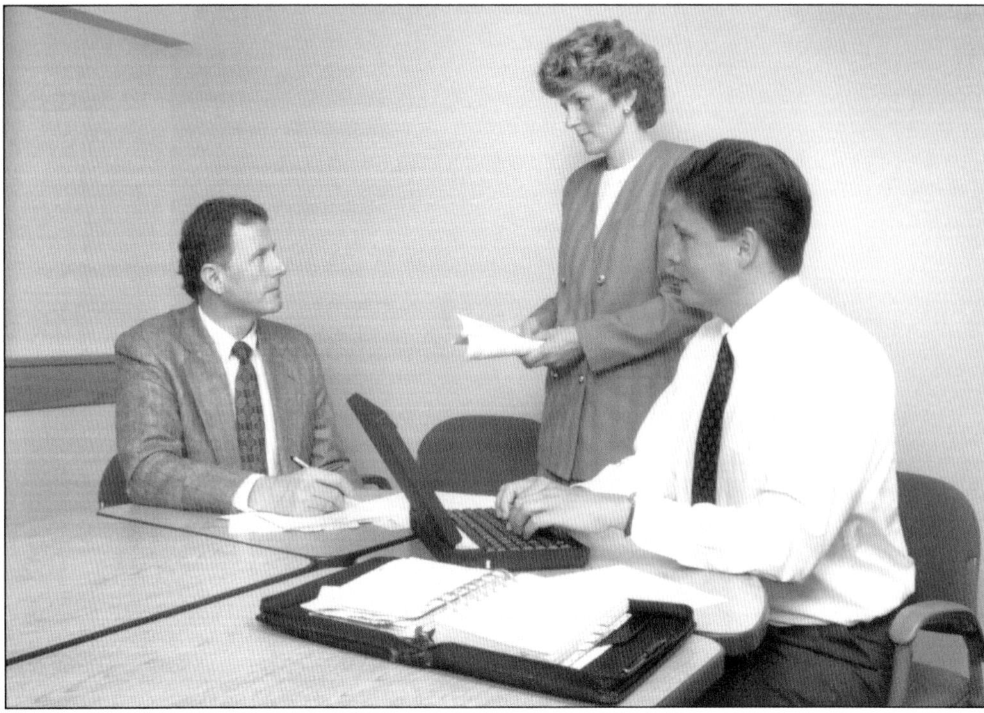

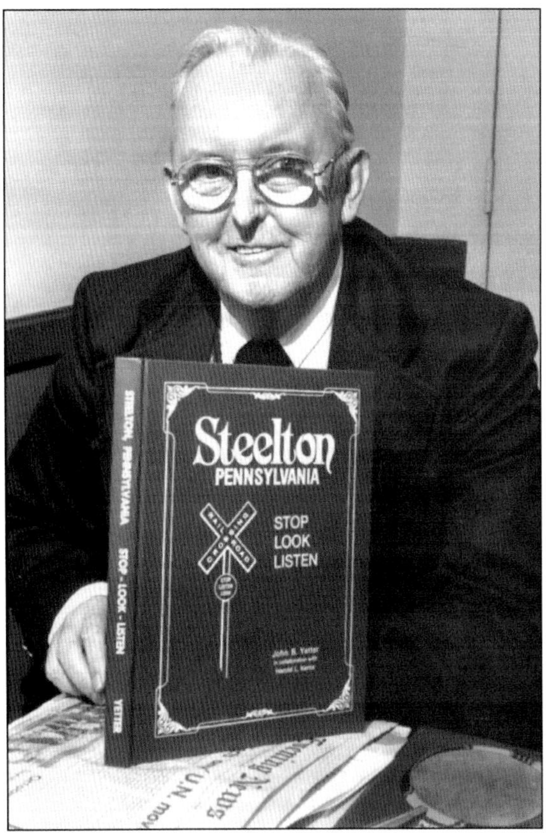

CONTINUING EDUCATION, C. 1990S. Continuing Education at Penn State Harrisburg complements the formal programs offered by the college and facilitates professional development opportunities that support lifelong learning. Established by Penn State in the 1950s, Continuing Education has had a presence at the Harrisburg campus since the 1970s. Pictured here are Dr. Edward Minnock (left), director of Continuing Education; Erin Shannon (center), and Mark Borger (right).

JOHN YETTER AND THE CENTER FOR PENNSYLVANIA CULTURE STUDIES, 1990. Established in 1990 by faculty in Penn State Harrisburg's School of Humanities and American Studies program, the center was created to facilitate the study of Pennsylvania's cultural heritage. One of the center's resources is the John Yetter Collection of Steelton Historical Materials, which contains over 2,000 photographs and publications compiled by John Yetter, shown here with his book, *Steelton, Pennsylvania: Stop, Look, Listen.*

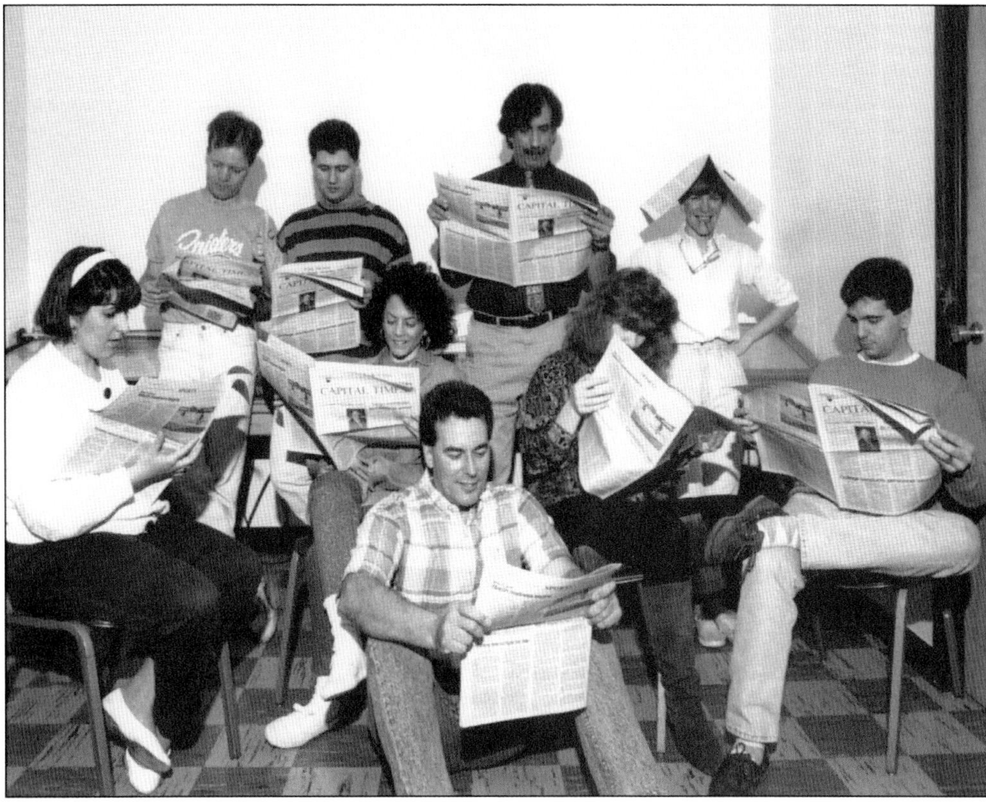

Staff at the *Capital Times*, 1991. During the early 1990s, few people had easy access to the Internet, and online news media outlets were still evolving. Traditional newspapers maintained their popularity as a form of mass media. The Penn State Harrisburg student newspaper, *Capital Times*, continued to publish local, state, national, and international news and kept the student body informed about current events. As evidenced by the number of students who posed for the above photograph, *Capital Times* featured a fairly large staff. In the January 25, 1991, issue of the newspaper (pictured at right), students' opinions and comments about the Persian Gulf crisis illustrate their support for the president and US military action.

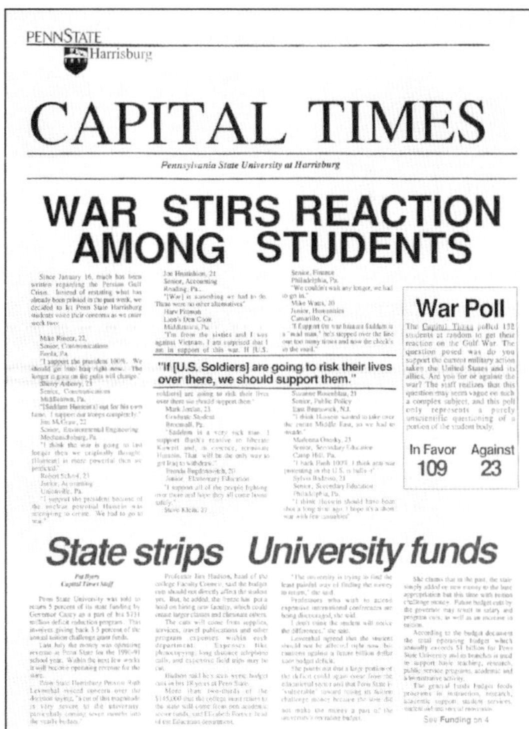

PENNSTATE Harrisburg

CAPITAL TIMES

Pennsylvania State University at Harrisburg

WAR STIRS REACTION AMONG STUDENTS

"If [U.S. Soldiers] are going to risk their lives over there, we should support them."

War Poll

The Capital Times polled 132 students at random to get their reaction on the Gulf War. The question posed was do you support the current military action taken the United States and its allies. Are you for or against the war? The staff realizes that this question may seem vague on such a complex subject, and this poll only represents a purely unscientific questioning of a portion of the student body.

In Favor	Against
109	23

State strips University funds

See Funding on 4

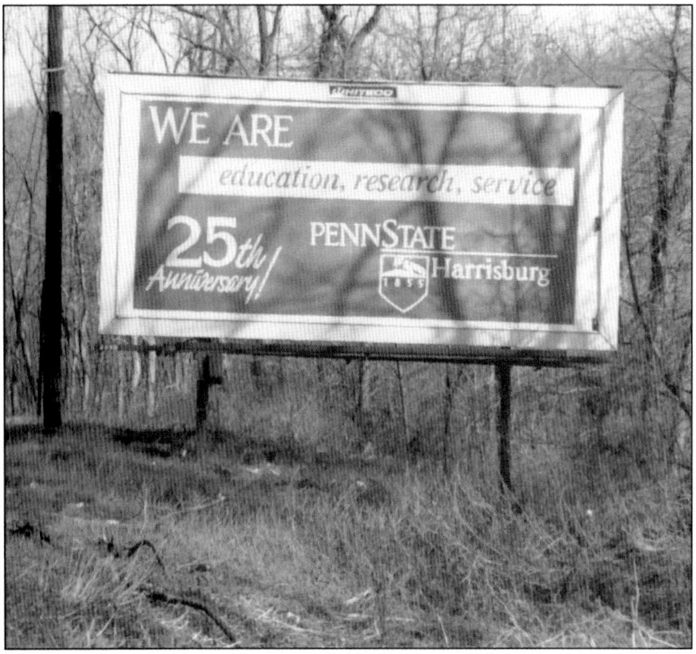

Twenty-Fifth Anniversary Sign, 1991. The year 1991 marked a milestone for the college: the recognition and celebration of 25 years of hard work that culminated in the college's evolution from a former US Air Force base to a bustling campus with 3,400 students and 16,000 alumni, as well as 20 undergraduate, 12 graduate, and 2 doctoral programs. The roadside billboard pictured here proudly announces the 25th anniversary of Penn State Harrisburg.

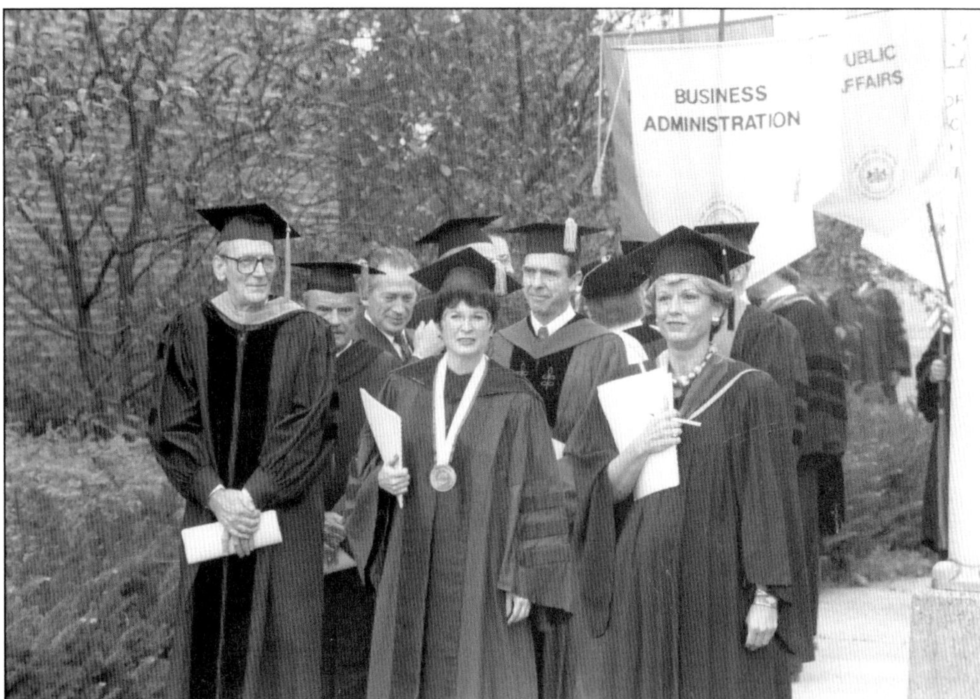

Twenty-Fifth Anniversary Convocation, 1991. This photograph captures the faculty processional that launched the college's 25th anniversary convocation ceremony, which was held on October 4, 1991, in the Sculpture Garden behind the Olmsted Building. Pictured here are, from left to right, Dr. Stanley Miller (acting provost and dean, 1984); Dr. George Wolf (dean of faculty, 1973–1978); Dr. Theodore Gross (provost and dean, 1979–1983); and Dr. Ruth Leventhal (provost and dean, 1984–1994).

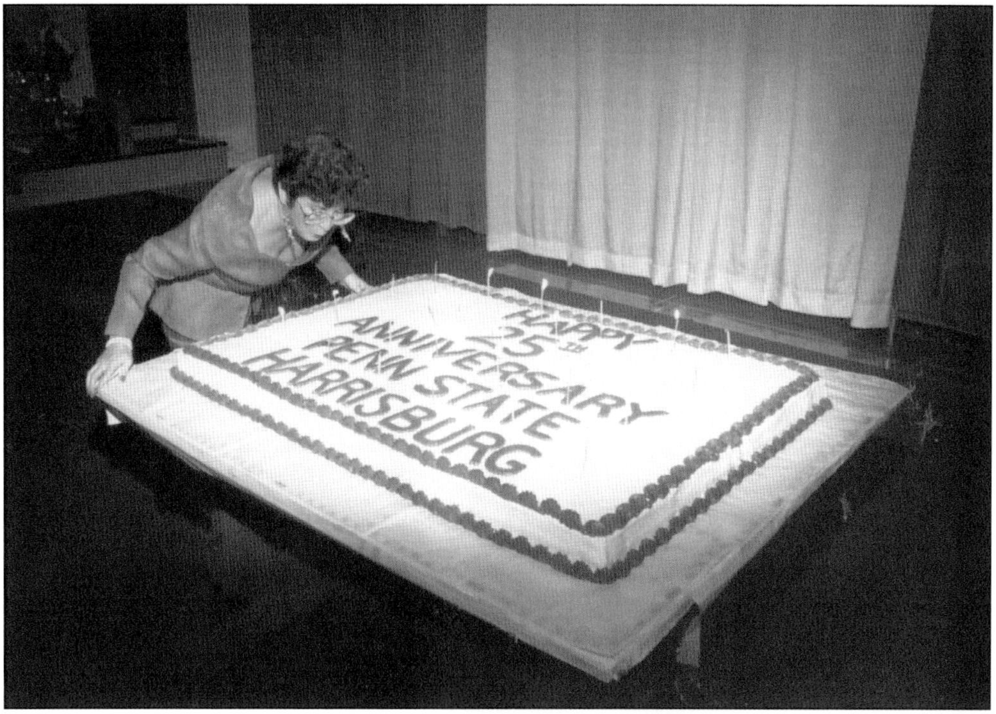

Twenty-Fifth Anniversary Cake, 1991. In addition to the convocation ceremony and speeches, the 25th anniversary celebrations included sporting events; a 3.1-mile race across campus; lunch on the Vartan Plaza that featured cheeseburgers, hot dogs, soft pretzels, and wet-bottom shoefly pie; and a gigantic festive cake, pictured here with Dr. Ruth Leventhal.

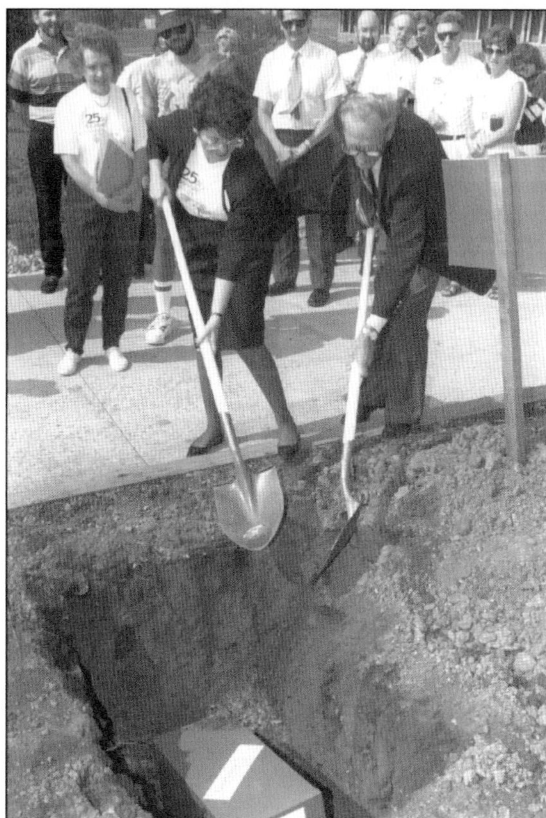

Twenty-Fifth Anniversary Time Capsule, 1991. A time capsule ceremony was held in the Vartan Plaza on October 4, 1991, as part of the college's 25th anniversary celebrations. Dr. Ruth Leventhal is pictured on the left holding a shovel to bury the time capsule, which contained various Penn State Harrisburg artifacts and memorabilia such as a 1991 fall class schedule, a calculator, and an issue of the student newspaper, *Capital Times*.

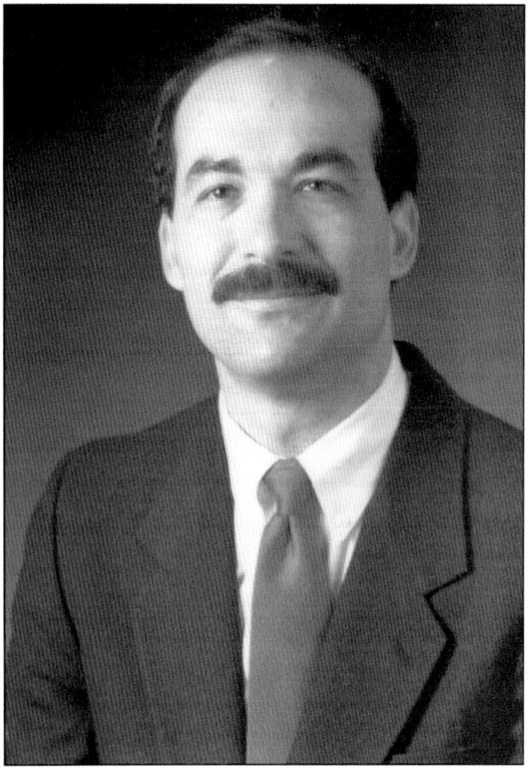

Dr. Simon J. Bronner, 1991. In January 1991, Dr. Bronner, a prolific author, scholar, and internationally acclaimed American folklorist, was named Distinguished Professor of American Studies and Folklore at Penn State Harrisburg. Dr. Bronner was the first professor from the college to earn this prestigious university title that recognizes a highly select group of faculty with outstanding achievements in teaching, research, and service.

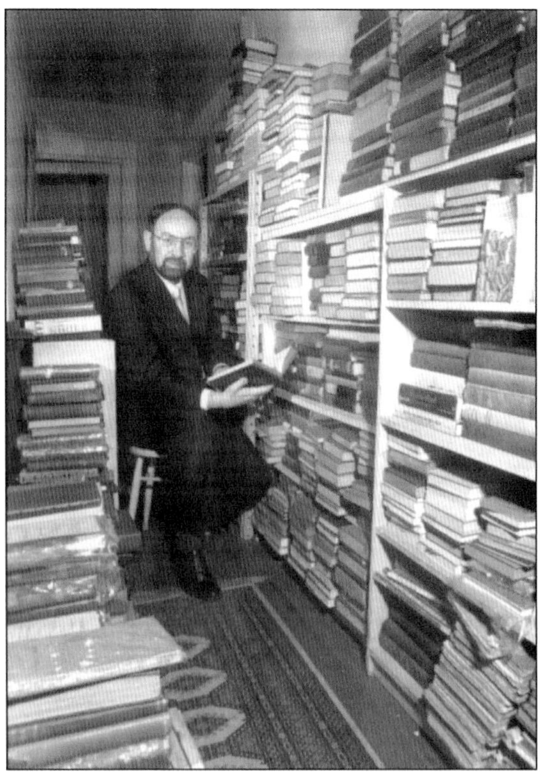

Dr. Harold B. Shill with Marshall Collection, 1991. After Dr. Charles Townley retired in 1990, a new division head of Library and Information Services was needed. Dr. Shill was appointed to this position on August 12, 1991. He is pictured surrounded by thousands of books and archival materials in the home of Alice Marshall, whose women's history collection was acquired by the Penn State Harrisburg Library in 1991.

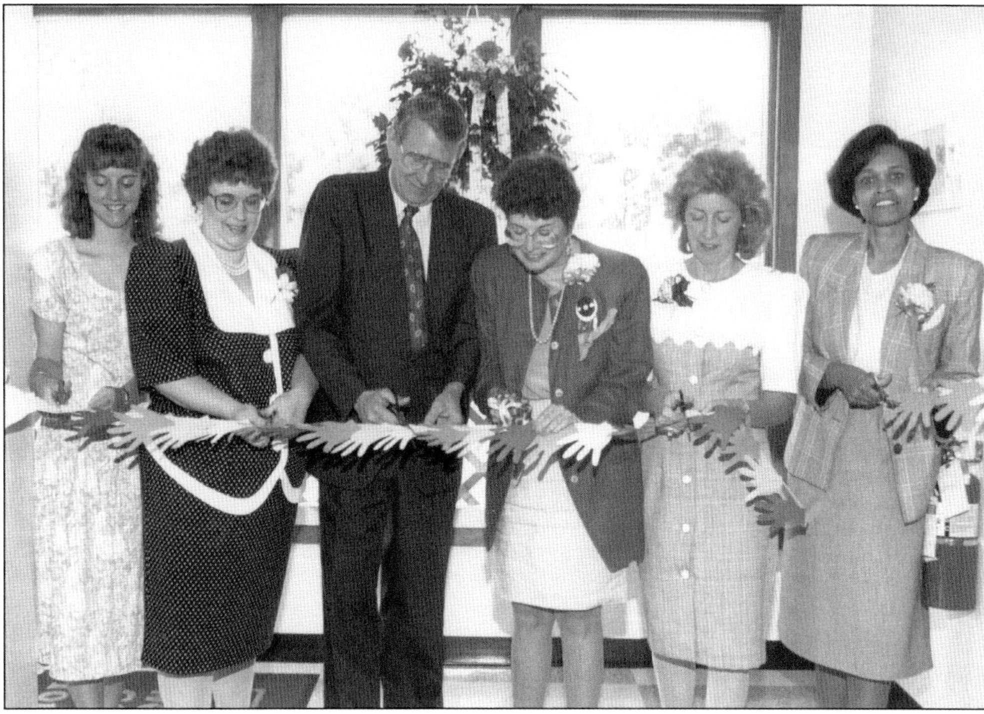

Childcare Center Dedication, 1991. After years of lobbying the college for affordable, convenient, and professional day-care services on campus, a childcare center was finally created by renovating the former Student Center near Wrisberg Hall. The Center was dedicated in 1991, with Dr. Ruth Leventhal (fourth from left) present at the ceremony. Today, it is called the Penn State Harrisburg Child Learning Center and operated by Hildebrandt Learning Centers, LLC.

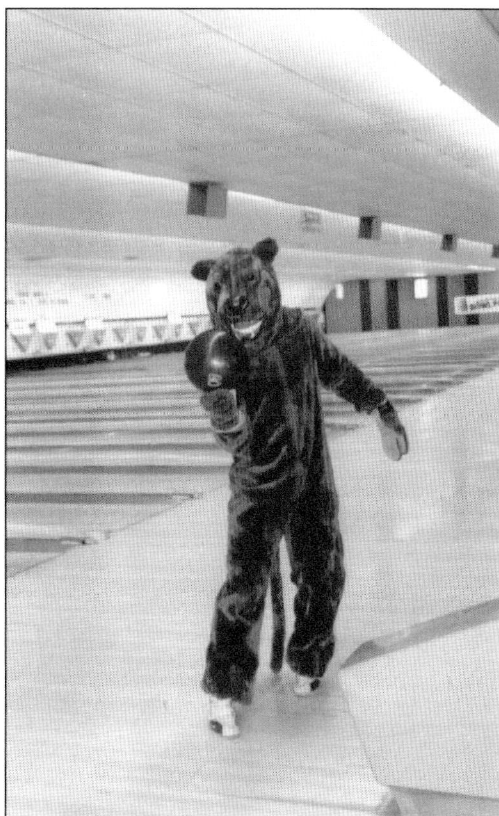

Bowling for Kids' Sake, 1990. Service to the community has always been important to students, faculty, and staff at Penn State Harrisburg. The Nittany Lion mascot made an appearance at the ninth annual Big Brothers/Big Sisters of America Bowl-A-Thon held in March 1990 at Trindle Lanes in Mechanicsburg, Pennsylvania. Staff and students turned out for the event, which raised over $2,200 for the organization.

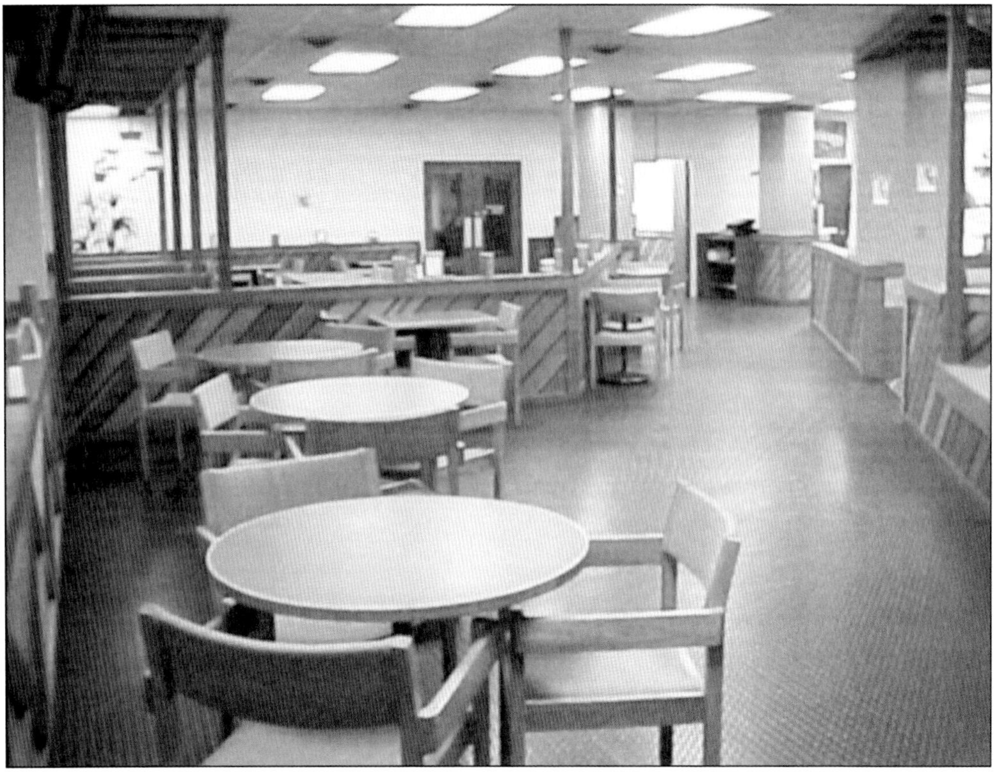

Lion's Den, c. 1991. Food service on campus was limited in the 1990s. A room located in the basement of the Olmsted Building provided hot and cold foods and held vending machines, which earned the room the name "Vendorville" until the early 1980s. In November 1981, with input from students, faculty, and staff, the cafeteria was renamed the "Lion's Den," pictured above.

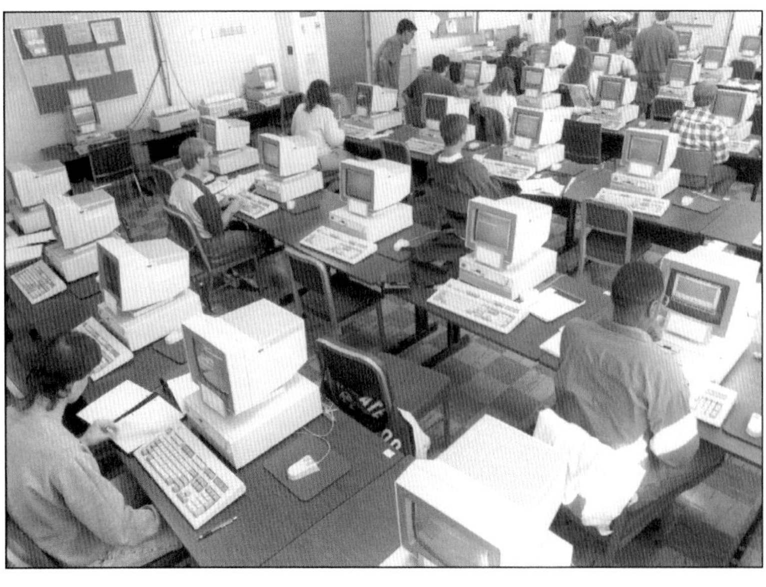

Computer Lab, c. 1991. Academic computing was embraced at Penn State Harrisburg and in full force by the early 1990s, as shown by this student computer lab located in the Olmsted Building.

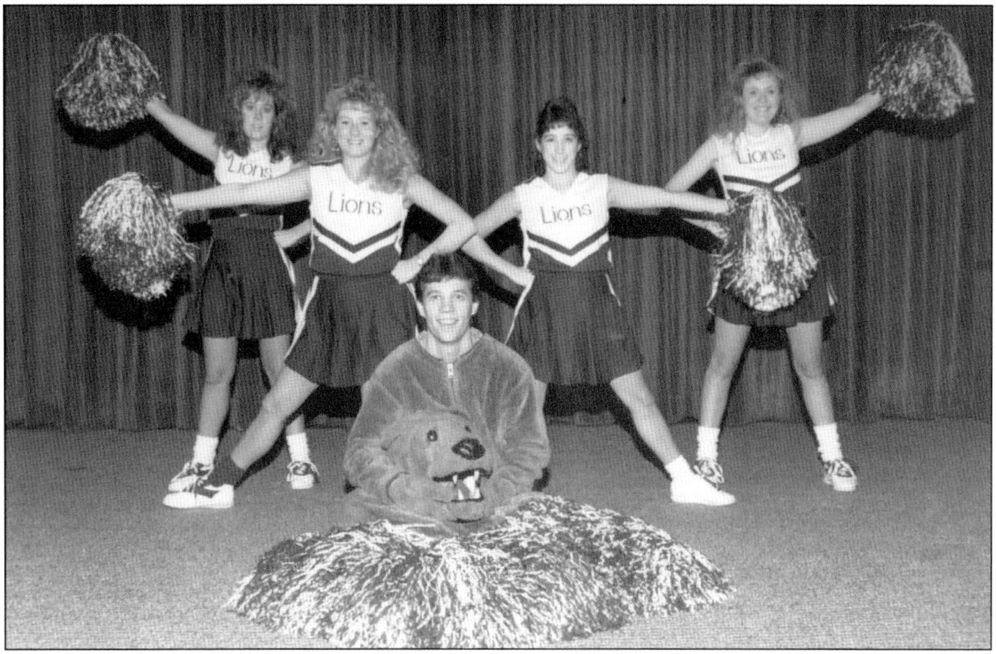

Cheerleading Squad, c. 1990–1991. Penn State pride and spirit were ever-present at athletic events on campus. This photograph of the Lions Cheerleading Squad includes the Penn State Nittany Lion mascot, whose handmade and valuable costume was donated to and is now part of the College History Archives located in Archives and Special Collections at the Penn State Harrisburg Library.

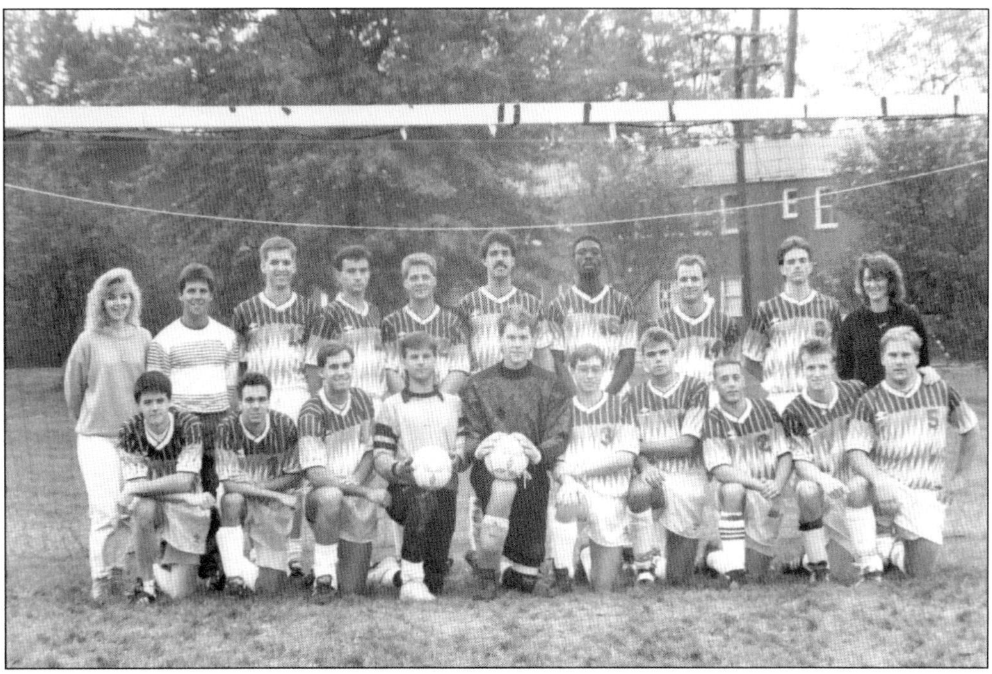

Men's Soccer Team, c. 1991–1992. This image shows the Penn State Harrisburg men's varsity soccer team from the 1991–1992 season.

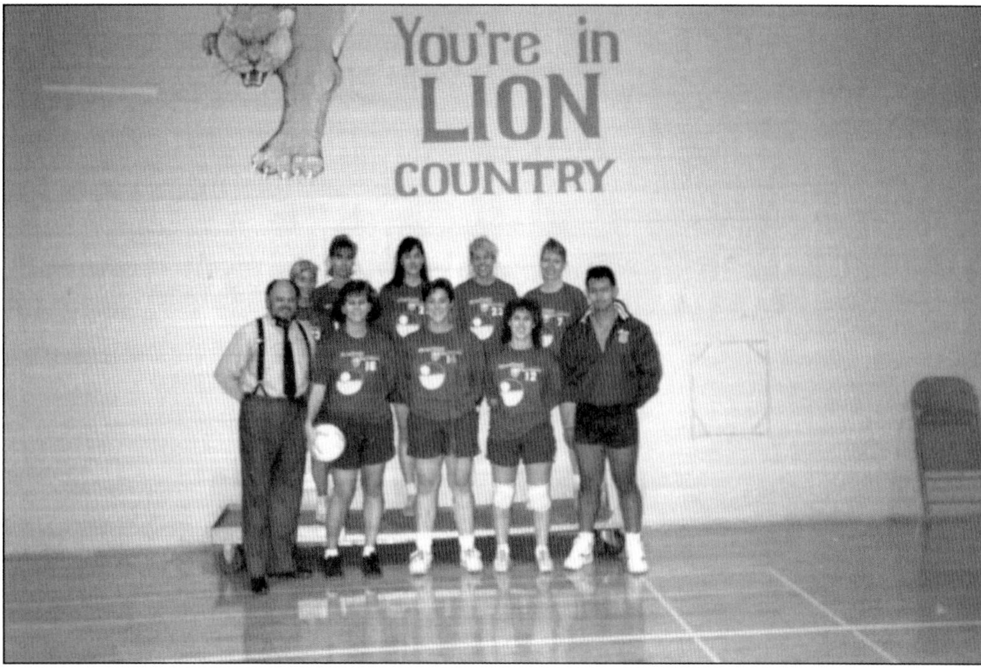

WOMEN'S VOLLEYBALL, C. 1991–1992. The college was well-represented in the 1991–1992 season by the women's varsity volleyball team, pictured above in the gym of the Capital Union Building (CUB). Note the mural on the wall that says, "You're in Lion Country." The photograph below captures a women's varsity volleyball game in action during the 1991–1992 season.

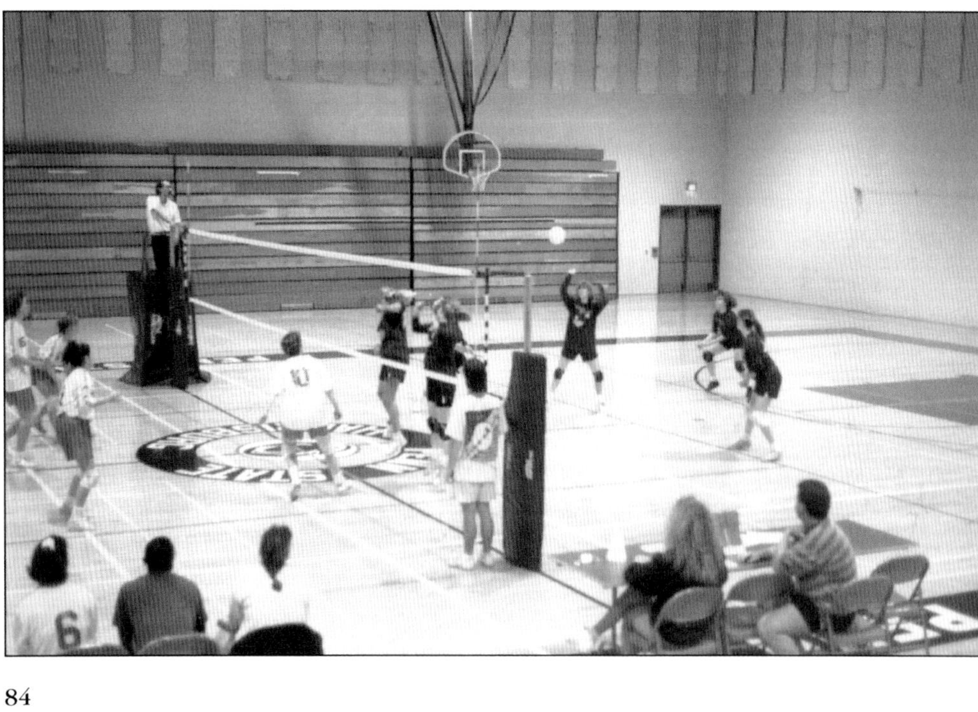

Cross Country Runner, c. 1991. A lone cross country runner takes advantage of the expansive trails and hilly terrain across the 218-acre campus at Penn State Harrisburg.

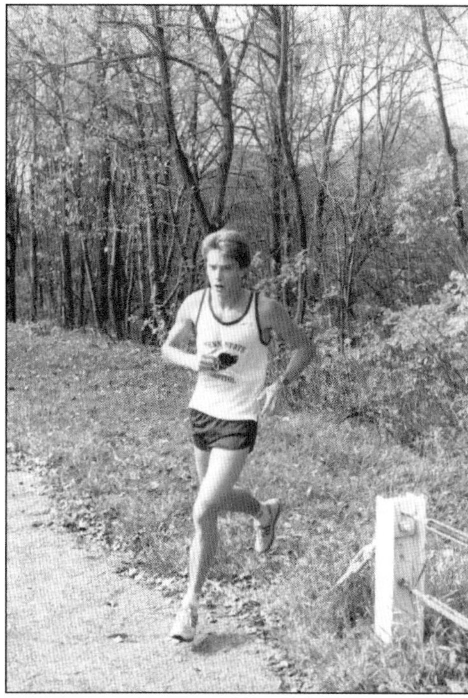

Men's Basketball Team, 1992. Historically, basketball has always been the most well-attended athletic event on the Penn State Harrisburg campus. This photograph of the 1992 men's basketball team, known as the Lions, reflects the continued interest from students in athletics as a part of rounding out the college experience. In 1995, Penn State Harrisburg began a 10-year hiatus from competing in intercollegiate sports, although intramural sports continued during the break.

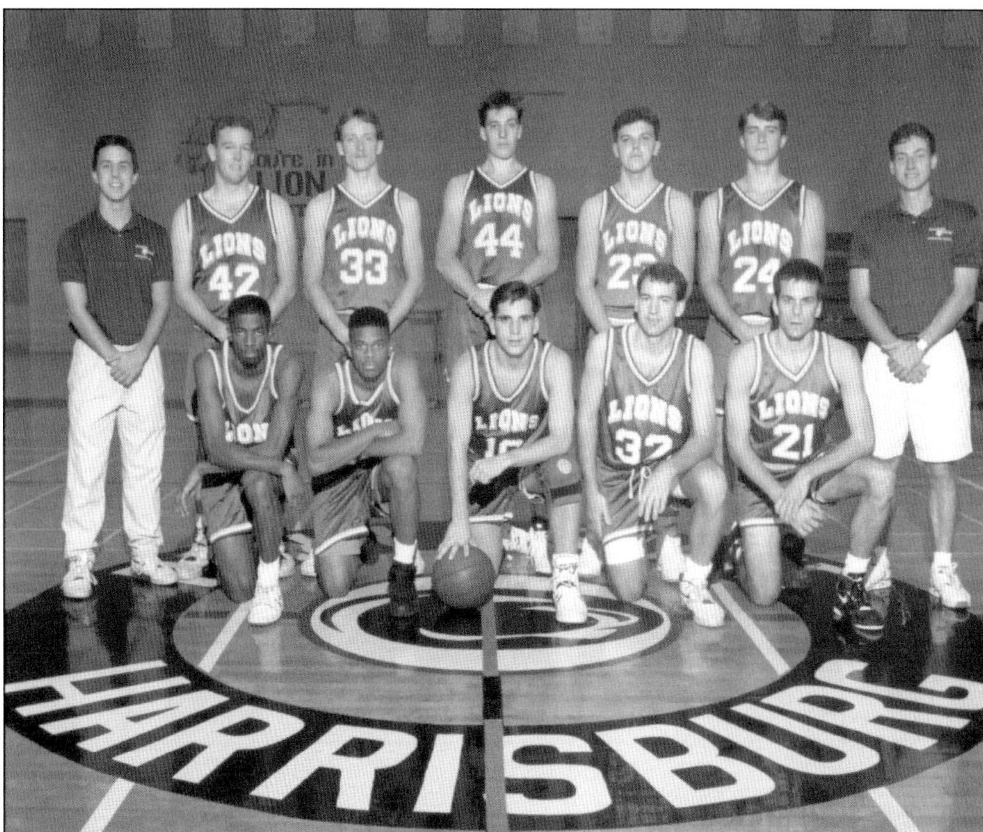

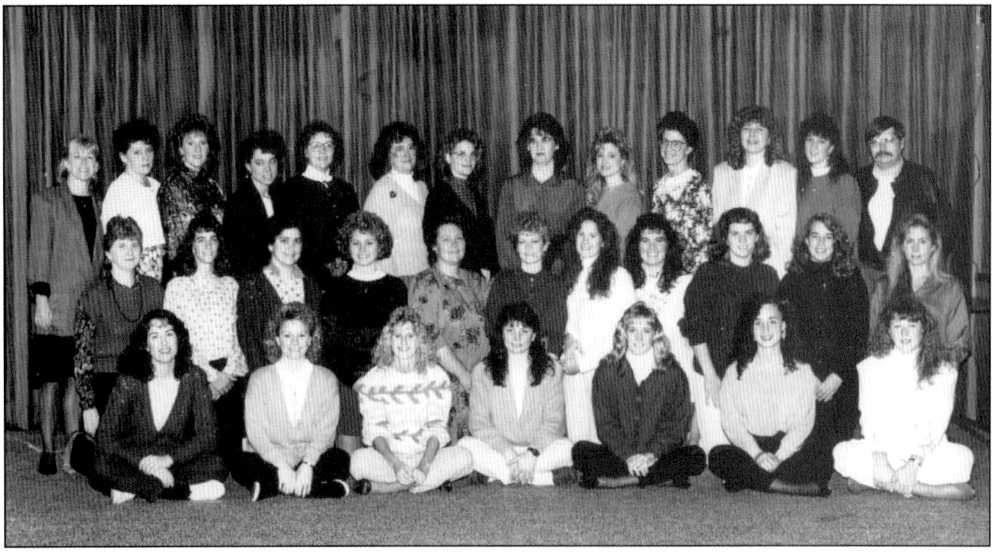

Kappa Delta Pi Members, 1992. Penn State Harrisburg's undergraduate and graduate programs have a strong reputation for excellence in education. Accordingly, the Kappa Delta Pi International Honor Society in Education was installed at Penn State Harrisburg in May 1990. The college is part of the Sigma Alpha Chapter of Kappa Delta Pi, the world's largest association of education and education-related professionals.

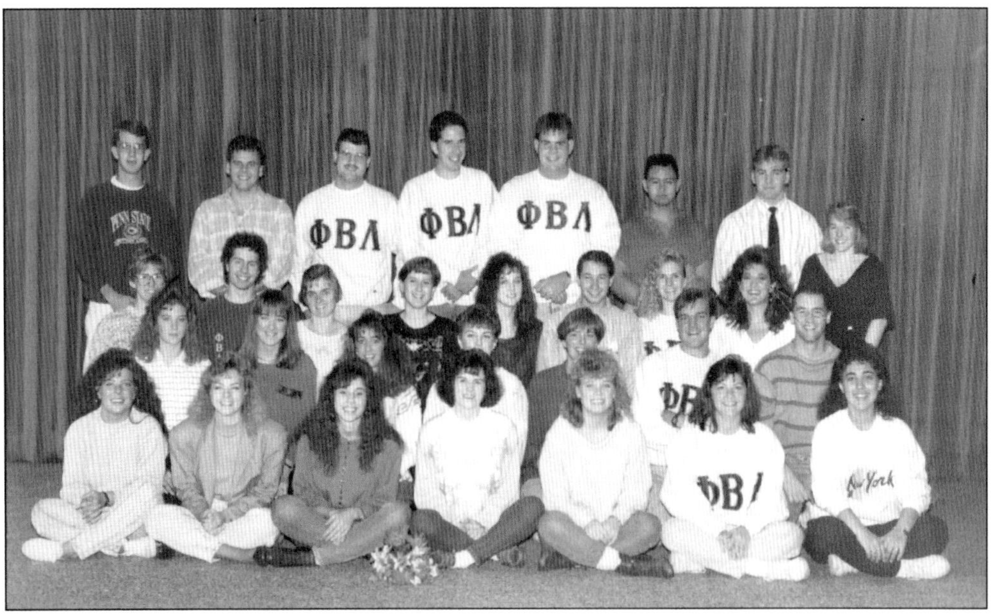

Phi Beta Lambda, 1992. In addition to its strengths in education, Penn State Harrisburg is well known for its business administration programs. Phi Beta Lambda, the collegiate version of the Future Business Leaders of America, serves the needs of business majors looking for a coed professional business fraternity. Penn State Harrisburg initiated this student organization in 1977–1978.

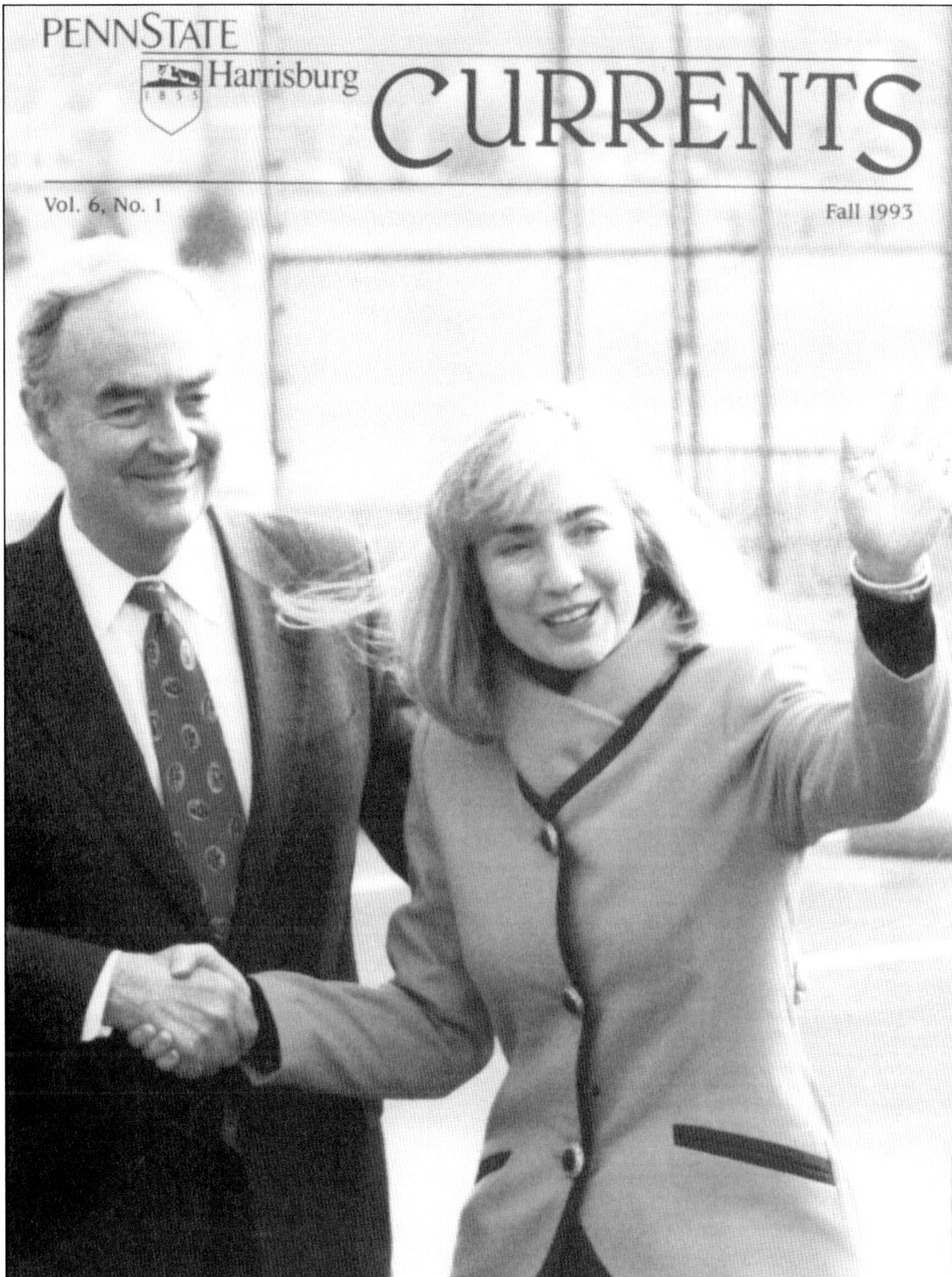

HILLARY CLINTON ON CAMPUS, 1993. On February 11, 1993, Penn State Harrisburg had a famous visitor—Hillary Rodham Clinton, the First Lady of the United States. She came to campus, along with Vice Pres. Al Gore's wife, Tipper, to attend Sen. Harris Wofford's Pennsylvania Health Care Conference in the Capital Union Building. While on campus for the day, the First Lady reported that her father and brother are Penn State alumni. Not surprisingly, media flocked to campus for her historic visit. The First Lady was prominently featured on the cover of the fall 1993 issue of *Currents*, Penn State Harrisburg's alumni magazine.

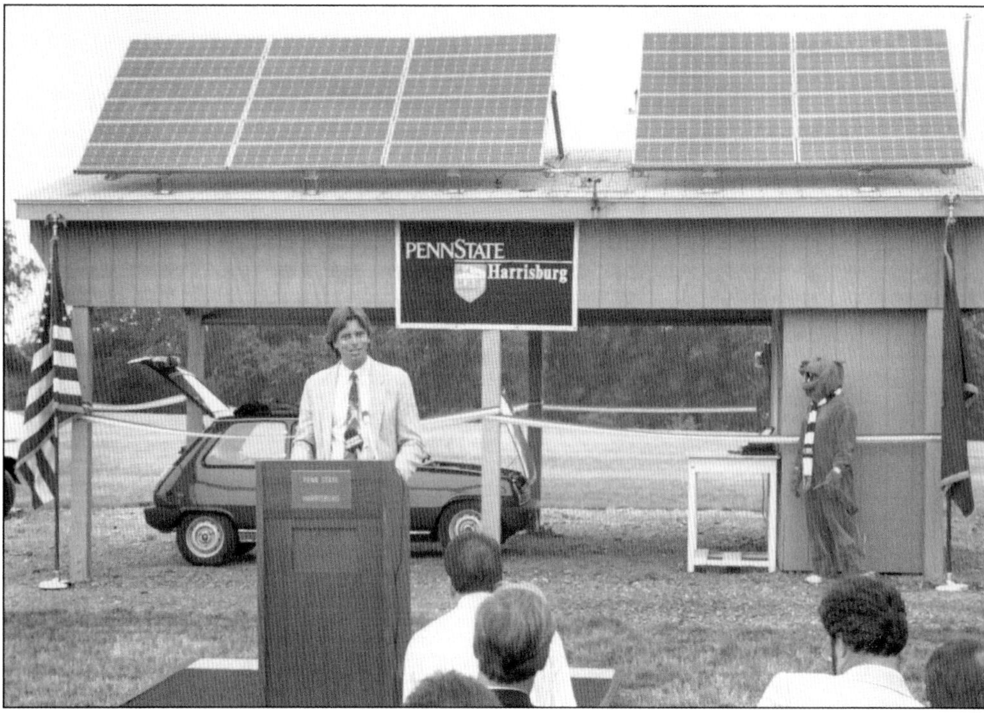

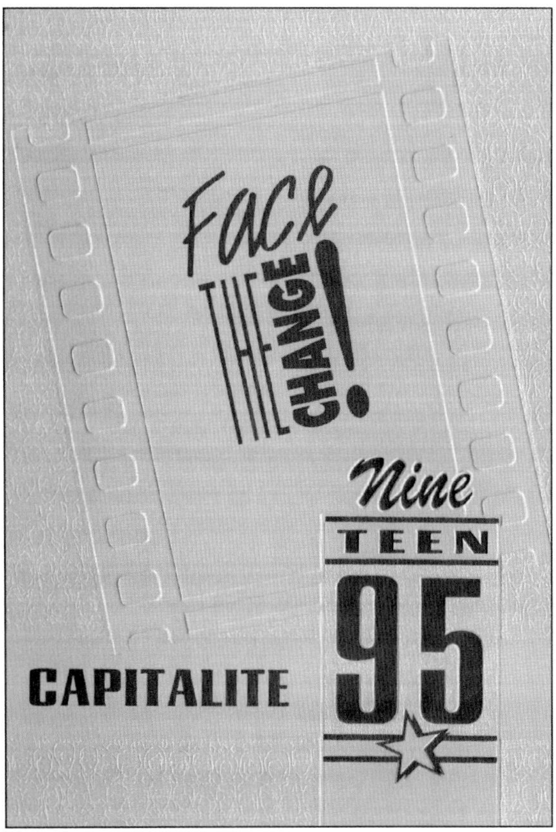

Electric Vehicle Charging Station, 1994. Ever a leader in the application of science, engineering, and technology, Penn State Harrisburg's SET faculty and students developed an innovative approach to recharging electric vehicles by using a solar carport. With the support of a grant from the Pennsylvania Energy Development Agency, Prof. Andrew Lau (pictured) developed the project and led the formal dedication ceremony of the charging station in June 1994.

The Final *Capitalite*, 1995. Students at Penn State Harrisburg produced a yearbook from 1968 until 1995, when it ceased publication. This image shows the last *Capitalite*, published in 1995. Student yearbooks are vital to understanding the history of Penn State Harrisburg because they serve as a primary record of students' lives, campus events, and activities that shaped the college community.

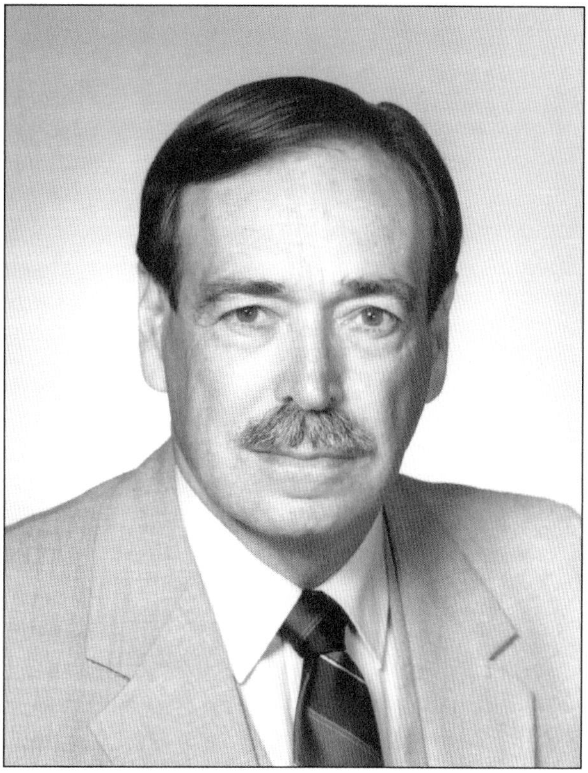

Interim Provost and Dean Theodore E. Kiffer, 1995. When Dr. Ruth Leventhal retired from Penn State Harrisburg in 1994, Dr. Kiffer came out of retirement to serve as interim provost and dean. He was in the US Navy during World War II and earned his MA and PhD degrees in English from Penn State. Dr. Kiffer is remembered for his down-to-earth administrative style and for living amongst students in Meade Heights.

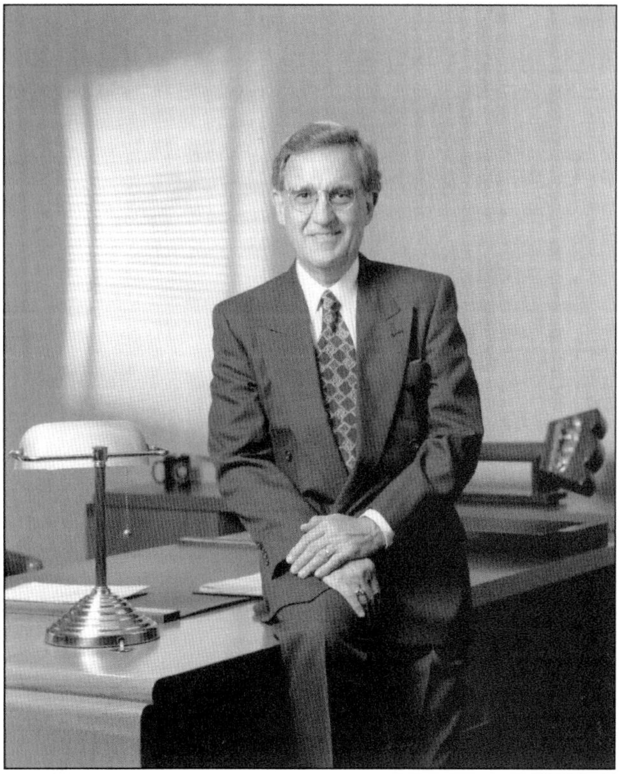

Provost and Dean John G. Bruhn, 1995. On September 21, 1995, Dr. Bruhn was inducted as provost and dean of Penn State Harrisburg. The event took place in the Capital Union Building. Dr. Bruhn served the college from 1995 to 1999. While under Provost and Dean Bruhn's leadership, the five academic units, previously labelled as "divisions," became "schools" at Penn State Harrisburg.

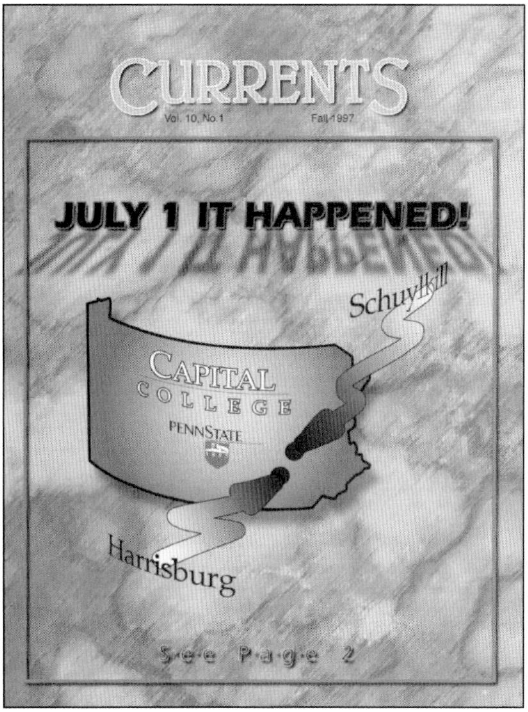

SCHUYLKILL MERGER, 1997. As a result of the university's desire to reduce costs, streamline operations, and realign relationships between campuses throughout Pennsylvania, Penn State Schuylkill decided to merge with Penn State Harrisburg to create a new, two-campus Capital College, as illustrated on this cover of the alumni magazine, *Currents*. The merger was effective on July 1, 1997, and resulted in the sharing of administration, faculty, and course offerings. It was dissolved by 2005.

LIBRARY OF THE FUTURE, 1998. Overcrowded materials and insufficient study spaces in the Heindel Memorial Library, located in the Olmsted Building, had been a challenge since the late 1970s. In April 1998, ground was broken for the new library at Penn State Harrisburg. This photograph of the "Library of the Future" sign on campus represents over a decade of work by administrators, faculty, staff, and students.

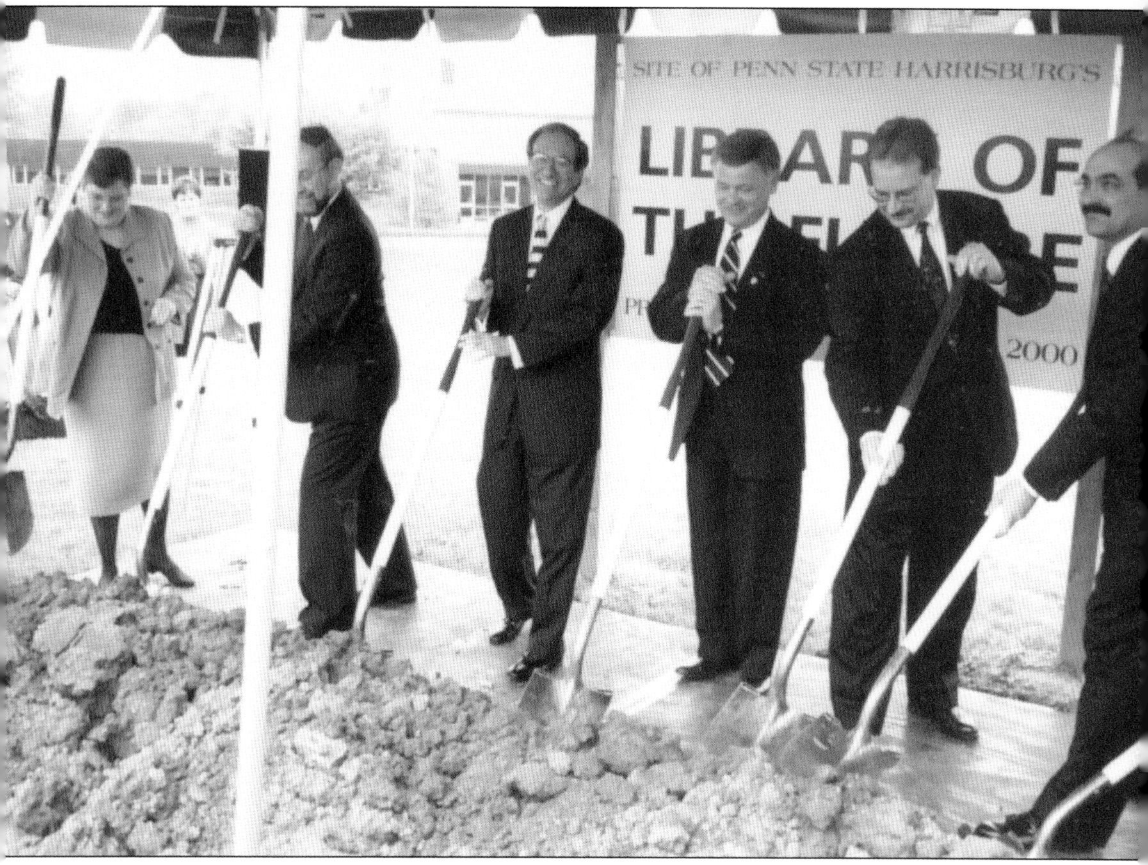

Library Ground-breaking Ceremony, 1998. On April 30, 1998, the ground-breaking ceremony for the new, $17.3-million, 115,000-square-foot, state-of-the-art library was held at Penn State Harrisburg. In attendance to dig the first shovels of topsoil were, from left to right, Nancy L. Eaton, dean of the University Libraries; Dr. Harold Shill, director of the Capital College Libraries; Gerald Morrison, immediate past chair of the College Board of Advisors; Gary Crowell, secretary of the Pennsylvania State Department of General Services; Jeffrey McKinney, president of the Penn State Harrisburg Alumni Society; and Dr. Simon J. Bronner, Distinguished Professor of Folklore and American Studies at Penn State Harrisburg. By this time, student enrollment had increased from over 2,600 (in the late 1970s) to more than 3,500. A new library was urgently needed to accommodate the changing needs of the expanding college, as well as the increasing demand for technology-enhanced classrooms, videoconferencing, and access to the Internet.

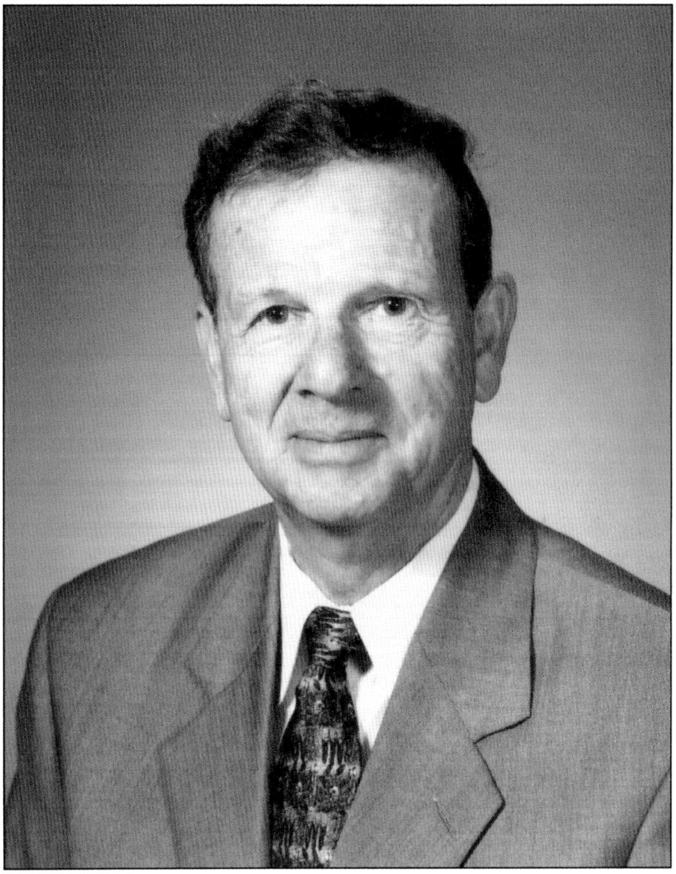

Interim Provost and Dean John Leathers, 1999–2000. Dr. John G. Bruhn announced his retirement from the college in 1999. Shortly thereafter, Dr. Leathers was appointed as interim provost and dean. Dr. Leathers served the college for one year and will be remembered for engaging with student organizations on campus, such as the Student Government Association, which demonstrated his philosophy that "students come first."

Six

Breaking New Ground 2000–2009

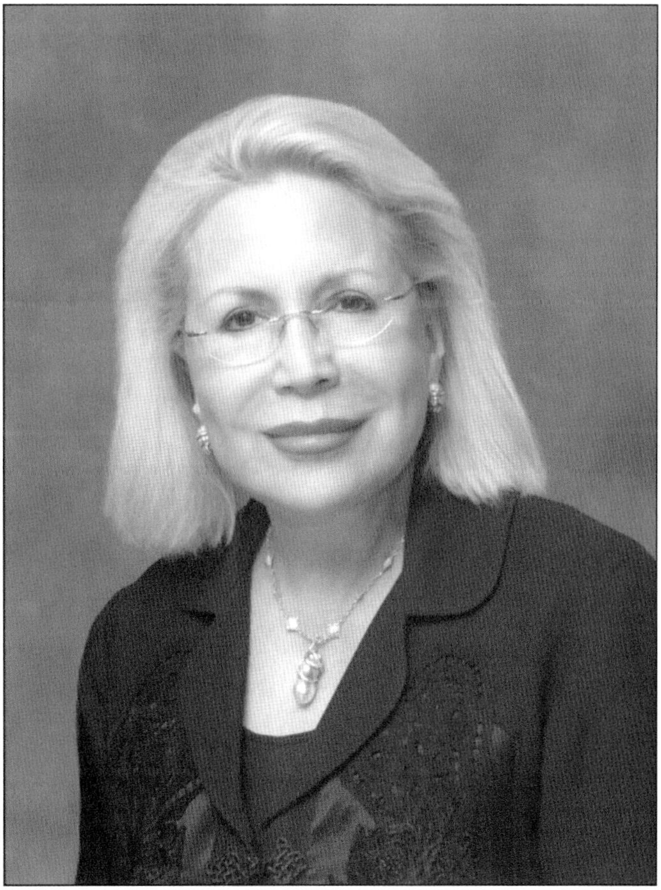

Chancellor Madlyn L. Hanes, 2000. The appointment of Dr. Hanes as provost and dean (later renamed chancellor) of Penn State Harrisburg took place on January 21, 2000. During her 10-year leadership, Penn State Harrisburg thrived. The college experienced explosive growth in enrollments, celebrated the dedication of a new library, witnessed the addition of new student athletic facilities, and completed its transition from a campus to a college. In July 2010, Dr. Hanes resigned as chancellor of Penn State Harrisburg and was appointed Penn State's vice president for Commonwealth Campuses.

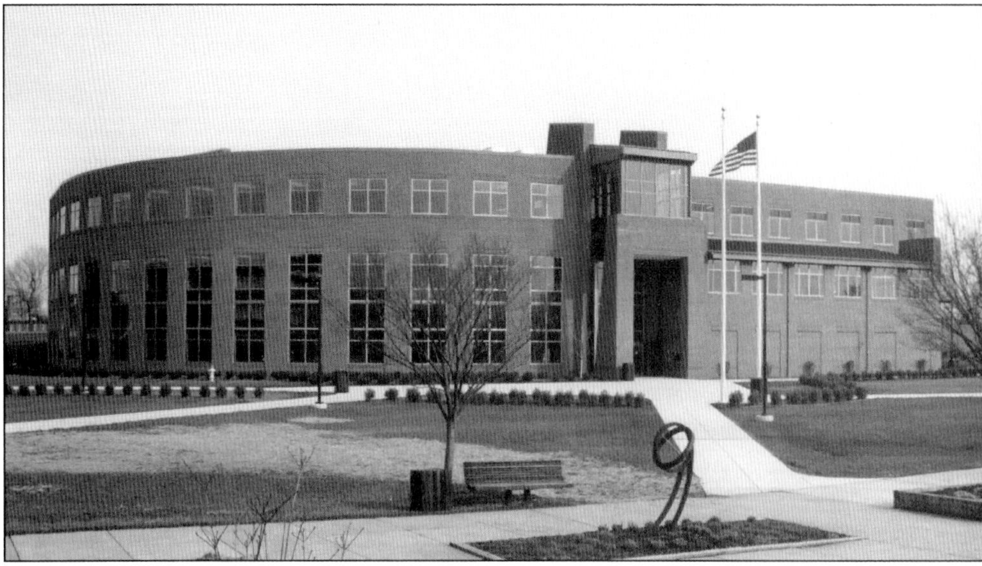

New Library, 2000. Occupying a prominent location in the heart of campus, the new library was a technologically advanced facility when it opened in January 2000. Designed collaboratively by Boston-based Shepley Bulfinch Richardson & Abbott, Inc. and Altoona-based Hayes Large Architects, LLC, the "Library of the Future" had the capacity to house 500,000 volumes, 180 computers, data ports throughout the building, group study rooms, an exhibition space, and the Cyber Café.

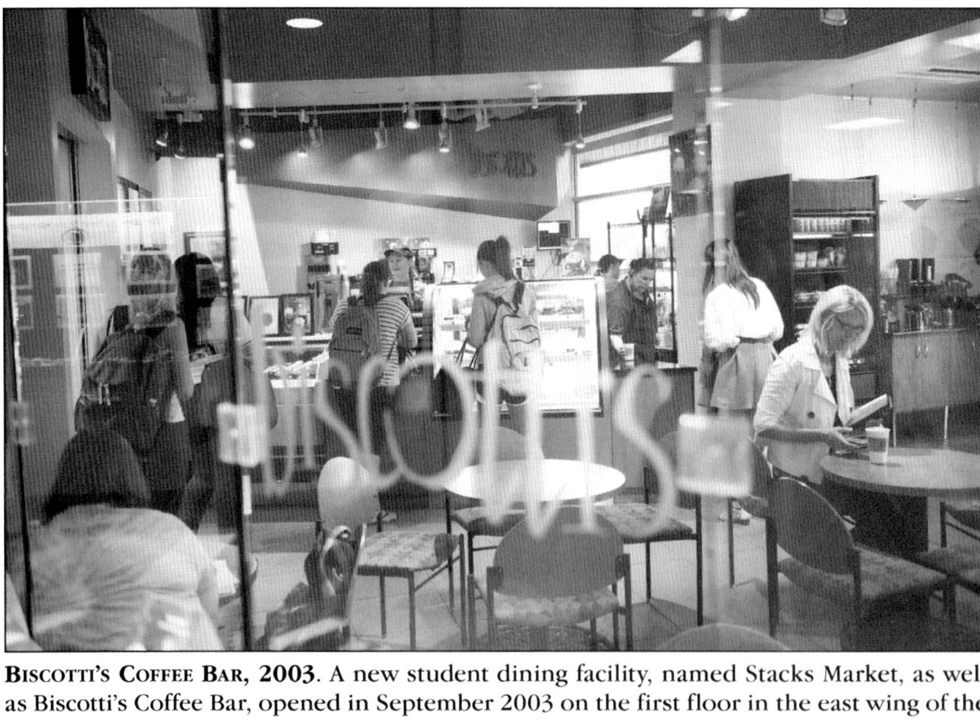

Biscotti's Coffee Bar, 2003. A new student dining facility, named Stacks Market, as well as Biscotti's Coffee Bar, opened in September 2003 on the first floor in the east wing of the Olmsted Building. Stacks Market was appropriately named after the former stacks or shelves that housed the college's library from 1966 to 1999. Penn State Harrisburg proudly serves Starbucks coffee and Pepsi-Cola products in Biscotti's and Stacks Market.

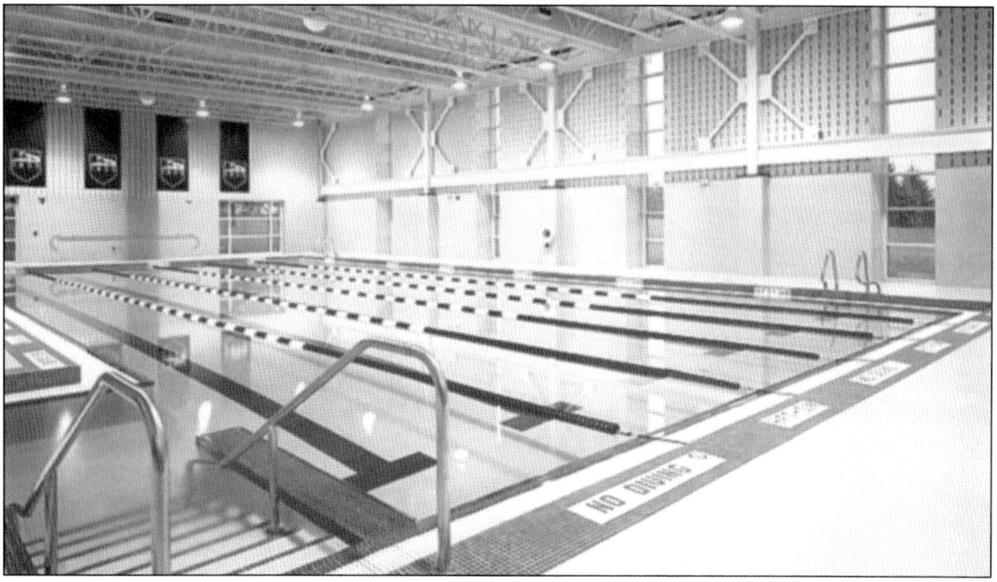

INTERIOR OF AQUATICS CENTER, 2004. The addition of a $2.3-million community aquatics center at the Capital Union Building strengthened ties with residents in Middletown and provided additional recreational options for a growing undergraduate student population. Designed by Allentown-based architects Breslin Ridyard Fadero, the 8,800-square-foot addition opened in fall 2004, the same time that Penn State Harrisburg admitted the college's first freshman class. (Courtesy of Breslin Ridyard Fadero Architects.)

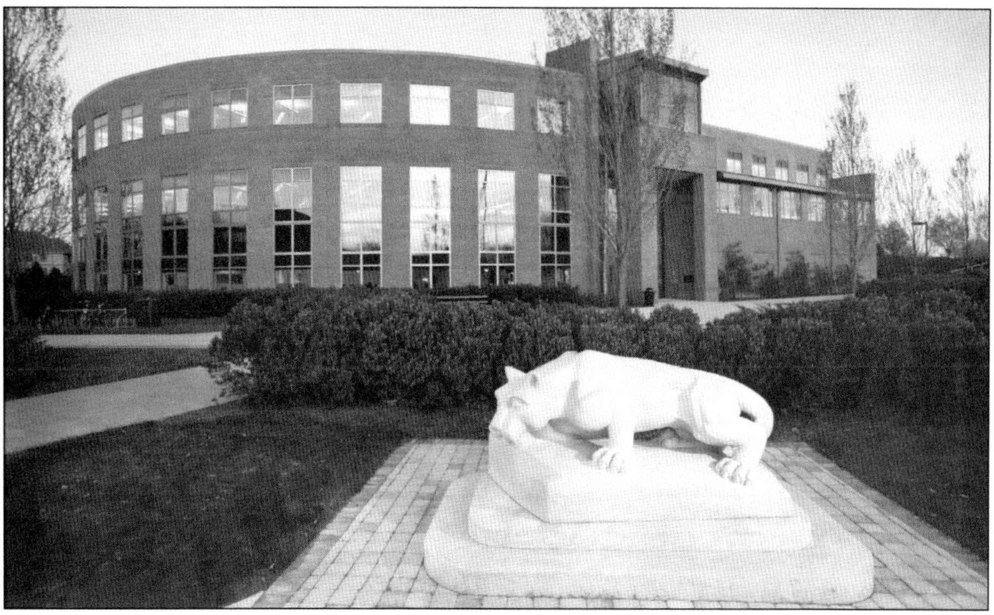

NEW *NITTANY LION SHRINE*, 2006. The Class of 2005 chose to purchase a large *Nittany Lion Shrine* as their class gift. In October 2006, the same month that the college celebrated its 40th anniversary, the 2,000-pound *Nittany Lion Shrine* was placed in Vartan Plaza and permanently fixed onto a concrete slab designed by the student chapter of Penn State Professional Engineers and Contractors (PSPEC) with the assistance of PSPEC faculty advisor Dr. Joseph Cecere and maintenance staff.

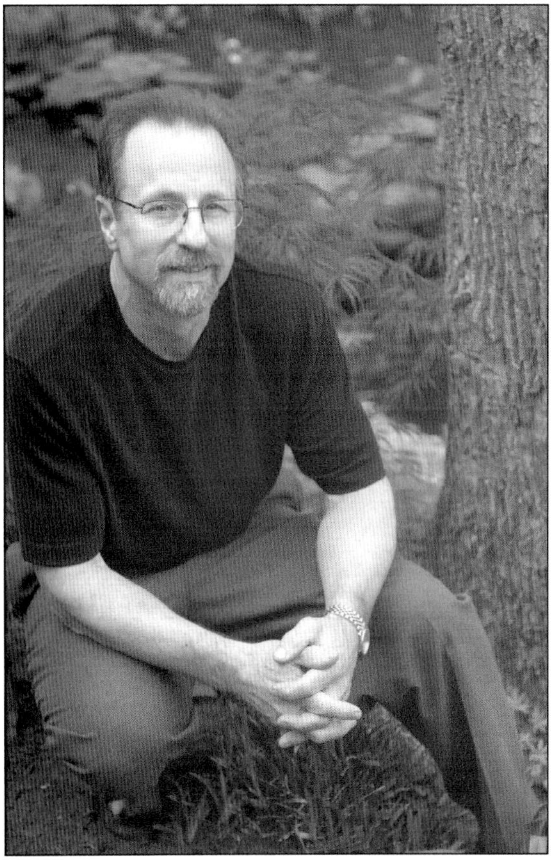

Ziegler Commons, c. 2005–2006. Richard Ziegler (left) was the recipient of the Honorary Alumni Award in 2006 for his volunteer service and generous support of the Ziegler Commons area (below) in front of the Olmsted Building. The Honorary Alumni Award is given by the Penn State Alumni Association to recognize people who are not graduates of Penn State but have made significant contributions toward its welfare, reputation, or prestige.

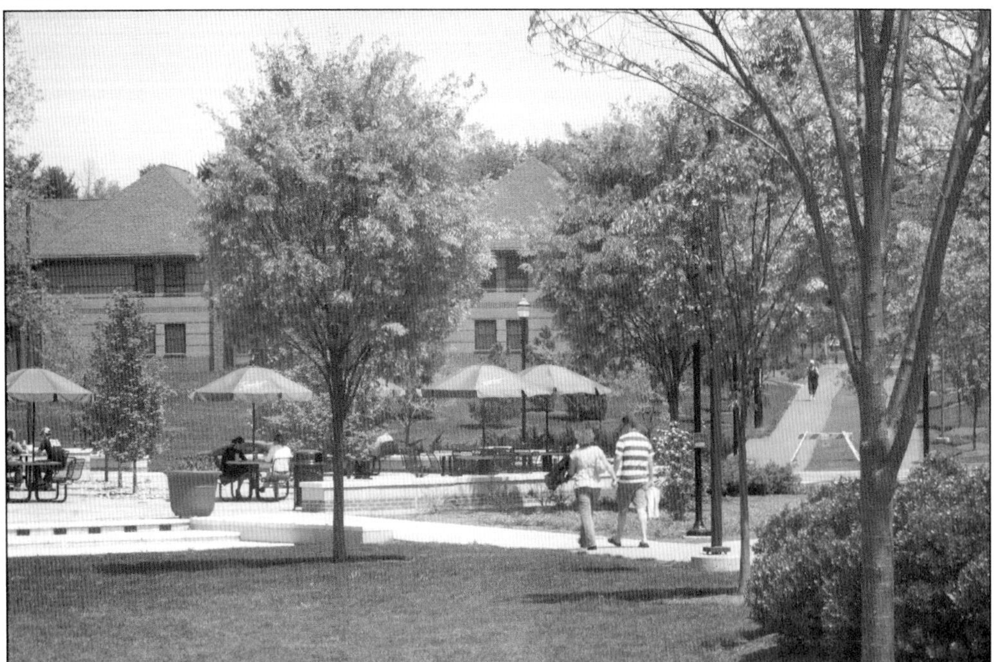

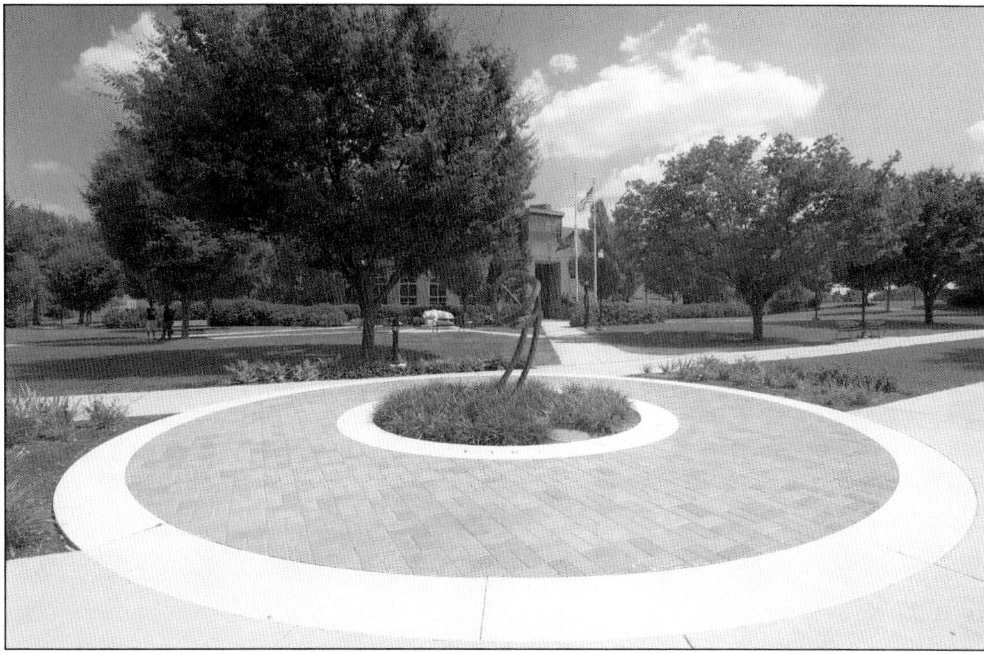

Vartan Plaza, c. 2005–2007. John O. Vartan, a 1973 graduate of the Capitol Campus, received a 1987 Alumni Fellow Award and was posthumously honored with a 2007 Alumni Society's Lifetime Achievement Award. Through his tremendous generosity, the college redesigned the mall (Vartan Plaza) in the heart of campus in the mid-2000s. The plaza extends from the front of the Olmsted Building to the opposite end of campus.

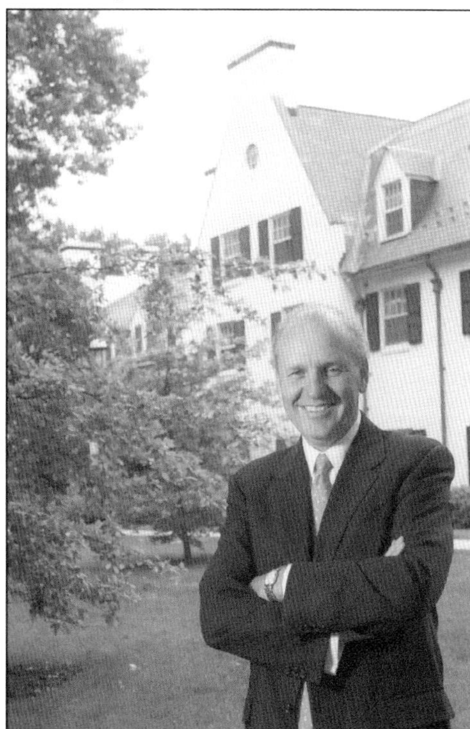

Distinguished Alumnus George R. Zoffinger, 2006. Zoffinger is a 1970 graduate of Penn State Harrisburg and a recipient of the 2003 Alumni Fellow Award, the most prestigious award given by the Penn State Alumni Association. The title of Alumni Fellow is permanent and lifelong. In 2006, Zoffinger also became the second Penn State Harrisburg alumnus to receive the Distinguished Alumni Award.

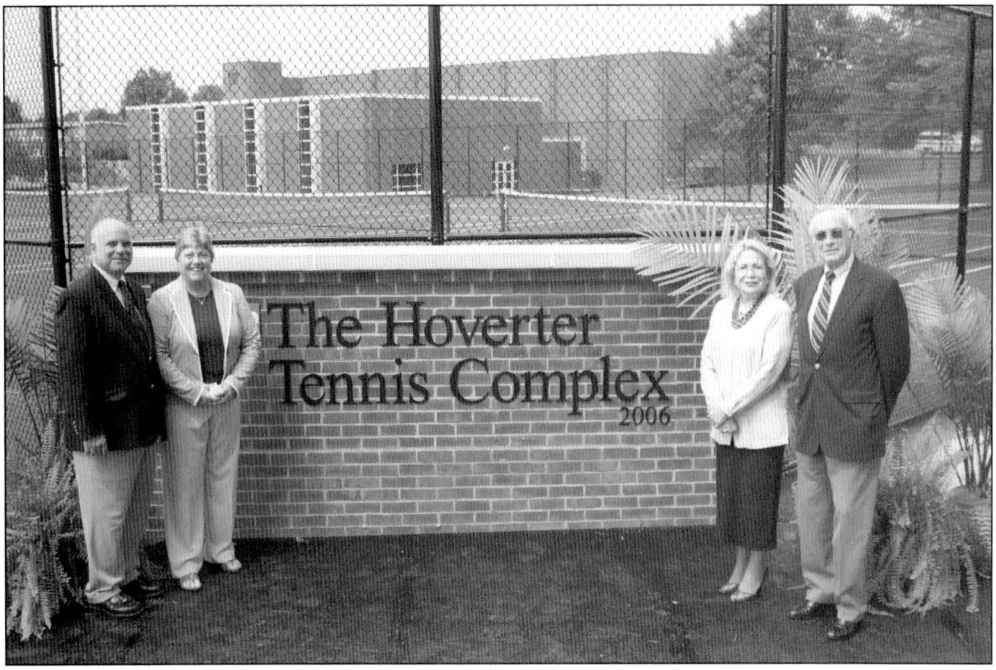

Hoverter Tennis Complex, 2006. Athletics on campus changed in fall 2005 with a call for the return of varsity athletics, which had been on hiatus since 1995. Penn State Harrisburg celebrated the renewal of competitions in the Penn State University Athletic Conference. In August 2006, the college also dedicated the new, eight-court Hoverter Tennis Complex, made possible with the generous gift of the Lawrence L. and Julia Z. Hoverter Charitable Foundation.

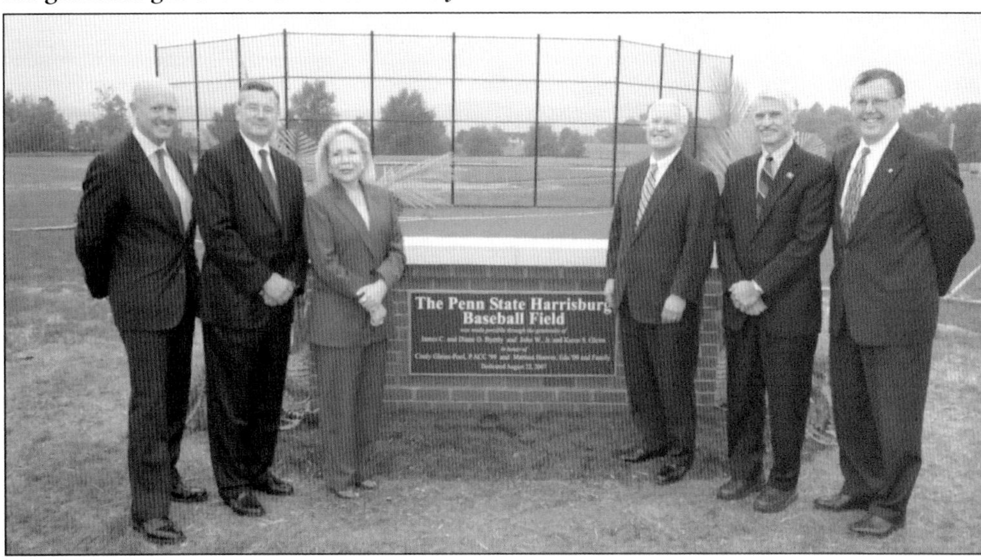

Baseball Field, 2007. The dedication of a new baseball field in August 2007 further expanded the athletic facilities on campus. Located next to the Capital Union Building and constructed thanks to the generosity of James C. Byerly and John W. Gleim Jr., the field's dedication ceremonies featured comments from Chancellor Madlyn Hanes and Bob Maschmeyer, Penn State Harrisburg's head baseball coach. United Concordia also funded construction of the home team dugout.

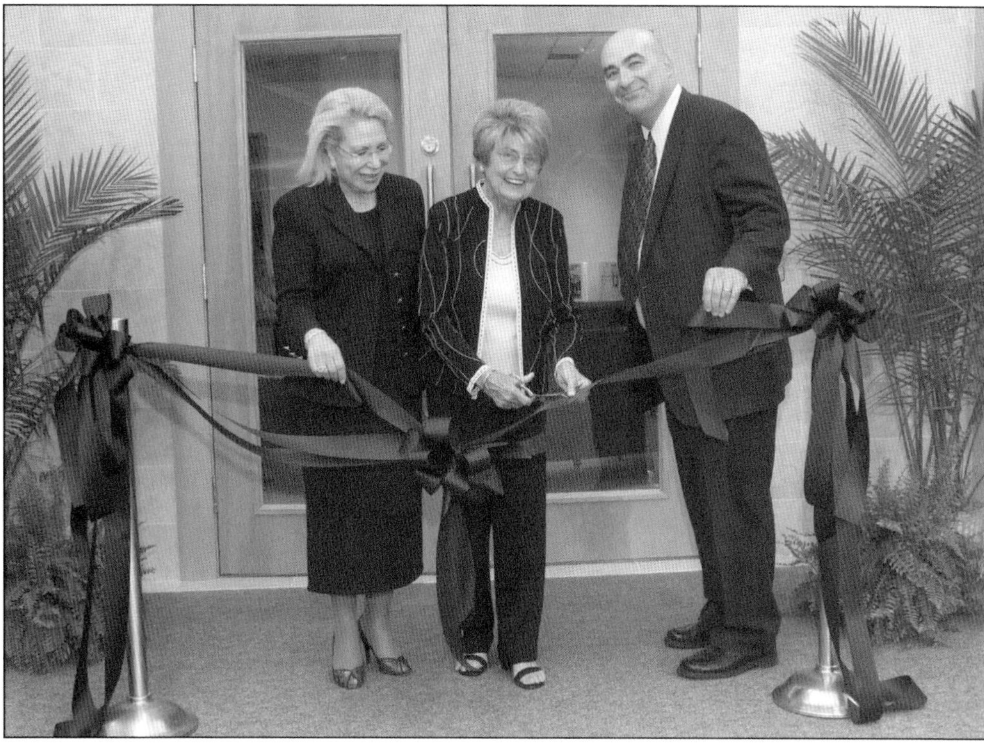

Holocaust Reading Room, 2007. With the generous support of Linda Schwab, a Holocaust survivor, the college unveiled the Linda Schwab Holocaust Reading Room in 2007. Pictured here at the ribbon-cutting ceremony are Chancellor Madlyn Hanes (left), Schwab (center), and Dr. Simon Bronner (right). Located in the library, the Holocaust Reading Room consists of a study space, seminar room, and exhibition space devoted to the study of the Holocaust.

New Olmsted Facade, 2008. The 47-year-old façade of the Olmsted Building was completely renovated—with new windows and a redesigned atrium—in 2007. It was completed and dedicated on April 1, 2008.

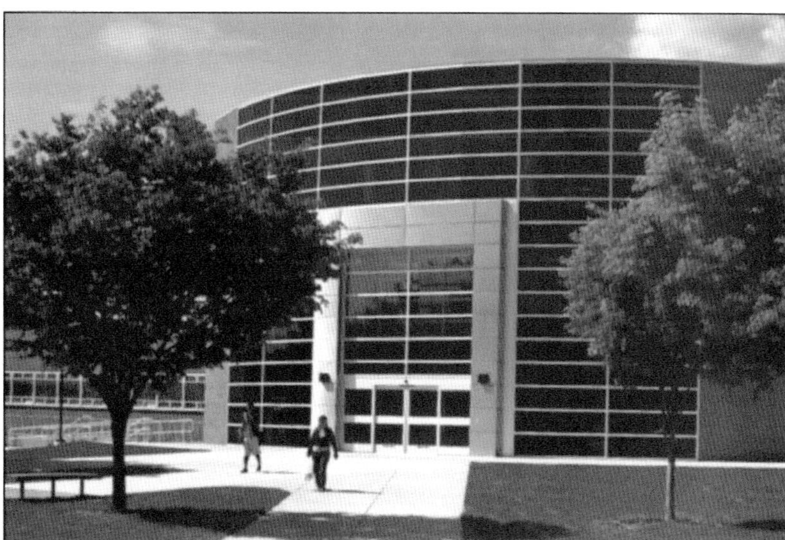

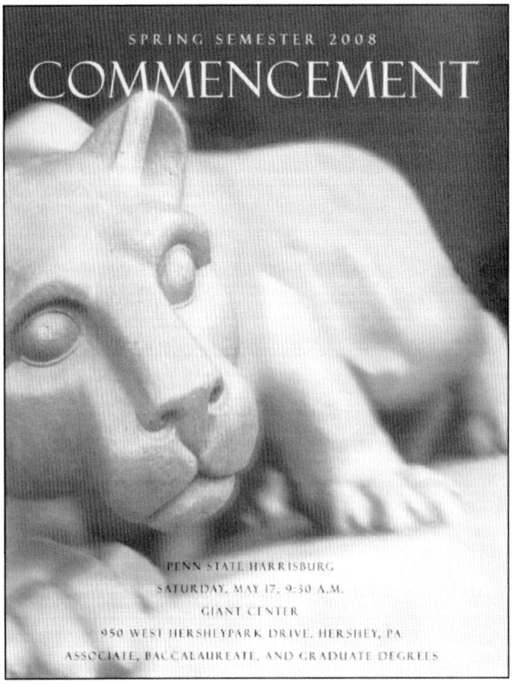

Spring Commencement Program, 2008. This photograph of the Penn State Harrisburg Spring 2008 Commencement program captures a historic moment in the life of the college—the first graduating class of undergraduates since Penn State Harrisburg began admitting freshmen in 2004. Graduation ceremonies were held in the Giant Center in Hershey, Pennsylvania.

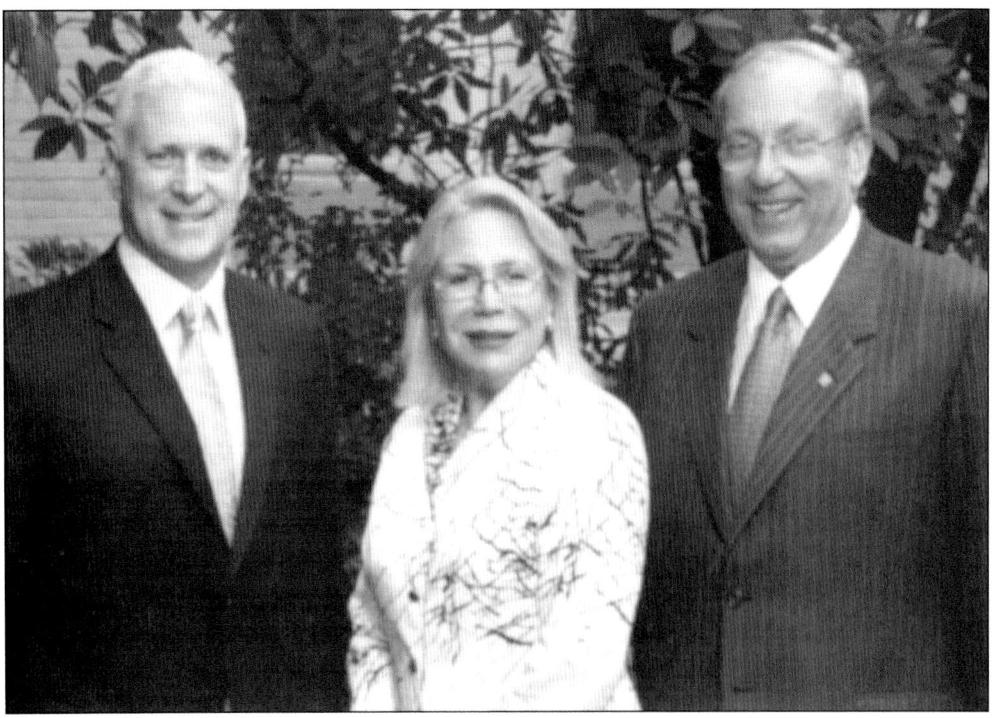

Distinguished Alumni Jeffrey B. Miller and Ralph J. Papa, 2009. In June 2009, the college recognized the third and fourth Penn State Harrisburg alumni to receive the University's Distinguished Alumni Award. Pictured here are Miller (left), a 2001 graduate with a master's degree in public administration; Dr. Madlyn L. Hanes (center), chancellor of Penn State Harrisburg; and Papa, a 1969 graduate with a bachelor's degree in social science.

Seven

Embracing Dramatic Change 2010–2015

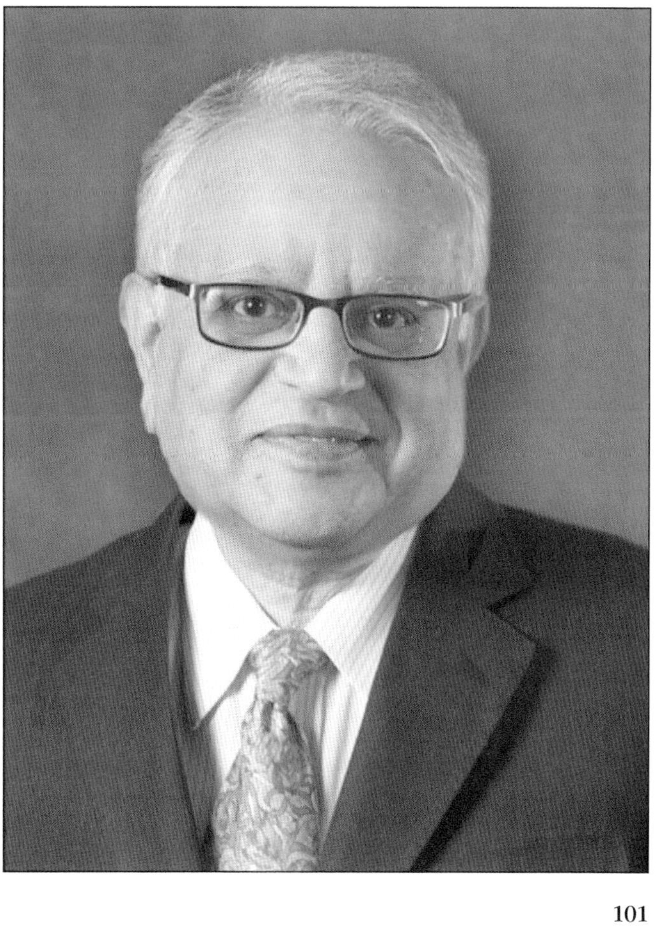

Chancellor Mukund S. Kulkarni, 2010. After Dr. Madlyn Hanes resigned as chancellor of Penn State Harrisburg and accepted a new position as Penn State's vice president for Commonwealth Campuses in 2010, Dr. Kulkarni served as interim chancellor from July to November 2010. He was subsequently appointed chancellor of Penn State Harrisburg on November 1, 2010. Under Chancellor Kulkarni's direction, the college has continued on a path of dramatic growth and positive transformation.

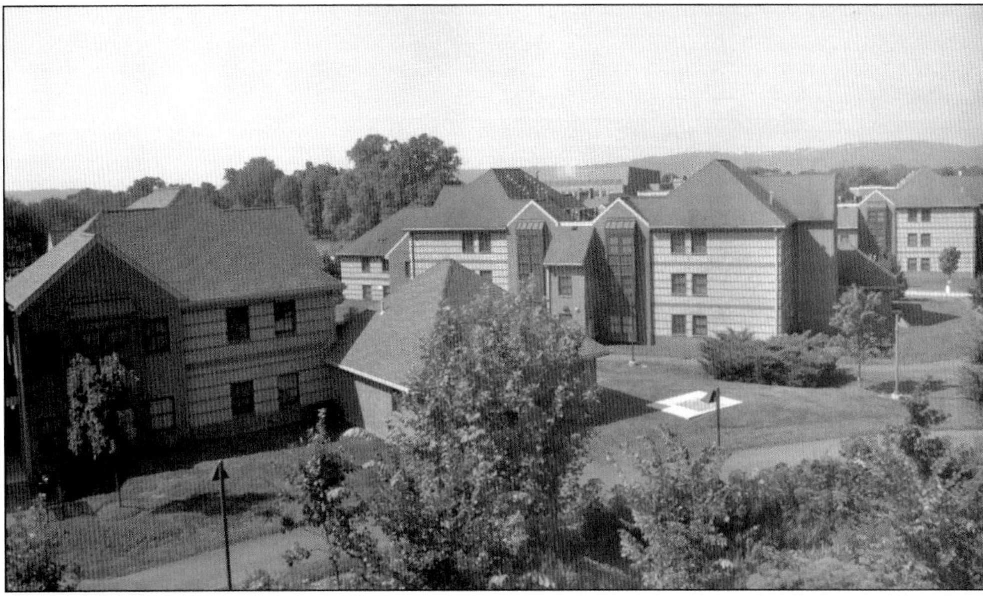

VILLAGE HOUSING, 2010. On-campus housing for residential students has grown tremendously in the past several years. Undergraduate students now have the option of living on campus in 1 of 10 different houses, known as Village Housing, that were built in 2010. Recently named after tributaries of the Susquehanna River, the houses can accommodate 430 students total. The complex includes the first LEED (Leadership in Energy and Environmental Design)-certified building on campus.

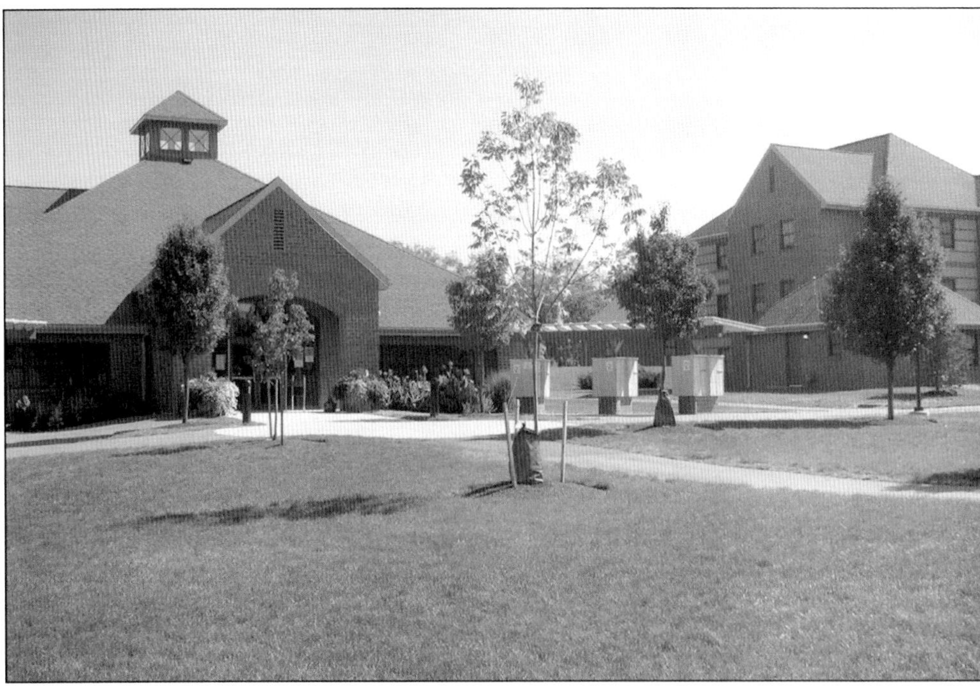

VILLAGE COMMUNITY CENTER, 2010. The community center in Village Housing provides students with a lounge area and meeting spaces centrally located near all of the housing in the complex.

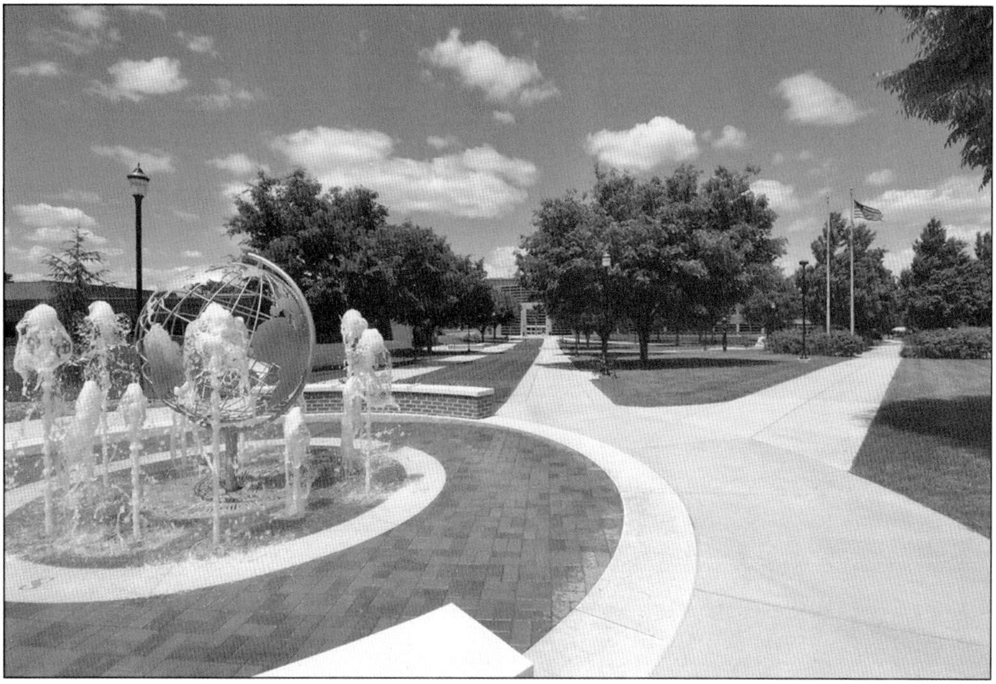

Campus Fountain, 2010. Located on the south end of the Vartan Plaza, this campus fountain features a globe as well as LED lights that change colors at night.

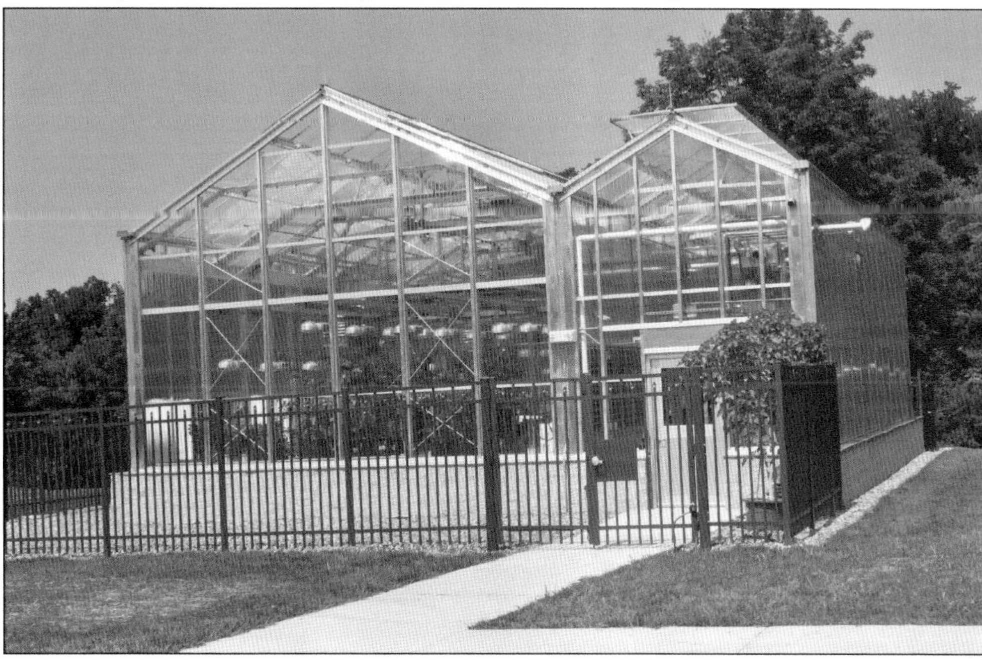

Greenhouse, c. 2010–2011. Located on the west side of campus and adjacent to Church Hall, the greenhouse is part of the $1.6 million Central Pennsylvania Research and Teaching Laboratory for Biofuels, which serves as a center for the study of second- and third-generation biofuels. The greenhouse is a 1,500-square-foot, climate-controlled facility approved for growing genetically modified plants. It was dedicated on September 15, 2011.

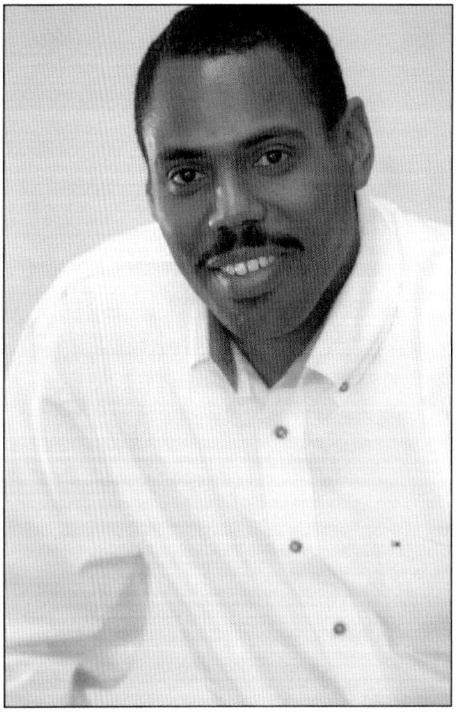

Dr. Shaun L. Gabbidon, 2010. In January 2010, Dr. Gabbidon was named Distinguished Professor of Criminal Justice in the School of Public Affairs at Penn State Harrisburg. Dr. Gabbidon was the second professor from the college to earn this prestigious title that recognizes a highly select group of faculty with outstanding achievements in teaching, research, and service.

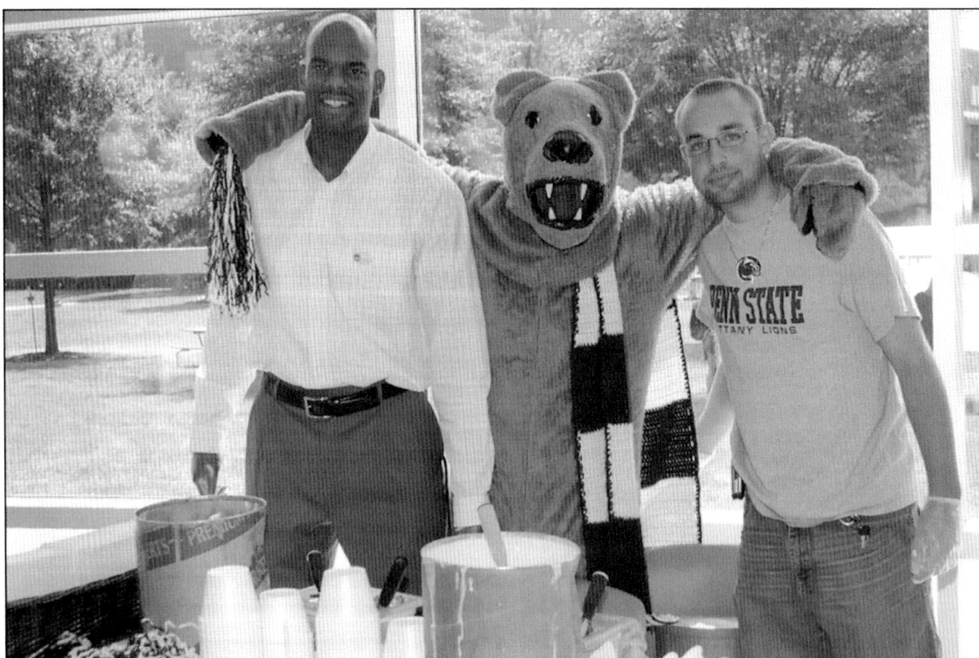

NCAA Division III Celebration, 2010. Eight years after the reintroduction of varsity athletics, Penn State Harrisburg gained NCAA Division III status in 2010. The college's 12 athletic programs became eligible to qualify for NCAA championship events beginning in 2010. At left in this photograph is Rahsaan Carlton, Penn State Harrisburg's director of athletics. In July 2013, Penn State Harrisburg also joined the Capital Athletic Conference.

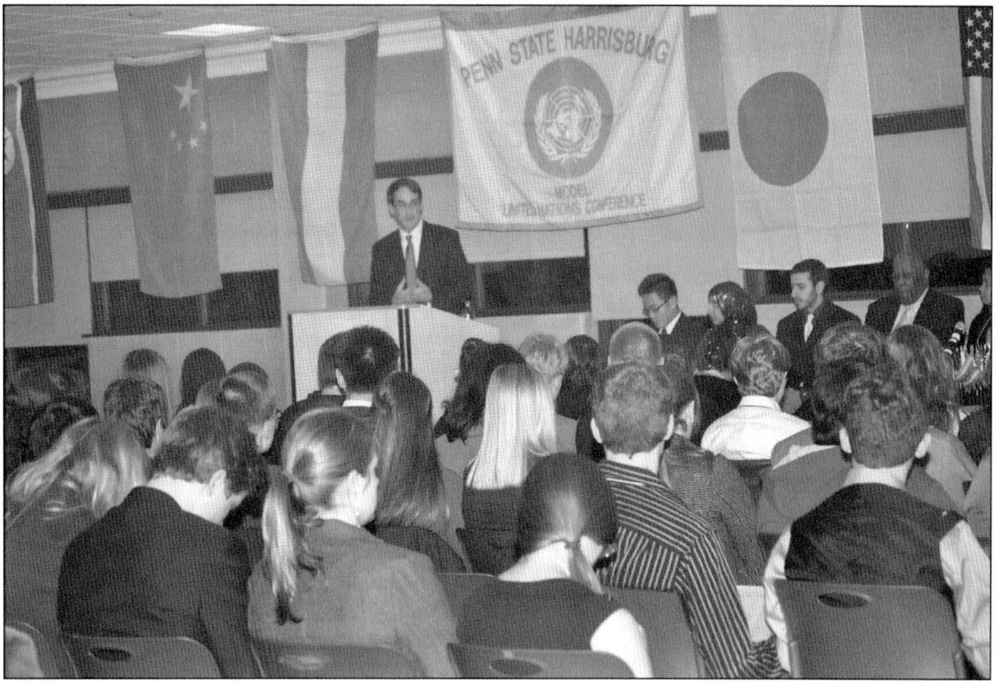

Model United Nations, 2012. With its long history of hosting Model United Nations, the college gathered over 200 high school student delegates from the region on February 16–17, 2012, for the 40th Anniversary Model United Nations. This photograph captures some of the attendants. The event, founded by Dr. Clemmie Gilpin, is organized each year by the college's student International Affairs Association with support from the School of Public Affairs.

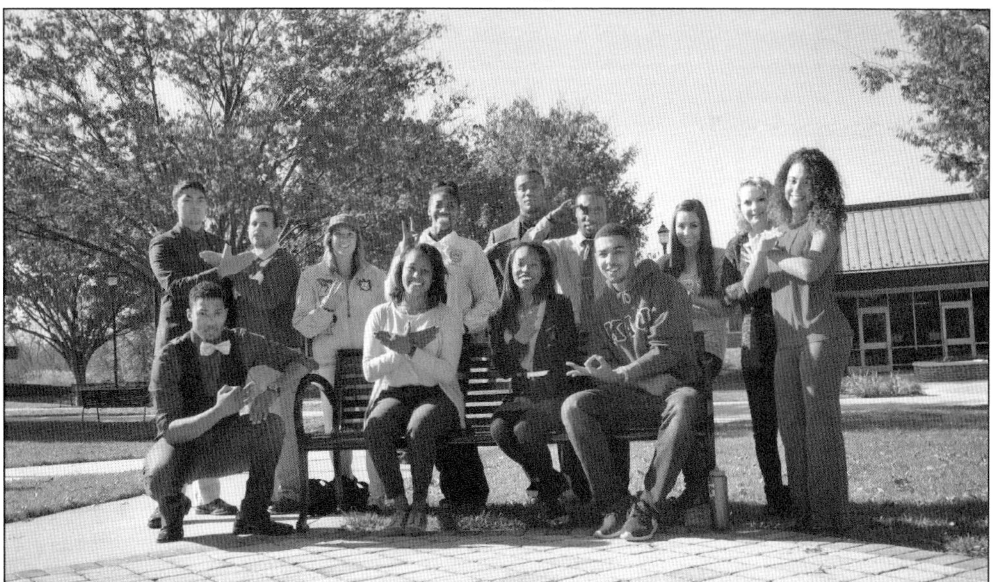

Greek Life, 2012. Aside from participating in athletics and a huge assortment of clubs and activities, students on campus can join a number of different fraternities and sororities, such as Kappa Alpha Psi, Kappa Beta Gamma, and Sigma Gamma Rho, which are officially recognized at Penn State Harrisburg.

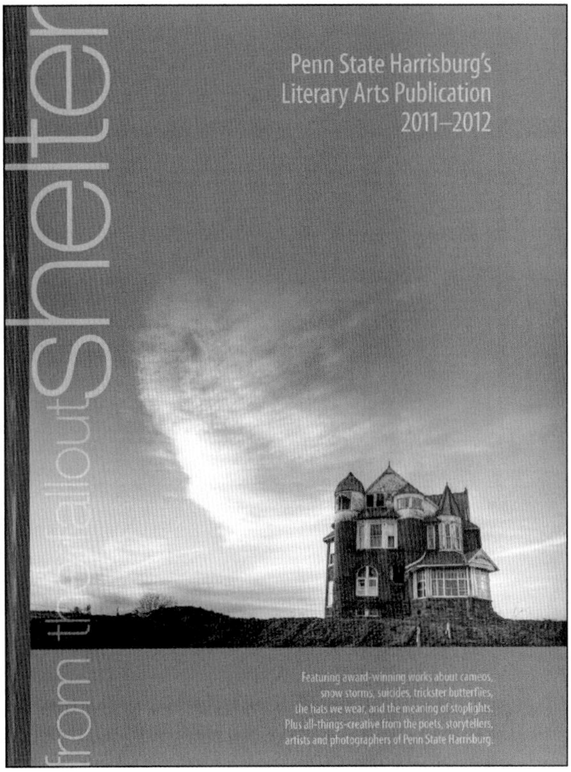

***From the Fallout Shelter*, 2011–2012**. The tradition of publishing a student yearbook may have ended in 1995, but Penn State Harrisburg's literary and arts magazine is still going strong. Under the creative advisement of Prof. Jen Hirt, the publication was reinvented in 2011 with a new design and name, *From the Fallout Shelter*, which is a nod to the bomb shelter that still exists in the basement of the Olmsted Building.

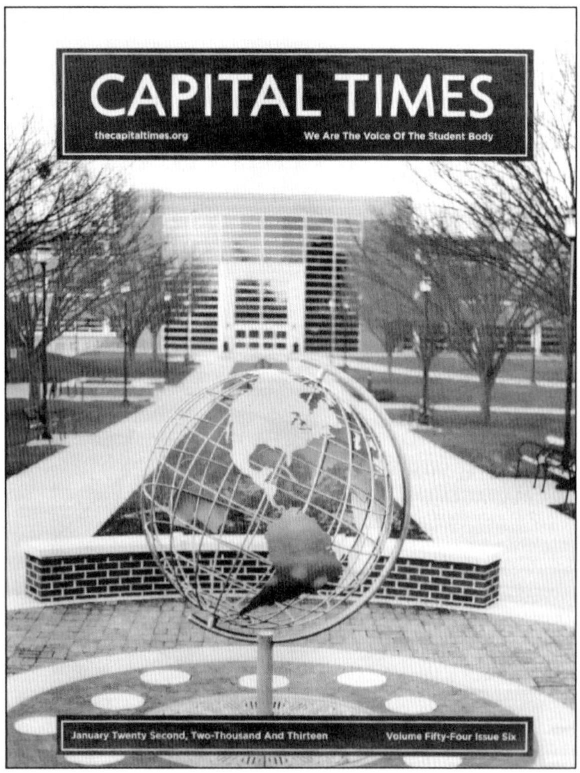

Redesigned *Capital Times*, 2013. Like *From the Fallout Shelter*, the student newspaper enjoyed a renewal in 2011, when editor-in-chief Paul Boger and assistant editor Chyna Geib brought their artistic talents and photography and writing skills to the campus and completely revamped the design of the newspaper. This January 2013 issue of the *Capital Times* captures a beautiful view of the fountain on Vartan Plaza.

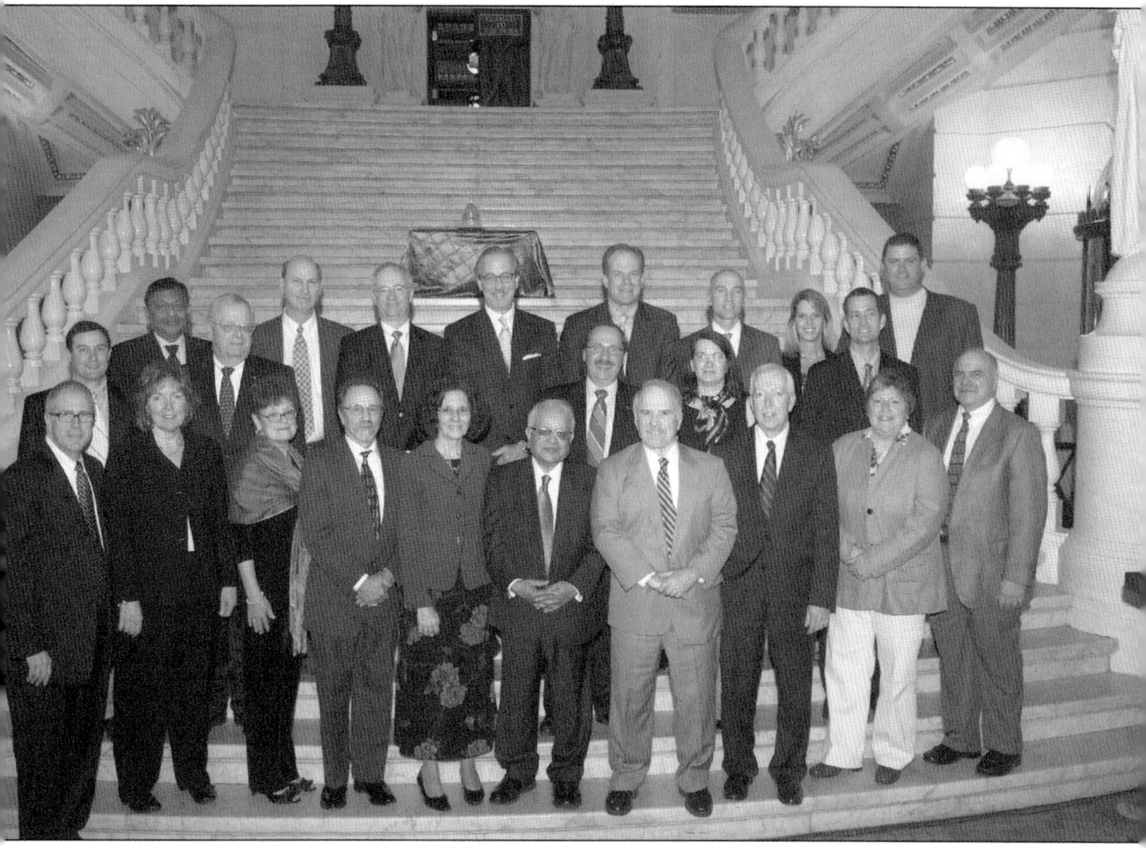

Penn State Harrisburg Capital Society, 2012. Created by Penn State Harrisburg in 2008, during Chancellor Madlyn Hanes's tenure, the Capital Society was created to honor and recognize those who share a commitment to the continuing excellence of Penn State Harrisburg.

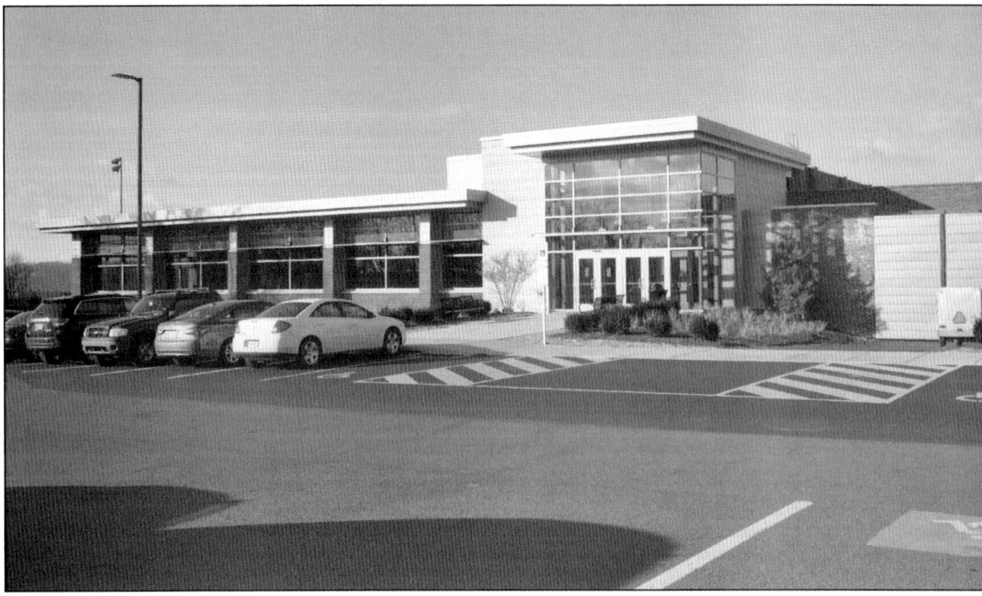

Capital Union Building Expansion, 2013. By 2011, the Capital Union Building (CUB) was beginning to show its age. Built in 1975–1977, it could no longer meet the needs of the expanding college community. A 12,560-square-foot addition to the CUB was completed in 2013 at a cost of $3.8 million. Featuring a welcoming new entrance and boasting a 6,000-square-foot student fitness center, the CUB is now an athletic destination on campus.

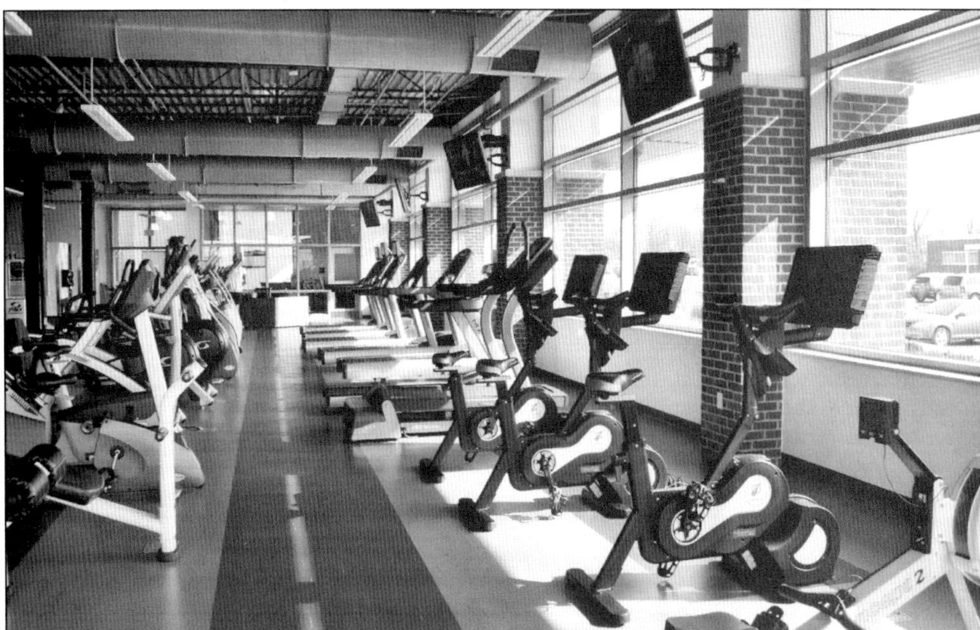

Interior of Capital Union Building, 2013. This image captures the interior of the new fitness center, which is one of Penn State Harrisburg's best-kept secrets. Dedicated on March 1, 2013, the second-floor fitness center includes an atrium, commercial-grade exercise equipment, flat-screen televisions, an information desk, and lockers. First-floor renovations provide additional locker rooms, along with laundry facilities and extra storage space.

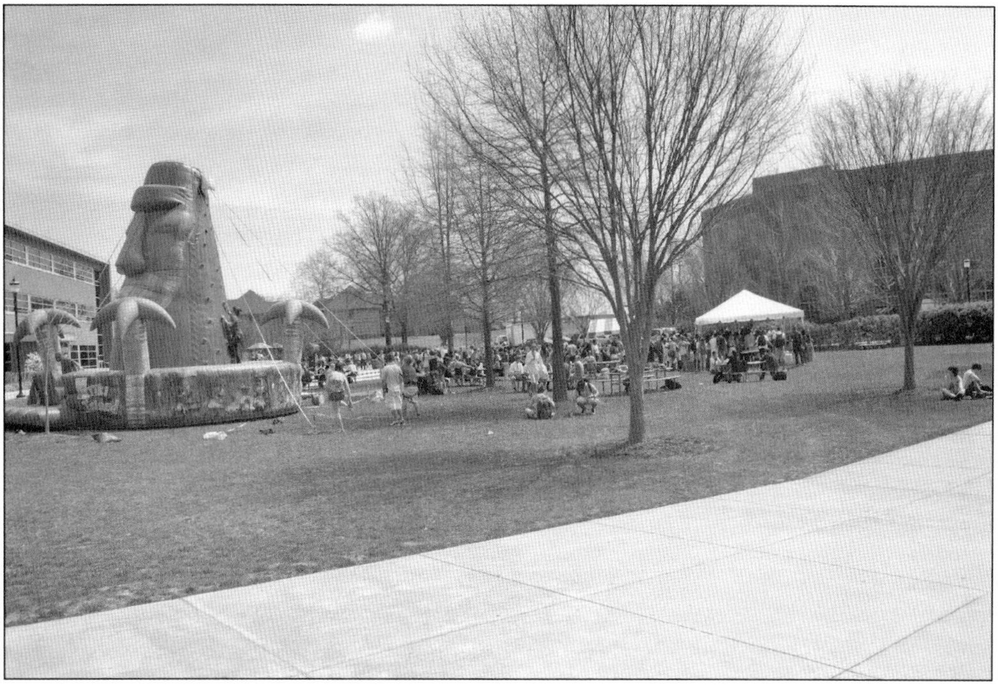

Spring Luau, 2013. The Rites of Spring tradition that began in the 1970s evolved to include a Spring Luau, which has created greater opportunities for undergraduate students to socialize and build a stronger sense of community on campus.

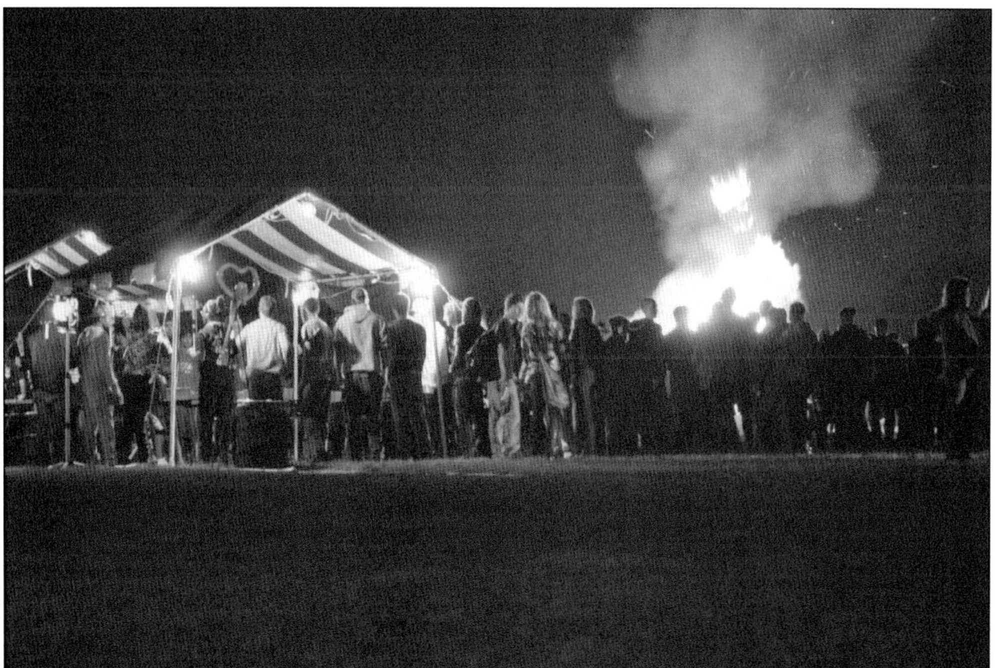

Bonfire in the 'Burg, 2013. The bonfire tradition has existed at Penn State Harrisburg since the early 1970s. One bonfire usually takes place during the fall semester. The latest incarnation of the event has been dubbed "Bonfire in the 'Burg."

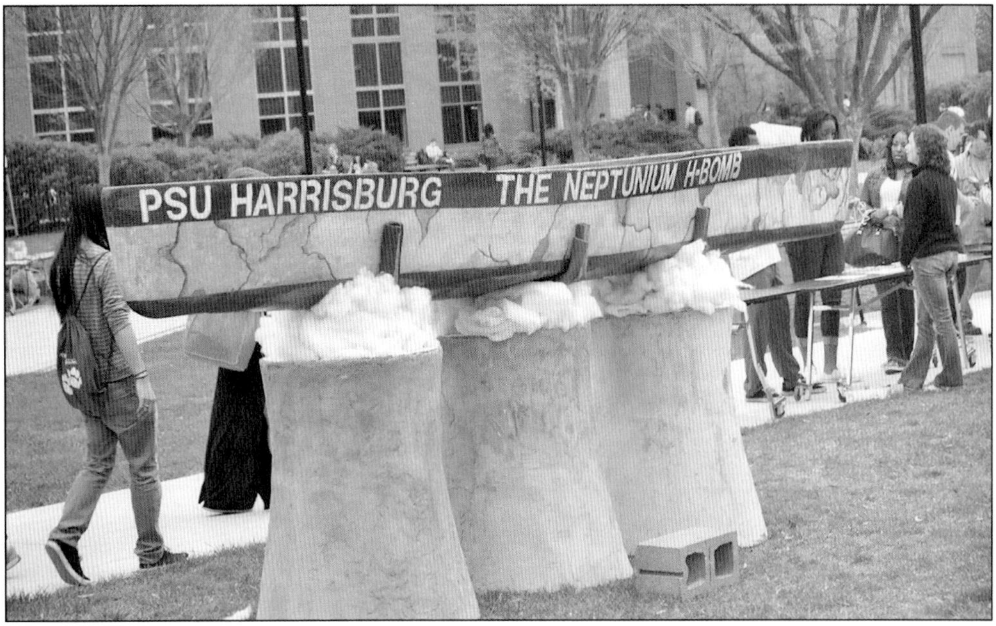

Earth Day, 2014. A tradition at Penn State Harrisburg since its official nationwide establishment in 1970, the annual celebration of Earth Day, held on April 22, grows bigger every year. This photograph of Vartan Plaza illustrates that students are still interested in learning about recycling and alternative energy sources, as well as promoting environmental education and activism.

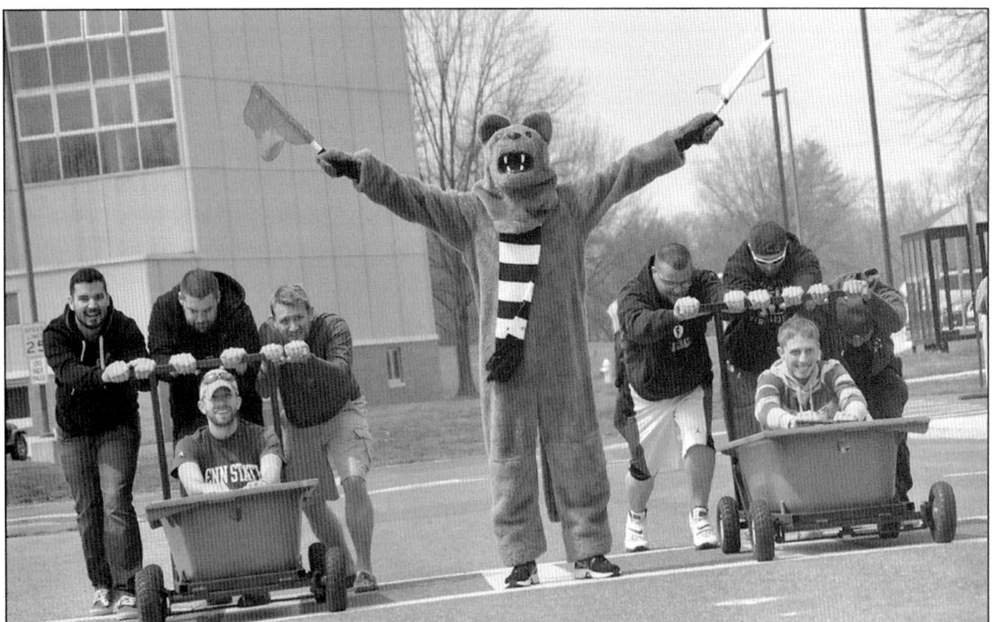

Bathtub Race, 2014. A campus event since 1972, the Bathtub Race is held during May in front of the Olmsted Building. (The race was previously staged near the Student Center on the west side of campus.) This photograph features students and the Nittany Lion mascot at the start of the race's 50-yard dash.

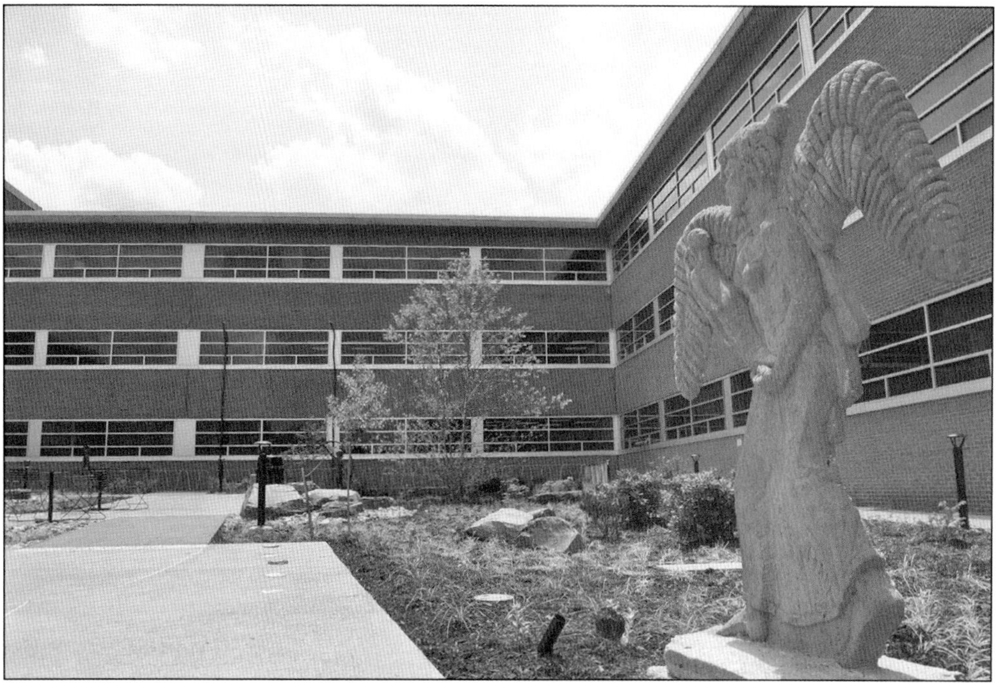

SCULPTURE GARDEN, 2014. The Bertha and Boris Blai Sculpture Garden is located behind the Olmsted Building. Renovated extensively in 2014, it features several sculptures created by Boris Blai and incorporates geographic references to Three Mile Island and other small islands in the Susquehanna River. Prominently featured in this photograph is the concrete sculpture *Angel in Flight*, designed by Harrisburg-area native Deborah Masters.

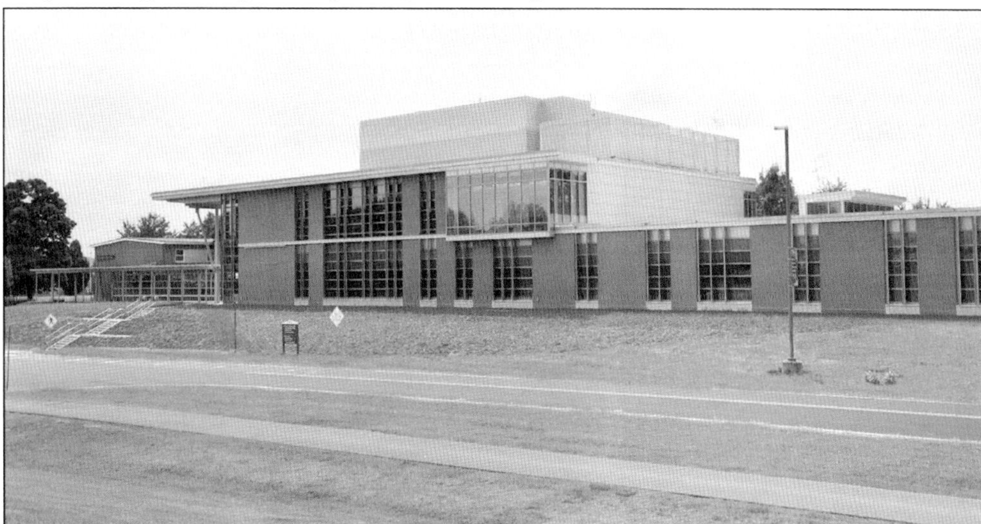

EDUCATIONAL ACTIVITIES BUILDING EXPANSION, 2014. The Educational Activities Building (EAB) was extensively renovated in 2013–2014. The $19.5-million project provided for a 51,500-square-foot addition, designed by Wilkes-Barre–based architectural firm Bohlin Cywinski Jackson, that now connects to the existing two-story building. It houses labs for civil, mechanical, and electrical engineering, as well as a multipurpose room, faculty research labs, offices, a computer laboratory, and tiered classrooms that can accommodate 120 students.

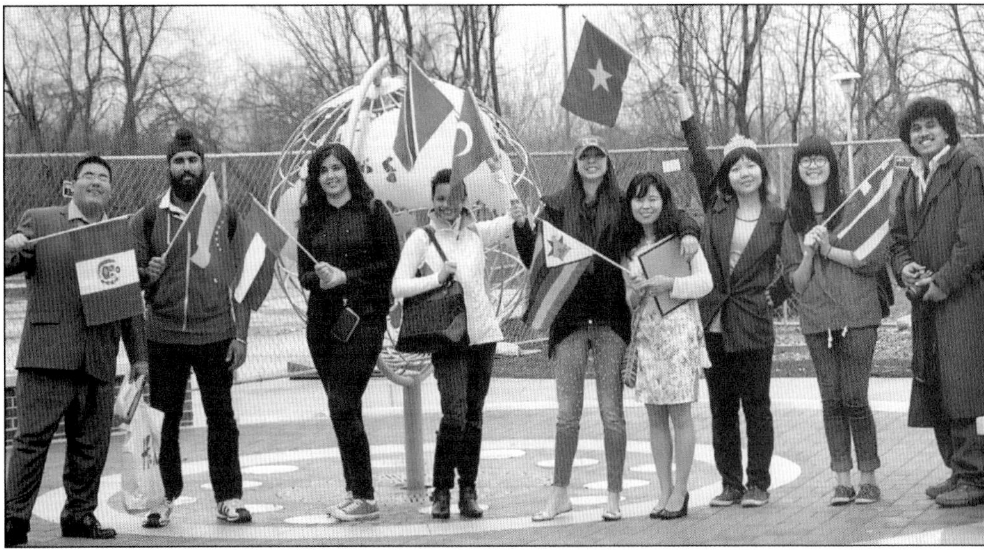

International Student Enrollment, 2014. One of the most dramatic changes on campus has been Penn State Harrisburg's increased international student enrollment, particularly students from China, India, and Korea. In 2008, the college enrolled just 70 international students. In just six years, that number has risen to 377 students from 38 countries. During fall 2015, the college enrolled 490 international students. This photograph shows international students with Anna Wei Marshall (fourth from right), the college's international student advisor, standing in front of the campus fountain.

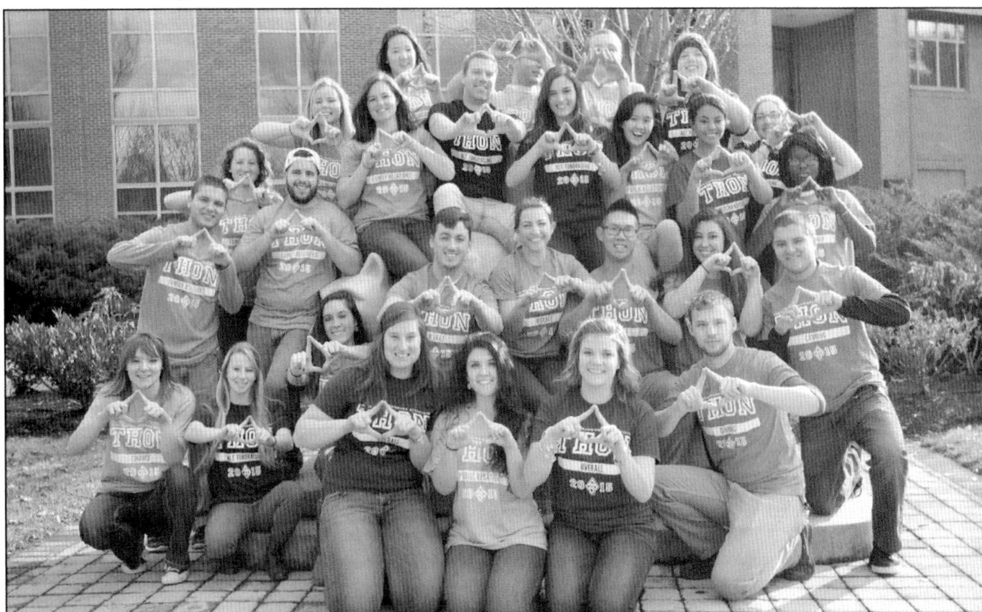

THON Committee, 2014. Penn State Harrisburg's THON Committee supports the Penn State IFC/Panhellenic Dance Marathon, which is the largest student-run philanthropic organization in the world. Every year, THON raises funds to help battle pediatric cancer and support affected children and their families. In 2014, Penn State Harrisburg's THON Committee raised nearly $50,000, contributing to the $13.3 million raised overall.

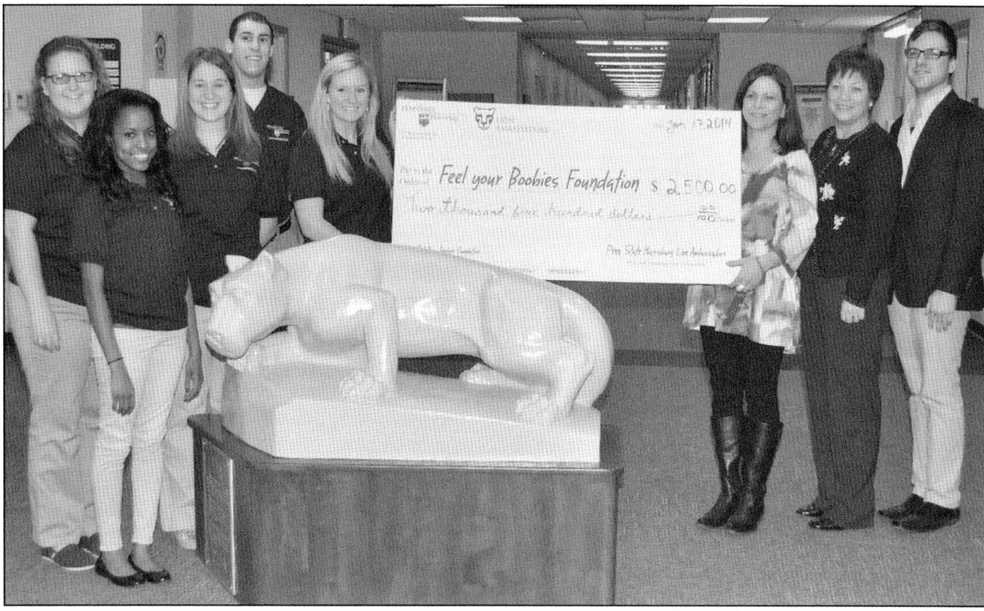

Boobies Ball, 2014. Established in 2006 by Penn State Harrisburg's Lion Ambassadors, Boobies Ball is a dance to support local breast-cancer awareness group "Feel Your Boobies" Foundation. Penn State Harrisburg was the first college campus to host such an event. The creator of the "Feel Your Boobies" Foundation is Middletown resident and former Penn State Harrisburg adjunct professor Leigh Hurst, who was diagnosed with breast cancer in 2004 at age 33.

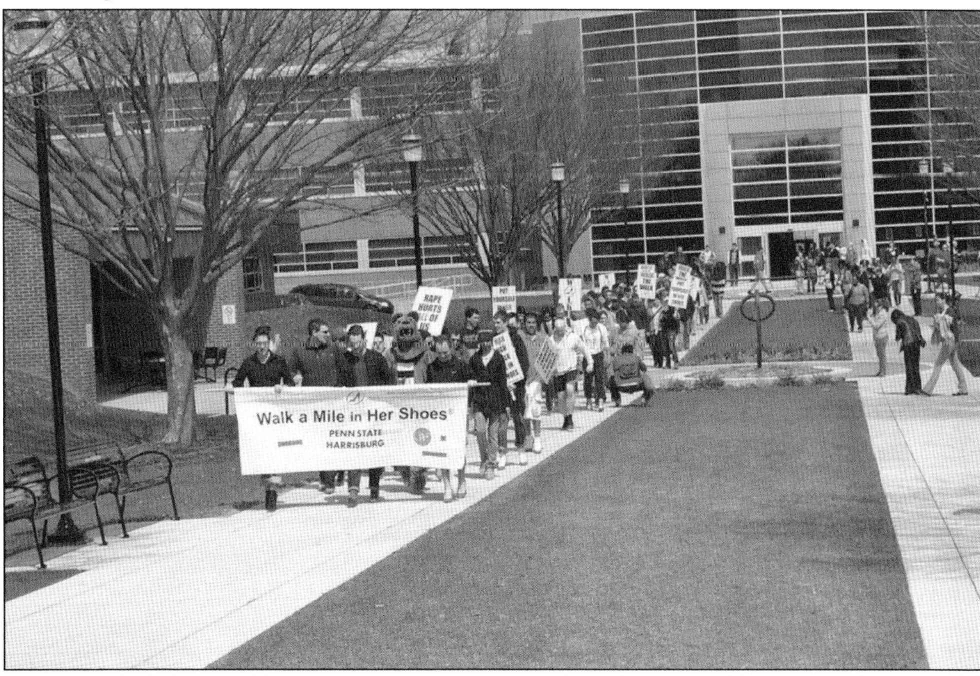

Walk a Mile in Her Shoes, 2014. A newer tradition at Penn State Harrisburg, the Walk a Mile in Her Shoes event offers men an opportunity to educate and rally the campus community to help prevent domestic violence and sexual assault.

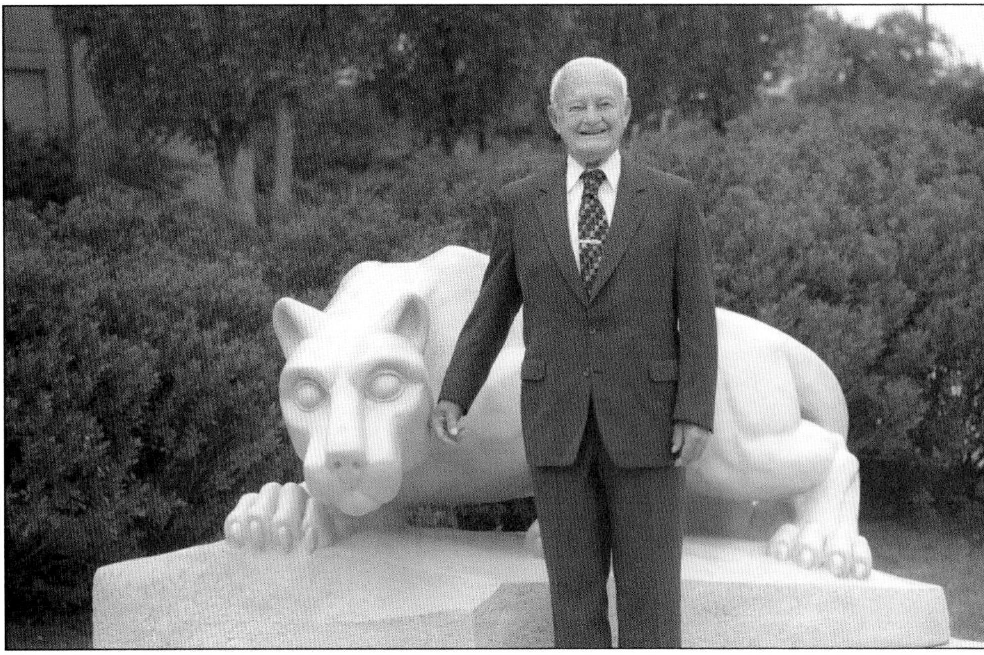

Russell E. Horn Sr. and Student Enrichment Center, 2015–2016. Horn (above), a 1933 civil engineering graduate of Penn State, has been a tremendous benefactor to the college over the past two decades. His generous gift of $1 million in 2012 assisted the college in building the new $30-million Student Enrichment Center (SEC). The architectural rendering of the SEC (below) highlights the 70,000-square-foot facility's curved design that will incorporate staff offices and space for student services. Designed by the Wilkes-Barre–based architectural firm Bohlin Cywinski Jackson, the new building is targeted for completion in August 2016. The SEC will also house a new Learning Center and a spiritual meditation center (funded in large part by Horn's donations), a new college bookstore, a 24-hour convenience store, a theater/lecture hall, and recreational space.

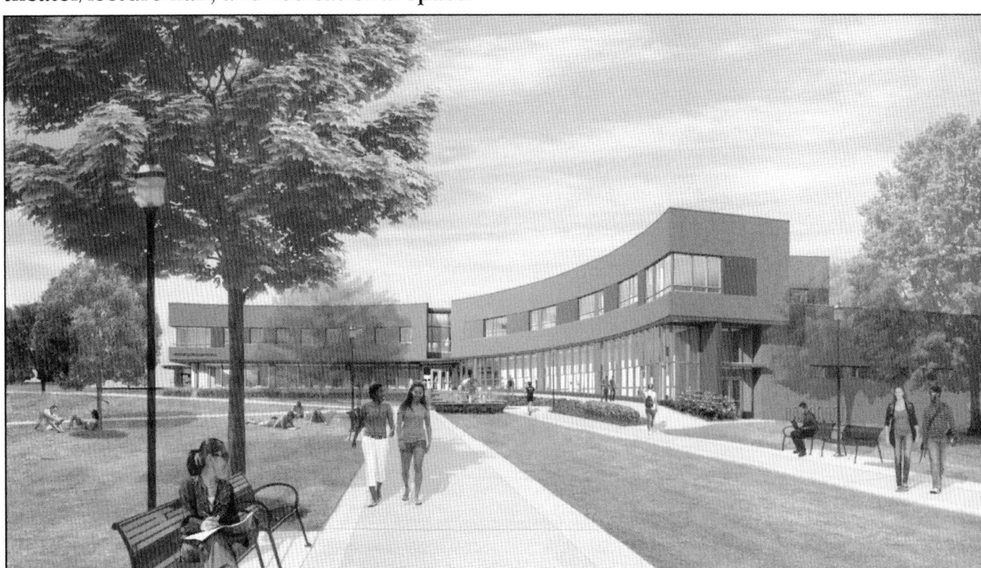

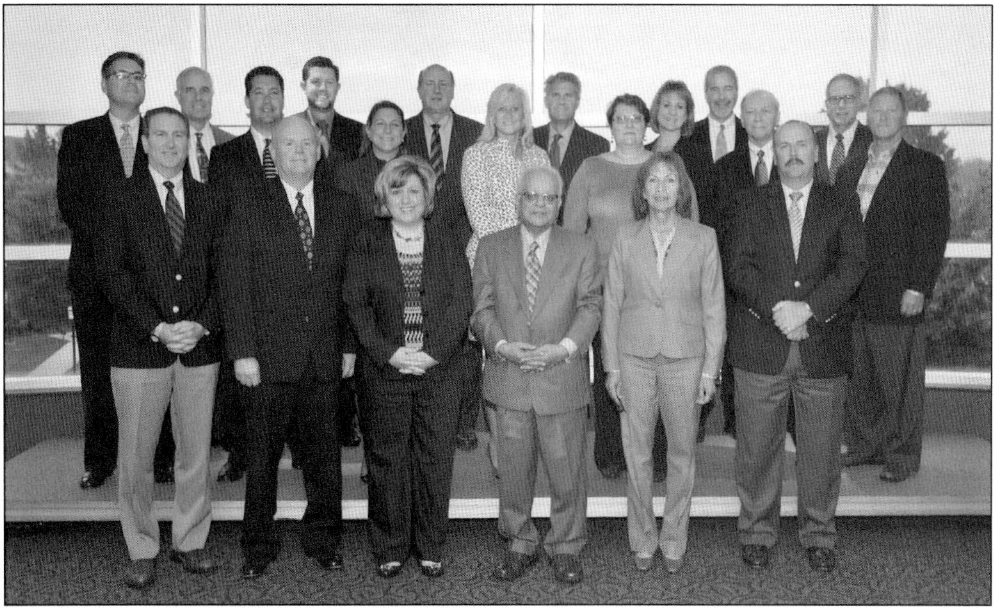

Board of Advisers, 2014. Penn State Harrisburg's Board of Advisers serves a vital function for the college and includes prominent business and government leaders, educators, and other regional experts who help identify and facilitate the school's strategic initiatives.

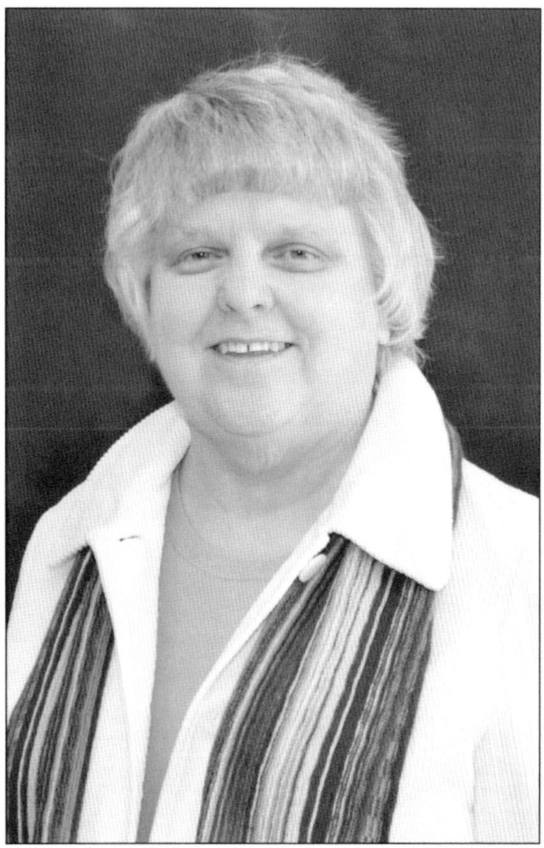

Dr. Beverly Cigler, 2015. In January 2015, Dr. Cigler was named Distinguished Professor of Public Policy and Administration in Penn State Harrisburg's School of Public Affairs. Dr. Cigler is the college's third scholar to earn this prestigious title that recognizes a highly select group of faculty with outstanding achievements in teaching, research, and service.

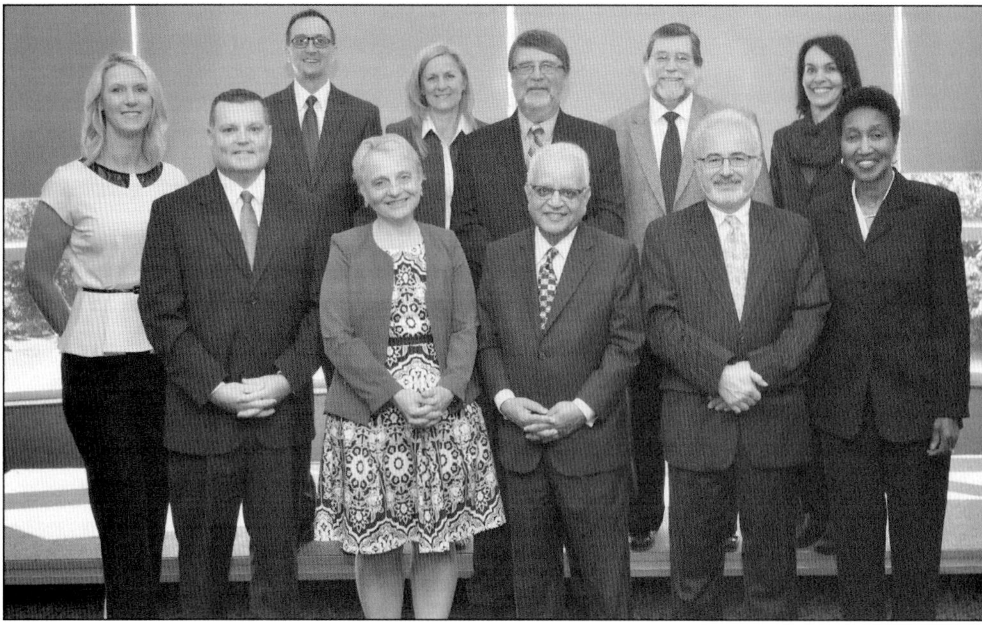

Chancellor's Council, 2015. Members of the Chancellor's Council pictured here are, from left to right, (first row) Marissa Hoover, Robert Coffman Jr., Dr. Susannah Gal, Chancellor Dr. Mukund S. Kulkarni, Dr. Omid Ansary, and Dorothy J. Guy; (second row) Jay Spiegel, Erin Shannon, Edward Dankanich, Dr. Donald Holtzman, and Marie-Louise Abram. Members Rebecca Gardner and Dr. John Hoh are not pictured.

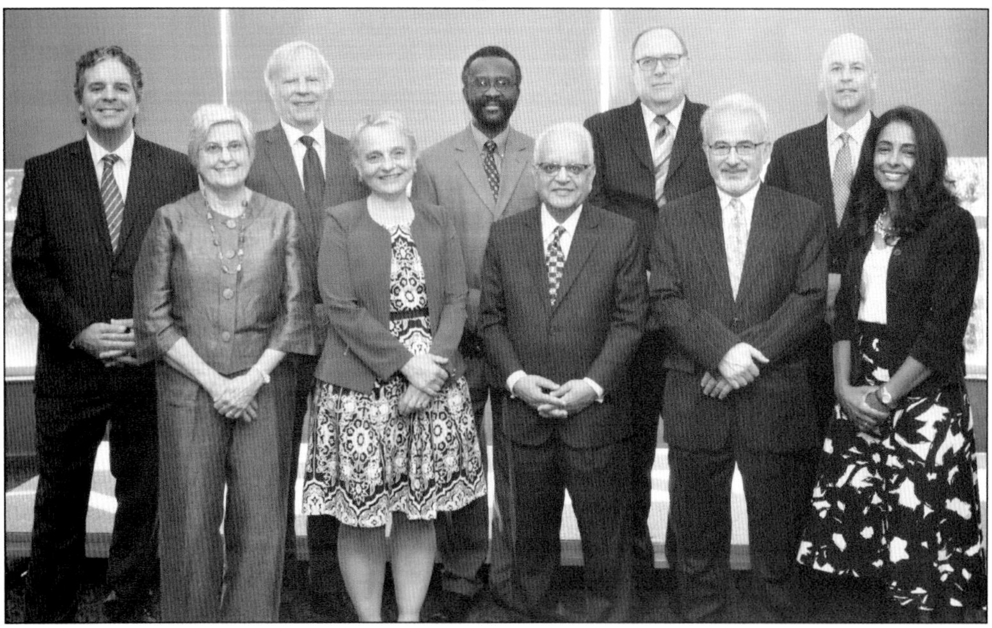

Academic Council, 2015. Members of the Academic Council pictured here are, from left to right, (first row) Dr. Catherine Surra, Dr. Susannah Gal, Chancellor Dr. Mukund S. Kulkarni, Dr. Omid Ansary, and Dr. Patria de Lancer Julnes; (second row) Glenn McGuigan, Paul B. Thompson, Dr. Peter Idowu, Dr. Gregory Crawford, and Dr. Stephen Schappe. Member Dr. Rafic Bachnak is not pictured.

Eight

PENN STATE HARRISBURG, THEN AND NOW 1966–2015

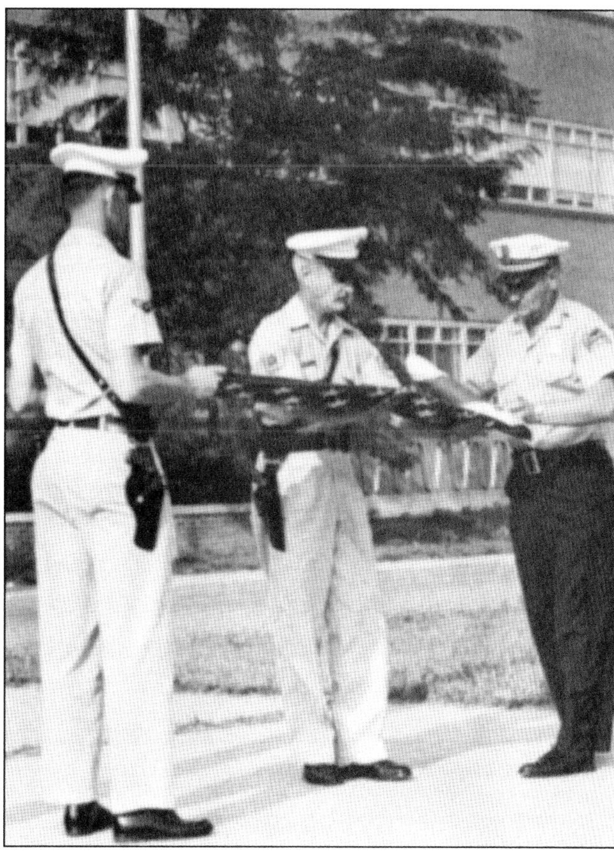

AIR FORCE'S LAST RETREAT, 1966. On August 28, 1966, the Olmsted Air Force Base held its last formal retreat in front of the Olmsted Building. The closure of the base was an economic blow to Middletown and the surrounding region. Although it was the end of one era, it marked the beginning of a new one for Penn State University.

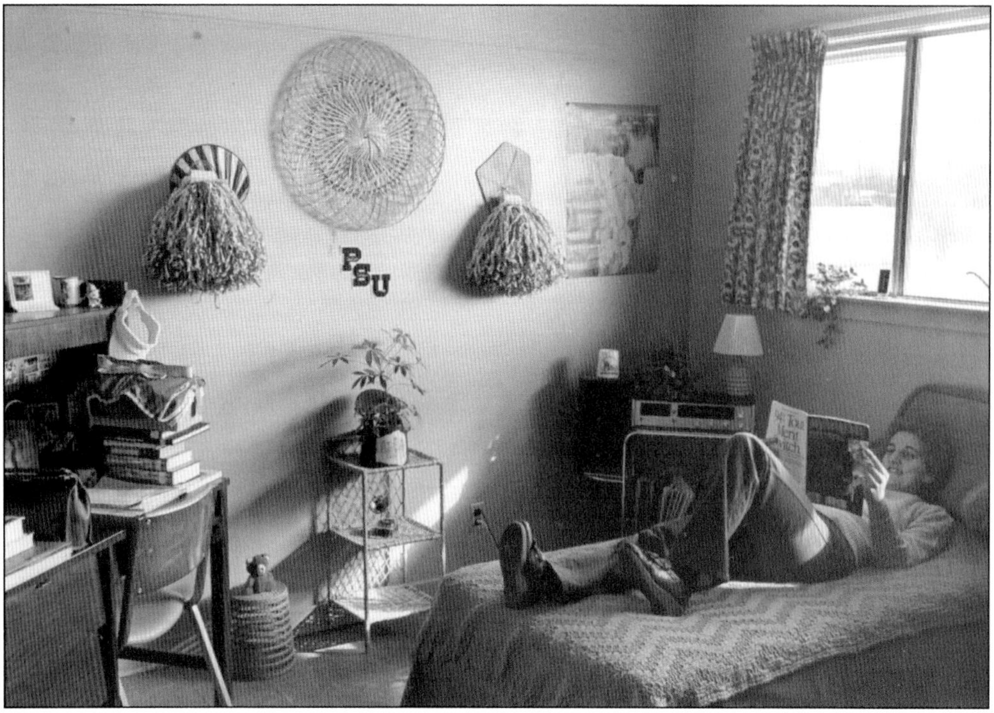

STUDENTS, 1970s AND 2010. Over the last 50 years, students and the tools they use to study have changed a hundredfold. This pair of images contrasts unidentified undergraduate students studying in their dormitories: the student above is pictured on her bed in Meade Heights in the 1970s, and the student below is shown studying at her desk in Village Housing in 2010.

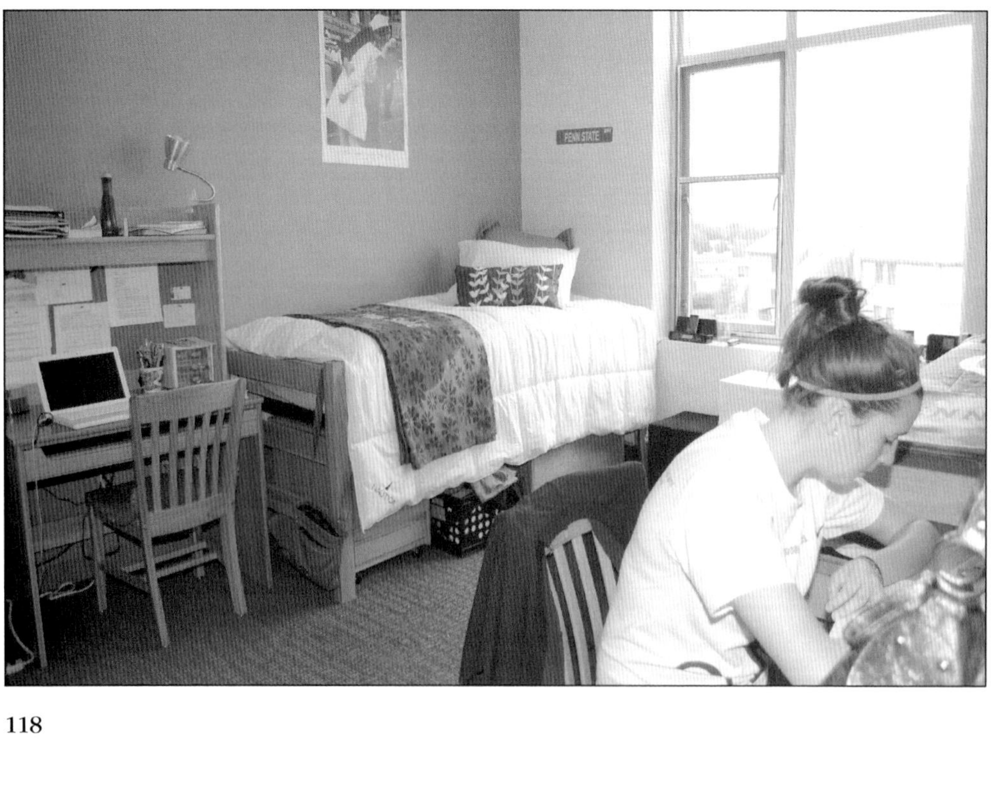

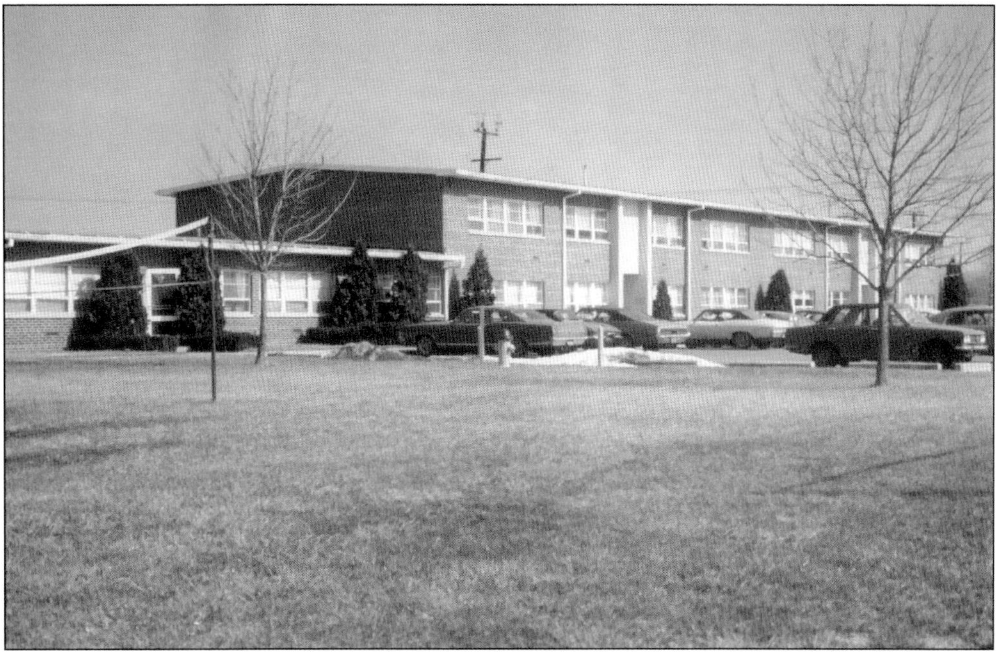

Residence Halls, 1970s and 2010. These two images reflect the dramatic way that student housing on campus has changed over the past 50 years. The above image shows the University Apartments (now part of the Educational Activities Building) around 1975. Below is a photograph of Juniata Hall, one of the state-of-the-art residence halls in Village Housing, from 2010.

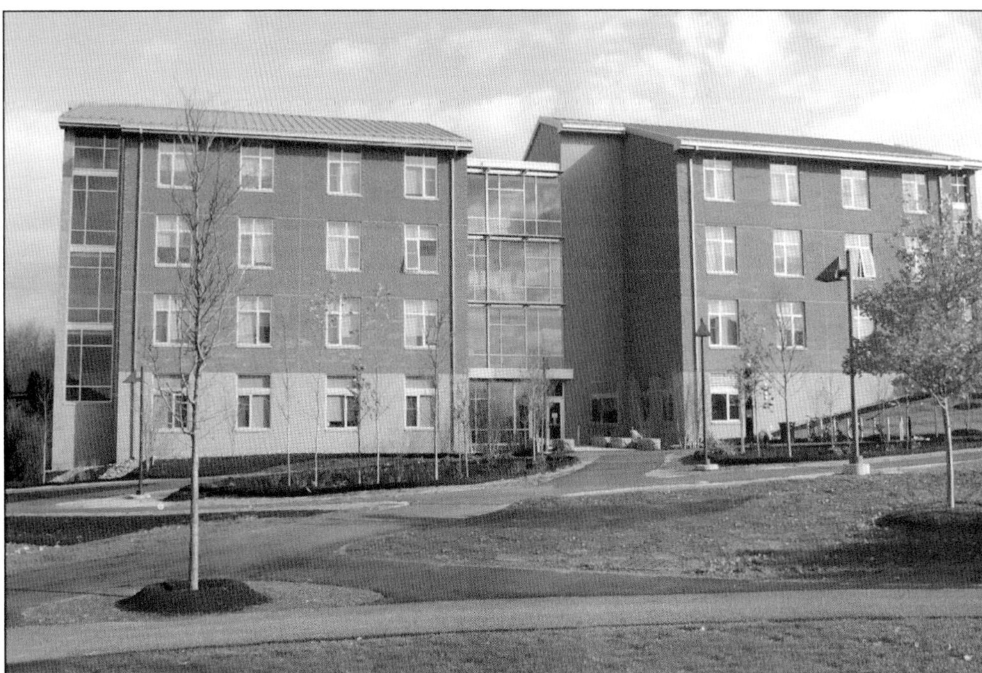

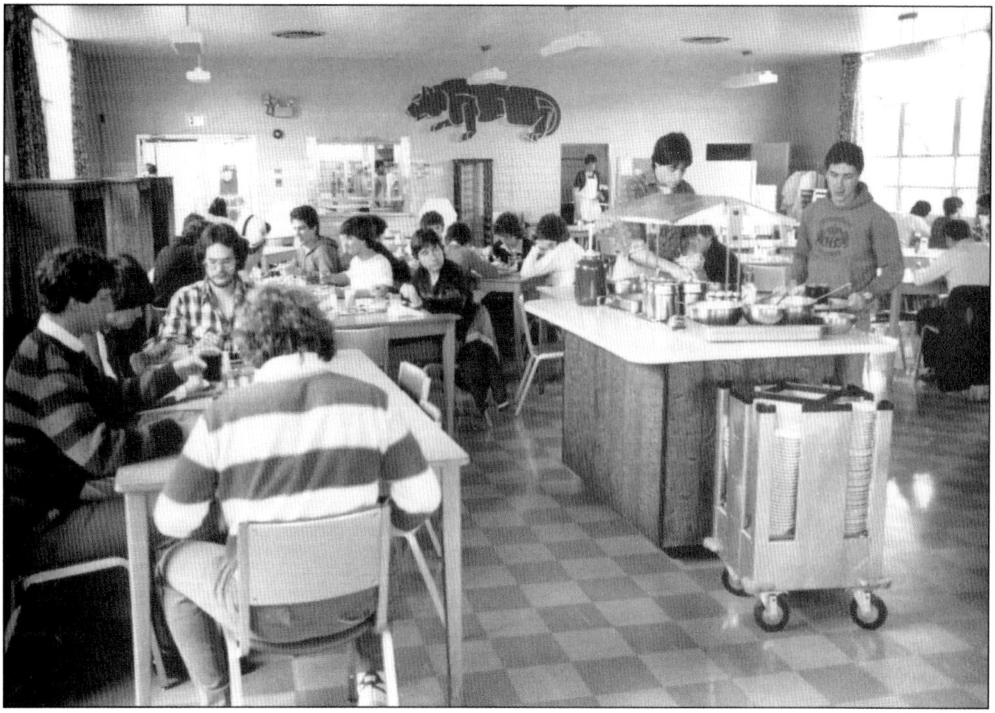

Dining Halls, 1980s and 2015. In addition to the dramatic difference in student residence halls between the 1970s and 2010s, the changes to student dining halls are striking. The above photograph dates to the 1980s and shows the dining hall located between Church and Wrisberg Halls. The below image shows Stacks Market, located in the Olmsted Building, in fall 2015.

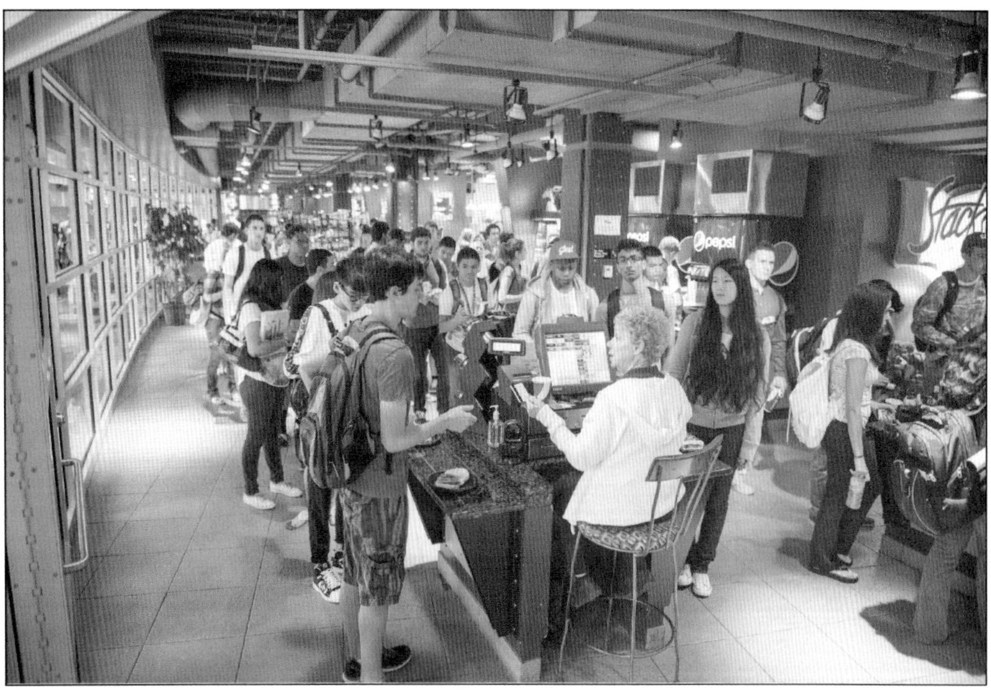

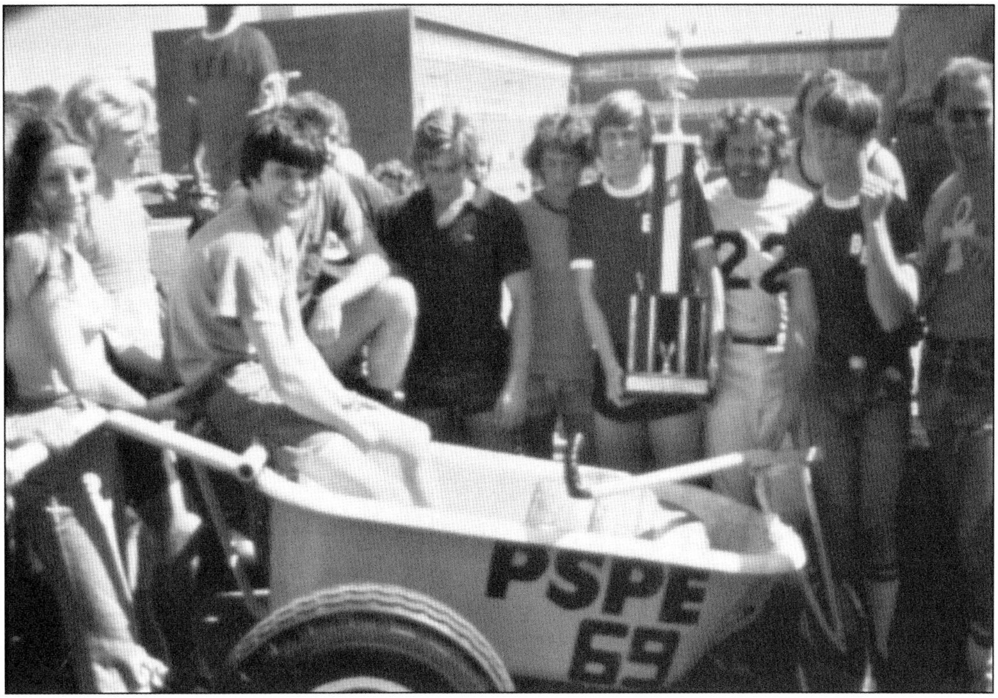

Bathtub Races, 1975 and 2014. The Bathtub Race tradition has persisted since the early 1970s and is still going strong. Every spring, students anticipate the race, which is typically held in May. Today, students race to win the coveted Bathtub Race trophy, which has changed over the years and is shown in both photographs.

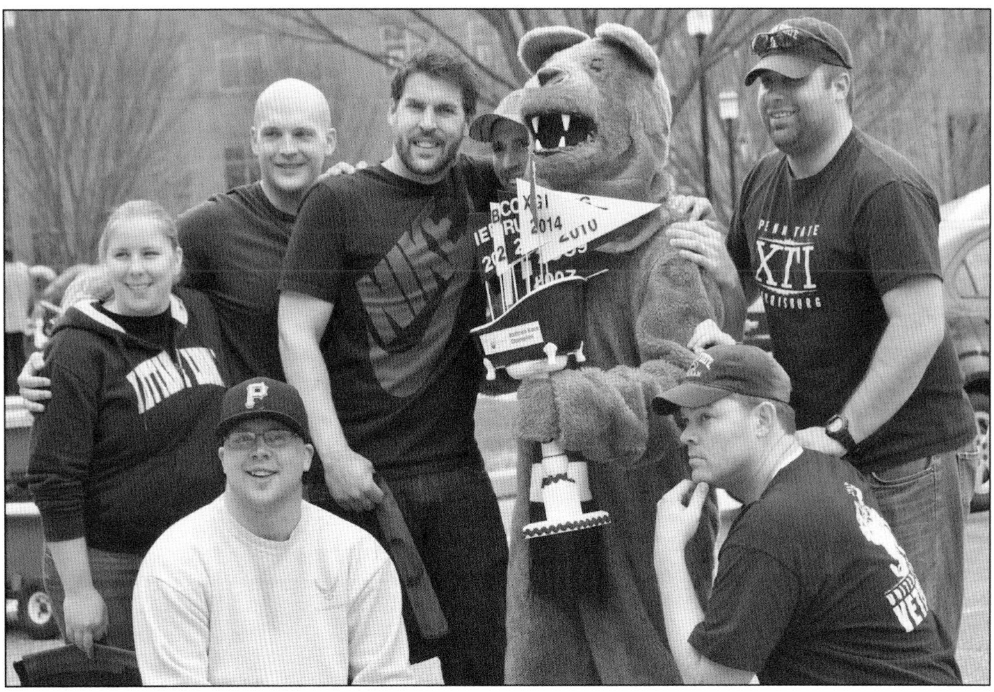

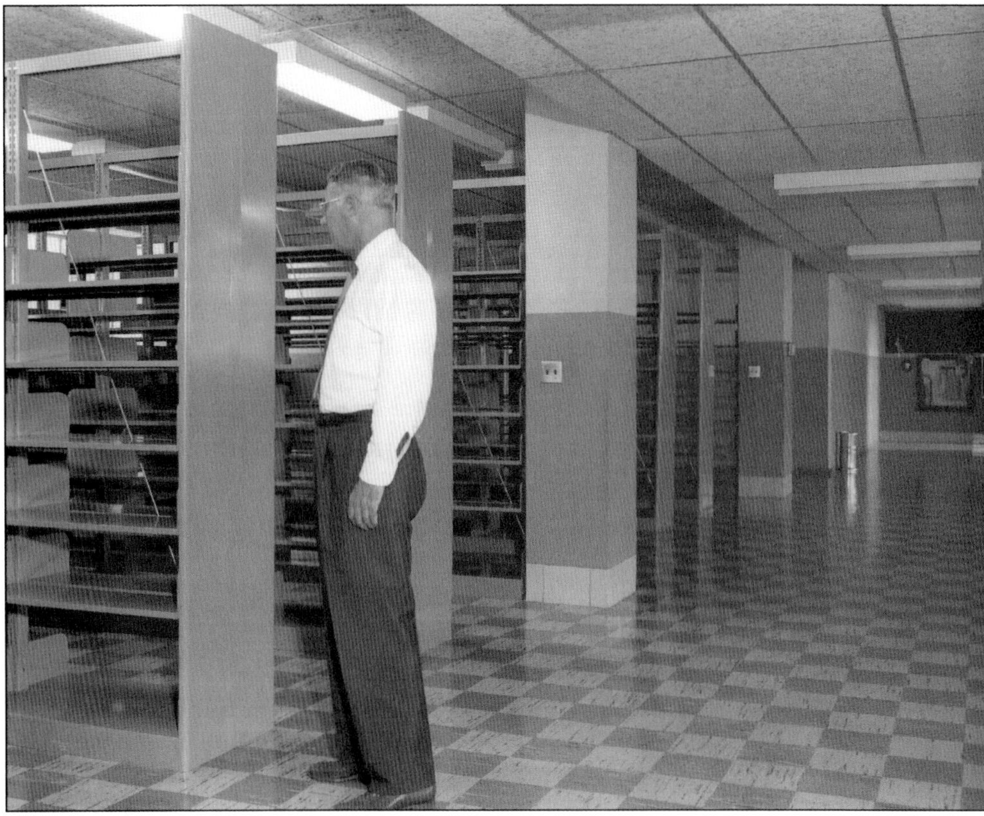

Library, 1966 and 2014. The above photograph of the first campus library, located inside the Olmsted Building, is from August 1966 and illustrates the empty shelves as a staff member awaits the arrival of books and journals. The photograph below, taken in 2014, shows the new library and emphasizes how much the library has evolved since the campus was formed.

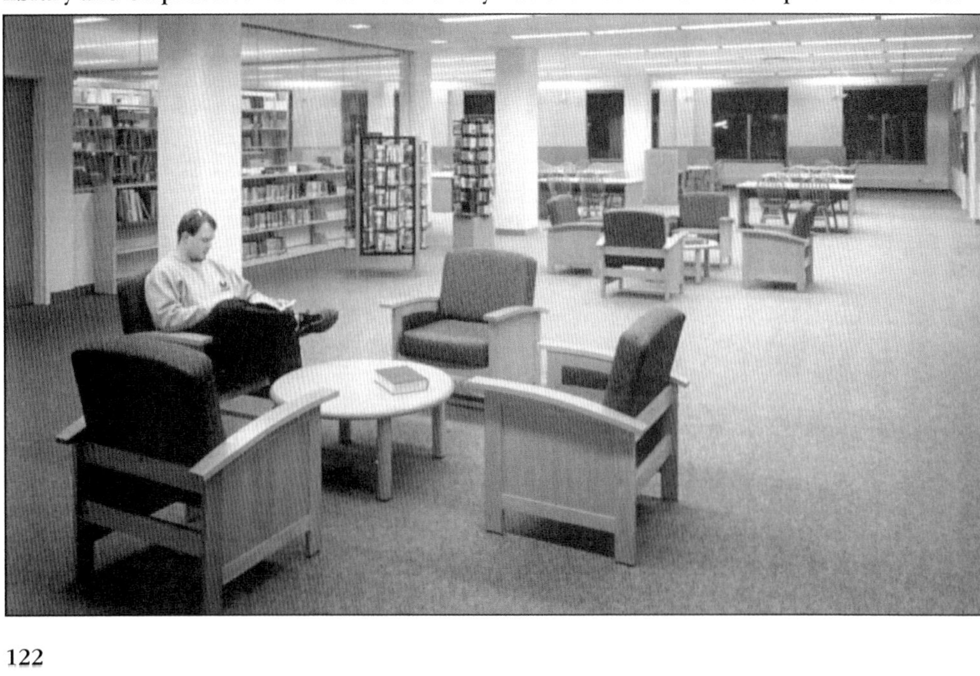

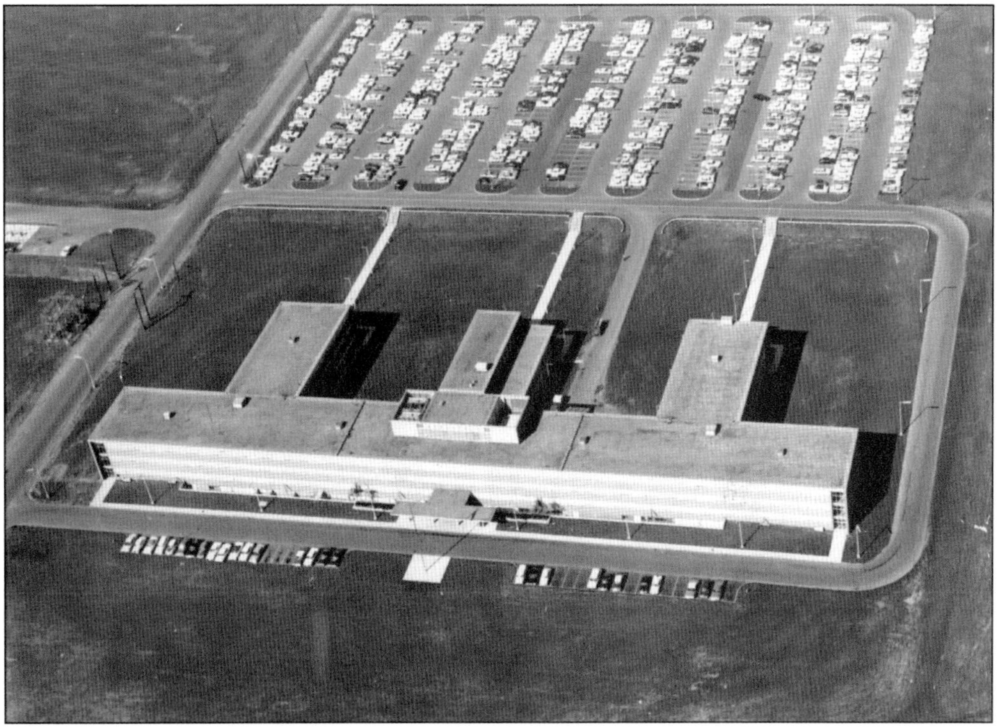

Olmsted Building, 1966 and 2015. This final, striking comparison features similar aerial photographs of Penn State Harrisburg and demonstrates the complete transformation of not only the Olmsted Building (above), but also the college's entire landscape design (below).

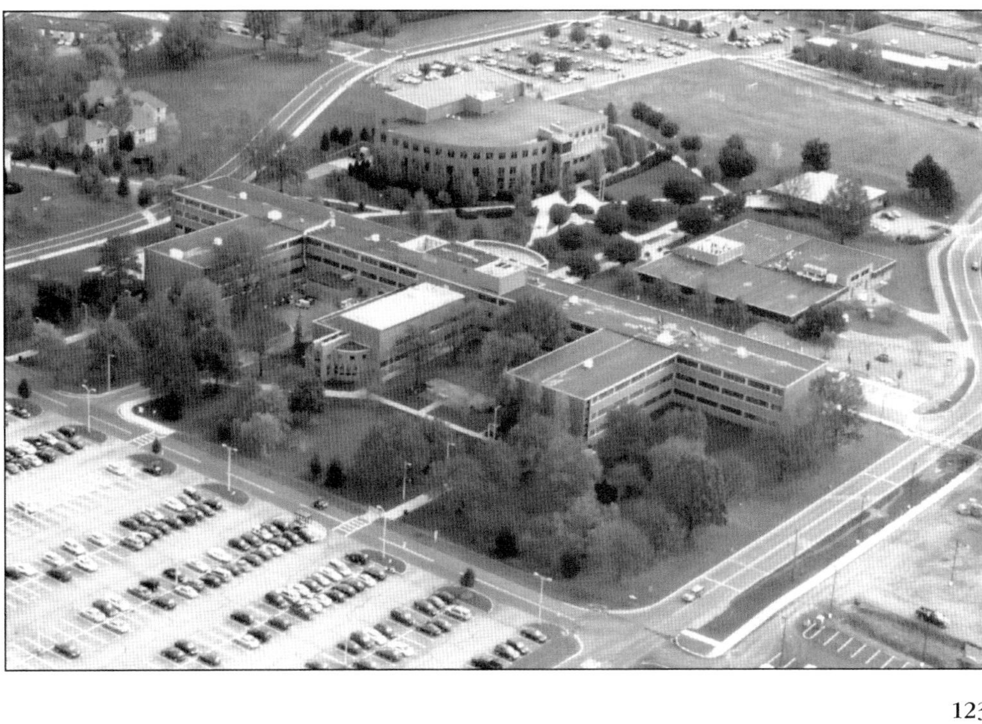

LEADERSHIP HISTORY

Dr. Mukund S. Kulkarni, Chancellor (November 1, 2010–Present)
Dr. Mukund S. Kulkarni, Interim Chancellor (July 1, 2010–November 1, 2010)
Dr. Madlyn L. Hanes, Provost and Dean (later renamed Chancellor) (2000–2010)
Dr. John L. Leathers, Interim Provost and Dean (1999–2000)
Dr. John G. Bruhn, Provost and Dean (1995–1999)
Dr. Theodore E. Kiffer, Interim Provost and Dean (1995)
Dr. Ruth Leventhal, Provost and Dean (1984–1994)
Dr. Stanley N. Miller, Acting Provost and Dean (1984)
Dr. Theodore L. Gross, Provost and Dean (1979–1983)
Dr. Robert E. McDermott, Provost (1972–1979)
Coleman Herpel, Director (1966–1972)

BIBLIOGRAPHY

Altman, Robert A. *The Upper Division College.* San Francisco, CA: Jossey-Bass, Inc., 1970.

Bezilla, Michael. *Penn State: An Illustrated History.* London and University Park, PA: The Pennsylvania State University Press, 1985.

"College History Archives," Archives and Special Collections, Penn State Harrisburg Library, Penn State Harrisburg, Middletown, PA.

Egle, William Henry. *History of the Counties of Dauphin and Lebanon, in the Commonwealth of Pennsylvania: Biographical and Genealogical.* Philadelphia: Everts & Peck, 1883. archive.org/details/historyofcountie01egle.

Esposito, Jackie R., and Steven L. Herb. *The Nittany Lion: An Illustrated Tale.* Foreword by Joe and Sue Paterno. University Park, PA: The Pennsylvania State University Press, 1997.

Everts & Stewart. *Combination Atlas Map of Dauphin County, Pennsylvania: Compiled, Drawn and Published from Personal Examinations and Surveys.* Reprint by the Dauphin County Historical Society, 1985. Philadelphia: Everts & Stewart, 1875.

"First Photographs of International Balloon Race Which Resulted in Five Deaths," Lammot du Pont, Jr. Aeronautical Photograph Collection, Hagley ID# 75360_00129, Hagley Museum and Library.

Hall, Henry, Ed. *America's Successful Men of Affairs: The United States at Large; An Encyclopedia of Contemporaneous Biography.* Vol. II. New York: The New York Tribune, 1896.

Hutchinson, C.H. *The Chronicles of Middletown: Containing a Compilation of Facts, Biographical Sketches, Reminiscences, Anecdotes, &c.; Connected with the History of One of the Oldest Towns in Pennsylvania.* Middletown, PA: Middletown Area Historical Society, 1906.

Sauers, Richard A. *Pennsylvania in the Spanish-American War: A Commemorative Look Back.* [Harrisburg, PA]: Capitol Preservation Committee, Commonwealth of Pennsylvania, 1998.

Schaeffer, Virginia M. *Early Middletown and Its Settlers.* Unpublished and unedited manuscript written for the Middletown Historical Society. Middletown, PA, 1976.

Snyder, Jackie. "Olmsted Expanding." *The Daily Collegian* 66.124 (May 13, 1966): 1.

Spancake, Lloyd S. "The History of Olmsted Air Force Base, Middletown, Pennsylvania." *Dauphin County Historical Review* 5 (1956): 4–15.

INDEX

About Penn State

Penn State Harrisburg, the Capital College, was founded in 1966 and is located in Lower Swatara Township, Middletown, Pennsylvania, just eight miles east of the capital city of Harrisburg. With student enrollments over 4,500 in 2015–2016, the Harrisburg campus serves as an undergraduate college and graduate school within the Pennsylvania State University (Penn State) and is one of 24 campuses located across the commonwealth of Pennsylvania.

Penn State was established in 1855 as one of the first colleges of agricultural science in the United States and originally focused upon the application of scientific principles to farming. It is Pennsylvania's only land-grant institution of higher education and the commonwealth's largest public university. The university employs 17,000 faculty and staff, enrolls nearly 100,000 students at campuses and in online programs through the Penn State World Campus, and provides care to more than one million patients annually in the Penn State College of Medicine at the Milton S. Hershey Medical Center. The university also supports more than 645,000 alumni through the Penn State Alumni Association, the largest dues-paying alumni organization in the world.

For over 150 years, Penn State has been a leader in providing higher education not only to Pennsylvanians, but also to a record number of international students. In 2013–2014, Penn State ranked 13th in the nation for attracting students from around the globe. Penn State has one of the largest graduate schools in the country, with enrollment over 13,500 and research expenditures of more than $813 million in 2014.

In addition to carrying out its mission of teaching, research, and service, the university also hosts the annual Penn State IFC/Panhellenic Dance Marathon, more commonly known as THON, which is the world's largest student-run philanthropic organization. In 2014, THON raised over $13 million for children and families impacted by pediatric cancer.

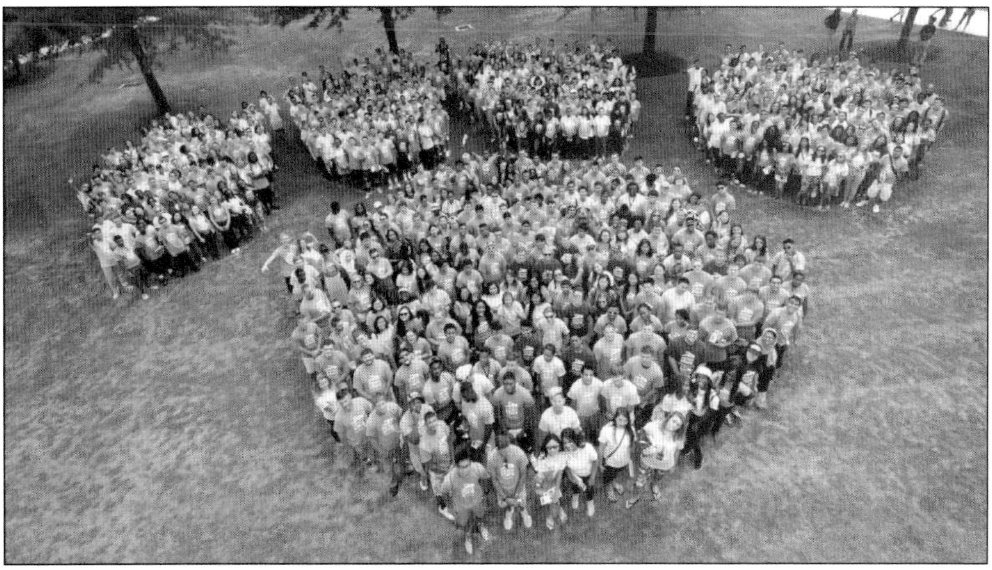

"We Are Penn State" Proud, 2015. On August 23, 2015, over 900 first-year students, as well as faculty and staff, came together on campus for the fall 2015 convocation, marking the beginning of the 2015–2016 academic year and welcoming students into the life and traditions of Penn State University. These first-year students have gathered in the shape of Penn State's famous Nittany Lion paw print symbol.